Center of Weight

ADVANCED LABANOTATION SERIES

EDITOR
Ann Hutchinson Guest
Director, Language of Dance* Centre, London, UK

Vol. 1, 1:
Canon Forms
by Ann Hutchinson Guest
and Rob van Haarst

Vol. 1, 2:
Shape, Design, Trace Patterns
by Ann Hutchinson Guest
and Rob van Haarst

Vol. 1, 3:
Kneeling, Sitting, Lying
by Ann Hutchinson Guest
and Rob van Haarst

Issue 4:
Sequential Movements
by Ann Hutchinson Guest
and Joukje Kolff

Issue 5:
Hands, Fingers
by Ann Hutchinson Guest
and Joukje Kolff

Issue 6:
Floorwork, Basic Acrobatics
by Ann Hutchinson Guest
and Joukje Kolff

Issue 7:
Center of Weight
by Ann Hutchinson Guest
and Joukje Kolff

Issue 8:
Handling of Objects, Props
by Ann Hutchinson Guest
and Joukje Kolff

Issue 9:
Spatial Variations
by Ann Hutchinson Guest,
and Joukje Kolff

Center of Weight

BY

ANN HUTCHINSON GUEST

AND

JOUKJE KOLFF

DANCE
BOOKS

Dance Books Ltd,
4 Lenten Street, Alton, Hampshire GU34 1HG

Printed in the United Kingdom by H. Charlesworth & Co.,
Huddersfield

ISBN: 1 85273 094 3

This book was written and produced at the Language of Dance® Centre:
The Language of Dance® Centre
17 Holland Park
London W11 3TD
United Kingdom
T: +44 (0)20 7229 3780
F: +44 (0)20 7792 1794
web: http://www.lodc.org
e-mail: info@lodc.org

Ann Hutchinson Guest

Joukje Kolff

v

Table of Contents

Introduction to the Series

The <u>Advanced Labanotation</u> series provides a detailed exposition of the many topics introduced in the chapters of the 1970 textbook *Labanotation - The System of Analyzing and Recording Movement*. To make the material immediately accessible to the reader, each book in this series begins at a basic level, thus avoiding the need for immediate reference to other texts.

Within the series each topic is published independently as soon as it is completed in order to make the information immediately available. Topics for which there is at present a lack of information available, and those for which there is an immediate need, are being presented first.

Detailed theoretical exposition is supported by appropriate notated examples, and, where needed, figure illustrations of the movements and positions. A selection of excerpts from choreographic scores illustrates the different points, with the examples taken from various sources and styles of movement. Finally, a detailed index facilitates rapid access to required information and, for the researcher, meticulous endnotes and a bibliography indicate background and sources.

Preface

Relationship to the pull of gravity is a constant in human life and, of course, even more so in dance, gymnastics and other specific physical activities which aim to defy or make specific use of gravity.

Balance and falling are encountered early in a child's development, they are aspects of movement for which awareness in placement of our center of weight is important. The specific center of gravity in a moving body may be hard to define but how weight is placed is central to any form of movement training.

This book looks at the larger changes in placement and movement of the center of weight as well as the minor, subtler changes, and defines how each is described in Labanotation and the logic behind such description. To some it seems surprising that a whole volume should be written on this aspect of movement, yet for both practical and expressive reasons knowledge of this subject can heighten one's technique as well as quality of movement.

Acknowledgements

Many sources have been investigated in researching the use of the center of weight in movement. Beginning with Laban's first general reference to the center of gravity in 1928, through Knust's specific analysis, consideration has also been given to the many major and minor applications and recent usages among fellow Labanotators.

We gratefully acknowledge the help given by our consultants Jacqueline Challet-Haas, Ilene Fox, János Fügedi, David Henshaw, Sheila Marion and Lucy Venable. Their detailed and judicious comments on working drafts of this material, and their active participation in discussions concerning issues and problems contributed much to the correction and clarification of the finished product.

We are much indebted to Rob van Haarst for his early research and collection of reading examples. We are also grateful to the notators of the reading materials, the choreographers concerned for giving permission to use the excerpts from their scores and to Veronica Dittman for her help in locating addresses and information.

Our thanks go to Traute Molik-Riemer for contributing the many figure drawings needed in this book and to Roma Dispirito for producing the Labanotation examples on *Calaban*. We are grateful to Helen Coxon for co-ordinating the compilation of the book. Particular appreciation and thanks go to Jane Dulieu who, with her knowledge and keen eye for accuracy, undertook the final checking of the book.

The research for this issue of Advanced Labanotation and its production have been made possible through funding from the National Endowment for the Humanities, the Arts and Humanities Research Board and the John Simon Guggenheim Memorial Foundation. We are grateful or their generous support.

We must also express appreciation to Andy Adamson who developed the *Calaban* software used to produce the Labanotation graphics.

Center of Weight

I BASIC CONCEPTS

1 Introduction

1.1. A range of movements concerned with centering the body weight, shifting it away from center and into falling, can be written in Labanotation using the symbol for center of weight: ● .[1]

1.2. In relation to these movements, attention is often focused on *balance* and *loss of balance*. This is particularly true in acrobatics or in a ballet or modern dance context. The body may be in perfect, centered balance on its point(s) of support. Balance may even be kept if the body is not in perfect alignment. It is possible to shift the weight off true center to other points and still be over the base of support without falling. The weight may intentionally be carried beyond the base of support into a fall. It is also possible to catch the weight and recover balance after a fall.

1.3. In the process of analysing these activities more closely, the terms *center of weight, center of gravity, balance, stability, line of gravity, line of balance, point of balance,* and *base of support*, are introduced here. For scientific needs, modern technological measuring equipment provides the means of determining the location of the center of weight and its displacement during a movement sequence.[2] However, for general purposes of movement analysis and notation more general statements suffice. Scientifically, there is a difference between *center of gravity* and *center of weight*, but we are advised by specialists in the field that for our purposes in recording movement there is no significant difference, hence use of the term *center of weight*.[3]

1.4. The term *balance* is generally understood in the sense of not losing one's balance, i.e. not falling. Balance may be *stable* or precarious. The pull of gravity is everywhere. The *vertical line of gravity* passes through any object and any part of that object, whether moving or still, this pull is ubiquitous. The *line of balance* is that vertical line, which passes through the body's center of weight when it is within the base of support. The *point of balance* is that central place within the base of support on the floor (or other object or partner) over which the performer is balanced and through which the line of balance passes. In perfect balance, the line of balance passes through the center of weight of the person or object and the center point of balance on the supporting base. This *base of support* may be very small or comfortably large depending on the body configuration as it supports on the floor. Balance is lost when the vertical line of balance through the body's center of weight passes beyond the base of support.

2 Center of Weight - Analysis

2.1. In any body configuration the *center of weight* (C of W) of a body or object is that point at which the body as a whole balances, no matter what the body configuration, in other words, that point about which all the parts of the body exactly balance (outweigh) each other.

2.2. The C of W of a perfect sphere or cube is exactly in the middle. In any solid object it is located at the geometrical center, provided that the object is entirely made of the same material (i.e. all of its parts have the same density). Determining the location of the C of W in the human body is more difficult because the body is a complex, segmented structure, heavier in some parts than in others, and capable of many different positions.

2.3. The precise location of the C of W depends on individual build and, in any given position, on the body configuration and on whether the performer is carrying any external weight. For a person of average build, in normal standing on two feet, arms hanging by the sides, the C of W is located in the pelvis in front of the upper part of the sacrum. It is usually lower in women than in men because of the narrower shoulders and heavier pelvis in females.

2.4. Changes in placement of the limbs and head affect location of the C of W. When the arms are raised, or an object is carried above the waist line, the C of W is located at a higher position and equilibrium is harder to maintain. Wrestlers lower their C of W by their stance and by pressing downward with belly and diaphragm muscles.

2.5. In **2a** the C of W is located at the intersection of the three lines. Each line represents a dimension; in each dimension there is as much body weight to one side of the C of W as to the other.

2.6. The C of W is not necessarily located within the body: if the body is curved, for instance, it may lie outside. In **2b** the C of W is located at the intersection of three lines. Due to the irregular body shape, it is no longer within the torso.

2.7. For our purposes of movement analysis and recording, the precise location of the C of W, the center of balance, the center of gravity, need not be known; general statements suffice. The C of W is not a part of the body; it therefore cannot move on its own, but can only be moved. There is no physical awareness of precisely where the C of W is, but awareness of balance, stability and falling is familiar. We learn how body movement can control balance or cause falling. It is not the small muscular adjustments which are written; instead a description in terms of C of W in relation to balance is given.[4]

Center of Weight - Analysis

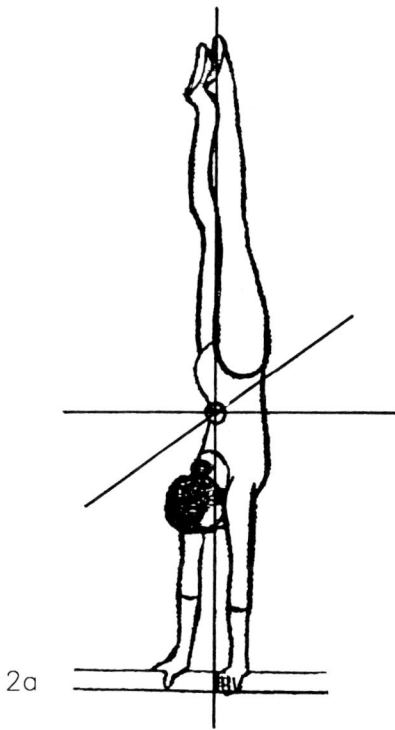

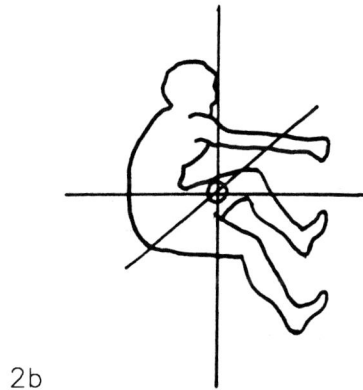

2a   2b

3 Line of Balance, Base of Support, Stability

3.1. This issue of <u>Advanced Labanotation</u> is mainly concerned with situations in which the body is supported by a horizontal floor. However, other situations are discussed in a separate issue on floorwork and basic acrobatics.

3.2. The *line of balance* is the vertical line passing through the C of W. When support is on a horizontal floor, the spot where this line intersects the floor is exactly below the C of W. Ex. **3a** shows the line of balance when standing in 2nd position; it intersects the floor between the feet.

3.3. The *base of support* is the supporting body surface or, if there is more than one point of support, the area on the floor delineated by all supporting body surfaces. In the following examples the base of support is the area within dotted lines, the x shows approximately where the centered line of balance will be located, if weight is equally distributed over the supports. In **3b** weight is on the left foot, so the base of support is the sole of this foot. Ex. **3c** shows the base of support in standing on two feet.

3.4. If a prop such as a cane is partially taking body weight, the area of support is enlarged. Ex. **3d** shows standing with some weight on a cane. In **3e** a position 'on all fours' is shown.

3.5. *Stability* of the body depends on:
  - the size of the base of support;
  - the height of the C of W from the supporting surface;
  - balance: i.e. placement of C of W and hence the line of balance
    within the base of support (see Section 4)
as well as in certain other circumstances.

3.6. **Size of Base of Support.** The larger the base of support the more stability. A 2nd position in ballet is more stable than a 1st position, and a 1st more stable than a 5th. There is increased stability in the progression from **3b** to **3e**.

3.7. **Height of Center of Weight.** A high object with a small base of support is more likely to be tipped over than a low object with the same base of support. Likewise, the human body is in a more stable position if the C of W is closer to the floor, for instance, if a dancer is in a *plié*. Conversely, if the center of weight shifts to a higher position, which occurs for instance when a man raises his arms, while lifting a partner, the body loses some of its stability. The difference in stability can be felt, for instance, when rising from bent legs on both feet to a small base, such as a balance on half toe on one foot.

3.8. The position of **3f** is very stable for two reasons. There is a large base of support (the triangle formed by the feet and each knee) and the C of W is close to the floor.

3.9. Some other factors that influence stability are the mass of weight (large people are more stable than small people), momentum or impetus gained from an outside force (stability is easily lost when jumping from a moving vehicle), visual and psychological factors (such as the effect of vertigo) and sliding friction[5] (instability in walking on ice).

Line of Balance, Base of Support, Stability

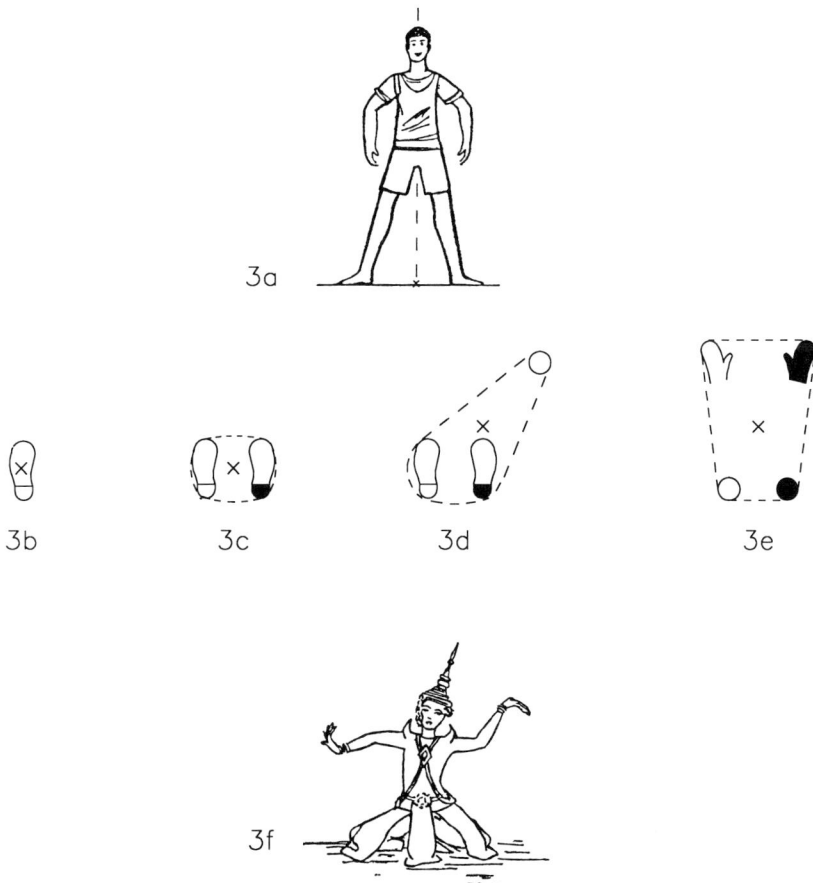

3a

3b   3c   3d   3e

3f

8

4 Balance

4.1. As previously explained, stability depends among other things on the relationship between the line of balance and the base of support. Therefore, balance is particularly an issue when the base of support is very small, as when on half-toe or a full-toe (*pointe*) support in ballet.

4.2. The body is in functional, stable balance if the line of balance intersects the base of support at its center, **4a**. In standing upright with feet closed, it is understood that, with good posture, the line of balance passes between the ears and hips and just in front of the ankle bones. This position is what performers usually strive for in upright standing.

4.3. In everyday situations the body constantly makes minor adjustments in its configuration and use of muscles in order to maintain balance. In carrying a heavy suitcase, it is common for the body to lean to the other side and for the free arm to move outward, **4b**, to provide counterbalance to the weight of the suitcase. When carrying a heavy pile of books, **4c**, the torso leans backward.

4.4. In tilting the torso forward, as in **4d**, a slight backward shift of the pelvic area usually takes place to counterbalance the displaced weight of the torso. Placing the arms forward in line with the torso, **4e**, increases the weight displacement so that the pelvis needs to counterbalance even more in the backward direction.

Balance

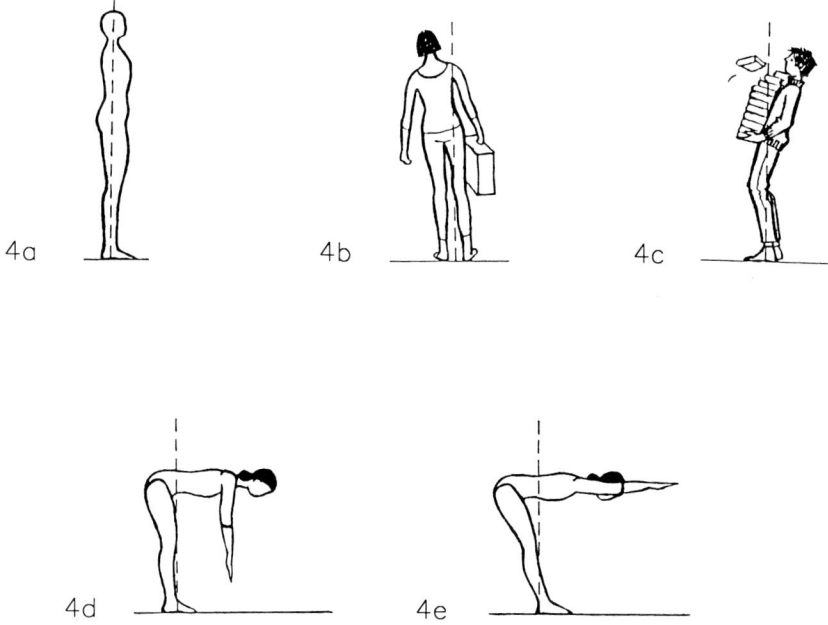

4a   4b   4c

4d   4e

4.5. Muscular control can prevent the need for many of these natural spatial adjustments. Specific muscular control makes it possible to perform **4f** instead of **4d** without falling forward. Certain dance techniques, Western contemporary dance, for example, train this kind of control for technical and aesthetic purposes. The natural tendency in **4g** is to counterbalance the weight of the right arm and leg by shifting the pelvic area or leaning the torso to the left; this can be prevented by muscular control, **4h**, as it is in ballet.

4.6. Aesthetic principles also play a role in activities such as gymnastics, where the prescribed ending position after a final jump is usually heels together, even though this is not logically the position in which stability is best regained.

4.7. Finally, we also use our experience of stability and balance when anticipating the impact of outside forces or the direction of the next move. If a rugby player knows he will be pushed from the front he will lean forward so as to 'give' in the opposite direction without losing balance. If the direction of the next move is unknown, as often is the case in tennis and other sports, for maximum moveability the C of W is best kept centered and lowered, often with the torso leaning forward and a wide base. In other instances it is the opposite of stability that is required. Swimmers waiting to start a race lean forward anticipating the loss of balance to give them impetus.

4.8. Such practical application of our physical awareness of balance and stability and readiness to adjust is of enormous importance to dancers, especially when learning new moves, when improvising or in partnering. In Contact Improvisation, for example, where improvising and partnering are central practices, constant awareness of balance and imbalance of oneself and one's partner(s) is important. In this form of dance one often challenges the boundaries of what feel like safe and stable movements, trusting the partner, ready to adjust, fall and catch. This physical consciousness may be less immediately needed in dance forms where choreography is predetermined and movements are practiced. However, even in ballet, it plays an important role in partnering.

4.9. When one person is carrying another, or when one is leaning against someone or an object, the analysis of stability and balance cannot be limited to the individual body. What matters in these cases is the C of W of the two bodies *together*, or in the case of leaning against an object, of the body and the object. (For leaning see Sections 21, 22.)

Balance (continued)

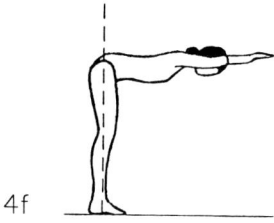

4f   4g   4h

5 Stability, Balance in Motion, Falling

5.1. The principles of stability and balance discussed so far have been applied to static *positions* of the body. If the body is *moving*, they apply to all the positions it passes through. Although it is difficult to determine the location of the C of W of the body in motion, for general purposes of movement analysis and notation it can be estimated at key moments in the movement sequence. The most salient feature is the relationship between the C of W and the center of the base of support, in other words, the degree of maintained balance or loss of balance.

5.2. **In Balance.** If the C of W is over the center of the base of support (i.e. the line of balance intersects the center of the base of support) the body is in perfect balance, as in **4a-4e**. If the C of W is closer to the margin of the base of support, the body can still be in balance, as in **4f** and **4h**. However, balance may have become precarious. Loss of balance occurs when the line of balance falls outside the margin of the base of support.

5.3. **Shifting the Weight.** Without moving the feet, the body weight can consciously be displaced a certain distance into any horizontal direction without loss of balance, for instance, to the right side, **5a**. This possibility increases with muscular ability. Here the line of balance intersects the base of support close to its margin. This activity is termed *shifting the weight*.

Shifting the Weight

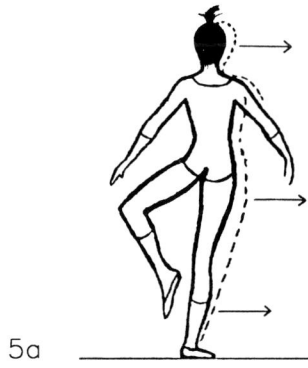

5a

5.4. **Loss of Balance, Falling.** Loss of balance or *falling* may occur to different degrees, ranging from slight instability, 'teetering' on the brink of loss of balance, to an uncomfortably heavy fall, as when one trips and falls flat on the floor.

5.5. In everyday movement sequences we often lose balance momentarily and unconsciously. In normal walking forward, with each step a preparatory weight shift causes the location of the C of W to move into the direction of the step, slightly beyond the base of the supporting foot. Because the other leg is already placed ready to 'catch' the weight, no actual falling occurs and the performer is usually unaware that a moment of instability has occurred. In fast steps and runs it is even less obvious. In landing from springing, depending on the style, the weight may be over the new support as soon as the foot touches the ground, or, in a traveling leap, for example, the weight usually becomes centered after the foot contacts the floor, during the cushioning knee bend. Because of the greater force that has to be countered in order to come to rest, we are usually more aware of the danger of falling after traveling aerial steps.

5.6. When sitting down on a chair, depending on its height and how far away it is, we usually pass through a brief moment of loss of balance even though we incline the torso to prevent this. We become aware of this brief instability when we sit down in a bus or train and the moment of loss of balance coincides with the moment the vehicle is set in motion.

5.7. The body as a whole falls whenever balance is lost and not immediately regained, i.e. when there is a noticeable time gap between loss of balance and recovery. In a planned fall, actions are taken to break the fall, or at least to soften it. The sooner these actions occur the smaller the fall. When falling from standing, for instance, the arms may be used to catch the weight and ease the torso to the ground. The falling action of **5b** is caught by a lunge, **5c**. The arms help to maintain balance until control is completely regained.

5.8. The state of falling, of being off balance, may occur in a single activity, or may be prolonged over several steps, as in a falling, stumbling run.

5.9. Unintentional falling may be caused by the action of an outside force, such as another person pushing, or one may miss a step when walking down stairs. Another reason may be sudden loss of friction as in stepping on an icy patch, the supporting leg sliding away from the line of balance, or the foot may be inadvertently caught by an object on the floor, **5d**.

5.10. Intentional falling is featured in many forms of modern dance. Doris

Humphrey, a representative of American modern dance, based much of her dance technique on principles of 'fall and recovery'. However, true falling is not always involved, the 'fall' is often more a matter of giving in to gravity in a swift movement sequence in which the C of W is continuously supported. Such lowering to the ground does not involve true loss of equilibrium.

    5.11. Ex. **5e** shows a sideward 'fall'. Lowering is aided by torso inclination and placement of arms into the opposite direction as one passes through kneeling and sitting into lying, the right hand taking some weight as it slides out to the side. In this kind of 'fall', actual loss of balance is prevented throughout by the succession of supports and counterbalancing in the body.

Loss of Balance, Falling

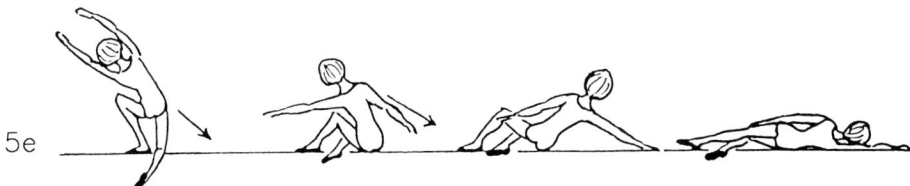

5b

5c

5d

5e

II WEIGHT CHANGES: BASIC DESCRIPTION

6 Weight Placement without Center of Weight Statement

6.1. In many movements, changes of weight placement can cause displacement of the location of the C of W. Where there is reason to attract the reader's attention to this displacement, C of W indications should be used. The positions and movements discussed in Part I can all be recorded in Labanotation without the C of W sign through writing slight tilts and shifts of various parts of the torso or larger tilts of augmented torso sections. Nevertheless, these examples are usually thought of and experienced as 'balancing', 'falling', 'shifting the weight', that is, in terms of weight placement and balance (see Sections 17, 18). Therefore, where this type of movement is concerned, descriptions containing the special symbol for C of W are usually more appropriate and easier to read, since they reflect the essence of the movement sequence more accurately (see also 7.1).

6.2. In most cases displacement of the location of the center of weight is not the focus of a given movement. In walking, kneeling or landing from a jump, for example, balance is retained or regained in the most comfortable manner, and so remains unanalysed and unwritten in the notation, as in the following examples.

6.3. In **6a-6d**, details of weight placement are understood even though the C of W symbol is not used. In **6a**, the torso automatically tilts slightly forward to counterbalance the movement backward and minimalise any instability occurring during transference into this foot-kneel position. This weight adjustment is understood in the notation; if desired, it can, of course, be spelled out.

6.4. The jump in **6b** is understood to be performed in such a way that the landing is smooth, balance is regained easily and risk of falling minimized. To some degree this will be aided by body configuration during the jump. A forward torso tilt at the moment of landing together with slight backward weight placement help to brake the forward momentum and avoid falling forward after landing.

6.5. In **6c** the weight comes to rest, after the second step, ending centered completely over the left foot. In **6d**, because the backward step is anticipated, weight will start moving backward where the arrow is indicated, or weight may have remained backward of centered placement, depending on the speed of the steps. This difference in weight placement is understood and need not be written with the C of W symbol. (See Section 16 for more detailed examples.)

Weight Placement without Center of Weight Statement

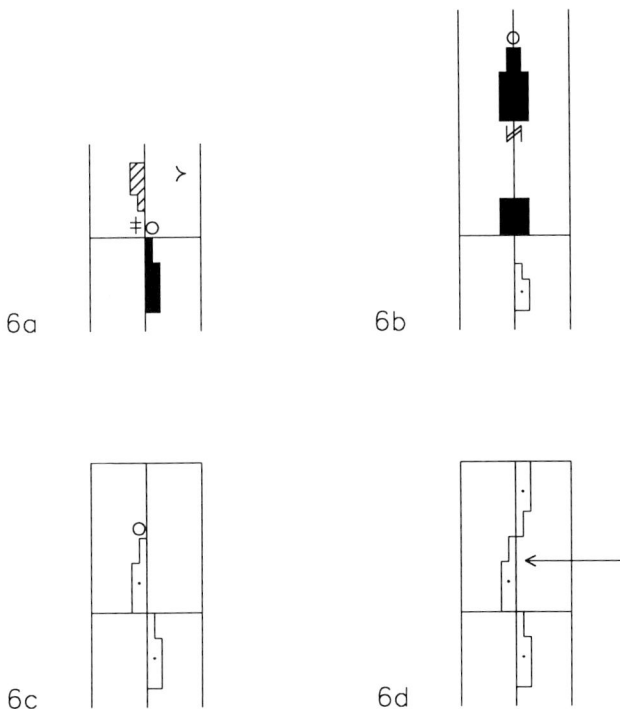

6a

6b

6c

6d

7   Center of Weight Indications

7.1.   A description in terms of C of W is only used when focus is on balance, stability, or falling. We recognize that the choice of description provides the reader with a key as to how to 'understand' and interpret the movement, therefore the choice should not rest on what is easy to write or to read, but on what is the essence of the movement.

7.2.   The symbol for center of weight, the focal point of balance in the body, **7a**, shares its basic meaning with the symbol for focal point, as used for focal point of a circle, **7b**, for a partner, **7c**, an object, **7d**, or part of the room, **7e**. Both signs are the same. What the sign refers to can be ascertained from context.[6]

7.3.   The four main categories of C of W indications are:
   - change of level of the C of W, **7f** (see Part III),
   - shift of weight without loss of balance, **7g** (see Part IV),
   - C of W leading, **7h** (see Part V),
   - leaning and falling, **7i** (see Part V).

7.4.   Indications for the C of W are usually placed on the left in the first outside column, as illustrated in **7f**, **7g** and **7i**. However, because the C of W symbol is used, it can appear in *any gesture column* but not in a support column.

Center of Weight Indications

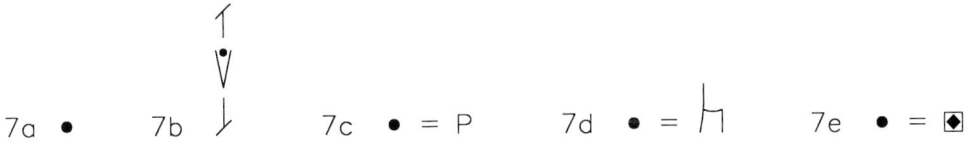

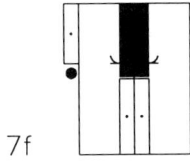

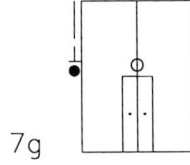

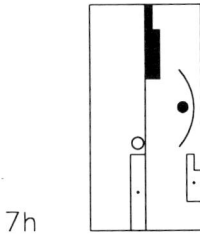

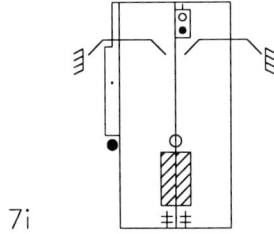

7a •   7b   7c • = P   7d • =   7e • = ◆

7f

7g

7h

7i

III CENTER OF WEIGHT - LEVEL

8 Analysis of Level for Center of Weight

8.1.   Level for the C of W is determined by the spatial relationship of the C of W to the point(s) of support. The degree of level is shown as a destination point, the distance from floor or other supporting object, these latter being the reference point. When the body is in the air, unsupported, no level exists for the C of W.

8.2. In simple rising or lowering of the body, the C of W remains centered over the base of support, i.e. the body remains in balance. The direction of the C of W remains 'place', i.e. on the vertical line; only its level changes.

8.3. In normal standing, the C of W is above the point(s) of support (the feet). It is thus in high level, **8a**. Note that what is place high for the C of W is termed middle level for the leg supports, **8b**.

8.4. The analysis established for sitting is that the C of W is at the same level as the point(s) of support (the sitting bones). Thus in **8c** it is in middle level.[7] As a convention it is also in middle level in a low kneel, **8d**, in a squat, **8e**, and also in a deep lunge, **8f**, since in these configurations the C of W is as close as possible to the point of support.

8.5. In hanging from the ankles, the C of W is below the points of support (the ankles); thus it is in low level, **8g**.

Analysis of Level for Center of Weight

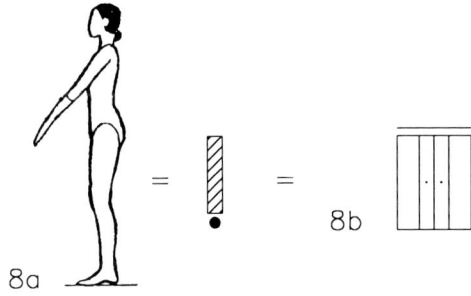

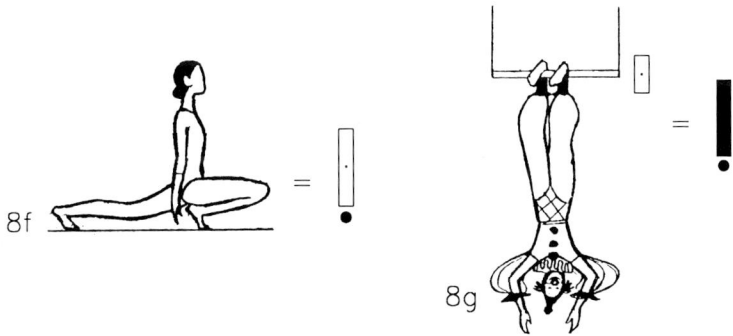

9   Distance from Point(s) of Support

9.1.   In measuring the distance between the C of W and the point(s) of support a 'rule of thumb' convention has been established for practical purposes. It is *not concerned with the exact location of the C of W*. The resulting general statements have sufficed for the needs met in dance, gymnastics, swimming, etc.

9.2.   The body is divided into three lengths.   Ex. **9a** shows that the lengths of the arms, the torso, and the legs are each equated to one so-called 'body-length'.[8]

9.3.   In the normal standing position of **9a** the C of W is one body-length (i.e. the length of the legs) away from the point of support.   The indication of **9b** states that the C of W is one body-length above the point(s) of support, as in **8a**. In **9c** it is one body length below the point of support as in **8g**.

9.4.   Other distances are shown by space measurement presigns based on the usual 6/6 scale.   In the case of the C of W, measurement is related to body-lengths, not to step-length.   The double wide sign, **9d** is used for a distance of 2 lengths, **9e** for $1\frac{1}{2}$ length, **9f** for $\frac{1}{2}$ length and so on (see also Section 10).
(For details on distance measurement see <u>Advanced Labanotation</u> *Kneeling, Sitting, Lying*, Sections 35, 36.   There is additional information in the issue on floorwork and basic acrobatics.)

9.5.   When hanging from the hands, **9g**, the C of W is 2 body-lengths below the point of support, the lengths of the arms and of the torso.   Similarly, in a handstand the distance of the C of W above the point(s) of support is two body-lengths, **9h**.

9.6.   A distance of $1\frac{1}{2}$ lengths occurs, when one is supporting on the elbows, an elbow-stand, as in **9i**.   The same distance occurs, when hanging from the knees, **9j**.

9.7.   In a high kneel, **9k**, the C of W is $\frac{1}{2}$ a body-length from the floor, i.e. half a leg-length.

Distance from Point(s) of Support

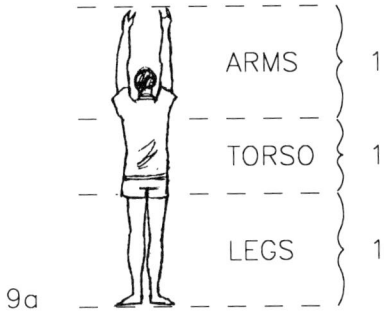

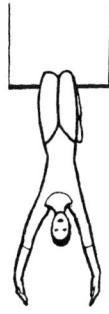

9a

9b 9c 9d 9e 9f

9g 9h 9i 9j

9k

10 Change of Level in Standing

10.1. Between standing and squatting, the lowering and rising of the body on the vertical line may be described in terms of degrees of leg contraction or of the distance of the C of W from the point of support. If the latter description is used, the six degrees of distance measurement correspond with the resulting degrees of leg contraction, as shown in the chart of **10a**.[9] Note that the point at which the heels need to be raised depends on individual ankle flexibility. Use can be made of the 8/8 scale for bending, thus providing additional degrees when needed; the 6/6 scale is the standard, the one generally used.

10.2. When a C of W description is used, reading is facilitated if the general level of support is indicated in the support column, **10b**.[10]

10.3. In **10b** nothing is stated about whether the heels should be raised; some individuals can squat[11] with the whole foot still on the floor. If heels down is required, it should be indicated, **10c**. In lowering from standing, arrival on the ball of the foot occurs at the end of the movement, hence the placement of the hooks in **10d**.[12] Similarly, in **10e** there is no reason to assume the heels lower to the ground, this should be stated, if needed.[13]
Note that, when no loss of balance occurs, change of level for the C of W is written with a 'place' direction symbol.

10.4. The C of W offers a choice of description. If the emphasis is on the action of the legs bending and straightening, contraction symbols are used as in **10f** for a full leg bend (as in a 'deep knee bend'). If concern is with awareness of the center lowering and rising, the C of W description is more appropriate, as for the squat in **10g**.

10.5. If the movement is performed with no particular emphasis either on bending the legs or lowering the weight, the common usage is degree of leg contraction, as in **10f**. In **10h** the C of W rises during two steps from middle level to a level half-way up from the floor in which the legs (i.e. the knees) are 90° bent.

Change of Level in Standing

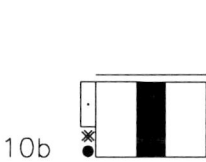

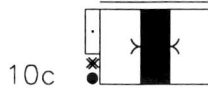

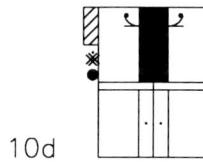

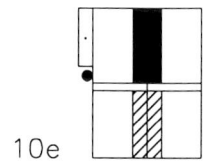

10a

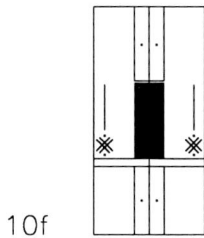

10b   10c   10d   10e

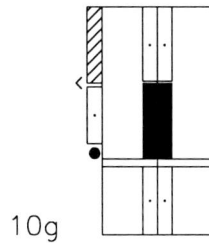

10f   10g   10h

10.6. A high support on the feet, as in **10i**, is understood to be an upward lift of the body as a whole, and not just placement of weight on the balls of the feet. Thus the statement of **10j** would be appropriate in showing this higher distance from the floor of the C of W when performing **10i**. However, the statement of **10j** is commonly used, when supporting on the feet.

10.7. The physical experience in lowering into a full knee bend (a full leg flexion) is just that, a sensation of lowering, going down. This sense of *motion* is not reflected in the notation of **10e** or **10g** because these describe the *destination* of place middle for the C of W.

If wanted, a description of motion downward can be indicated as in **10k** which states approaching the direction down. What is not stated here is the distance, the degree of this motion. Note use of the 'away' cancellation sign, which follows, stating that the previous indication is no longer in effect.

10.8. The motion can also be described as a path sign, as in **10l**, the direction of the progression being straight down.[14] Here again, distance is not stated, the path sign only provides a statement of motion. However, the addition of low level for the legs suggests a lower movement than **10k**. The rising in **10l** is indicated as an upward path (the direction of the progression). Again, how far is not stated, but in **10m** the return to normal standing (place middle symbols) for the supports on the feet conveys the message of a return to the normal place high situation for the C of W.

Change of Level in Standing (continued)

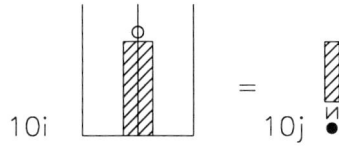

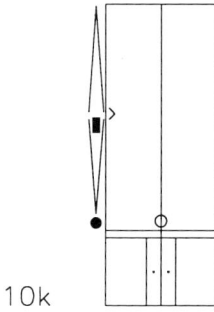

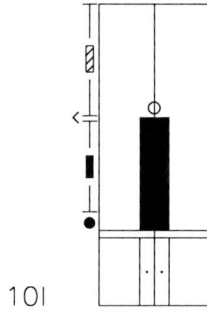

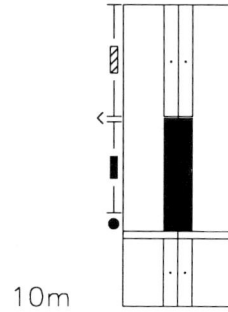

10i   =   10j

10k   10l   10m

11 Kneeling, Sitting and Lying

11.1. **Kneeling.** The recent introduction of angling (ICKL 1983 Technical Report, Appendix A; Hutchinson Guest and van Haarst, 1991) describes level in each possible direction for supporting on the knees. However, should a C of W description be preferable, the following analysis indicates the possible choices. In the 6/6 scale an upright, place high kneel would be indicated as 11.a, being half the leg-length from the point of support. The next stage in lowering is 11.b which produces a 60° angle between thigh and lower leg. A 30° angle results in **11c** with the lowest point being **11d** best described as C of W at place middle, although **11e** is also correct.

11.2. In moving from a high kneel to a low kneel, the physical sensation is of the pelvis (the weight) moving backward and downward. Because of this, the writer may think a backward direction symbol for the C of W would be appropriate. However, because the lower leg is there to provide a support for the balance during this lowering, the C of W is always *above a point of support* (some part of the lower leg) as it lowers. Therefore the direction for the C of W continues to be on the vertical line above a point of support and hence in balance. At the end weight is actually over the feet, but this support, this position, is still called a kneel.

In terms of *motion*, i.e. the direction of progression, lowering from a high kneel to a low kneel is a backward low path for the pelvis, **11f** in terms of *destination*, the body is at an in-balance situation at each moment. Similarly, rising to a high level kneel, as in **11g**, is experienced as a forward upward motion, but each stage is at an in-balance destination point.

11.3. **The 8/8 Scale.** The standard indications for kneeling levels - high, **11g**; middle, **11h**; and low, **11i** - suffice for general use. It should be observed that a middle level kneel, **11h**, illustrated in **11j** has a 45° angle at the knee between the thigh and lower leg. This level is not accounted for in the 6/6 scale of measurement; the 8/8 scale must be used, illustrated in **11k**[15] So, the 45° angle of **11h** could also be written as **11l**.

11.4. **Sitting and Lying.** In sitting, **11m**, or lying, **11n**, the C of W is considered to be *at the point of support*, therefore, if stated, the C of W is written as place middle (see also **8c**). As a rule, this C of W level is not written for sitting and lying, thus **11m** and **11n** would usually be written as **11o** and **11p** respectively.

Kneeling

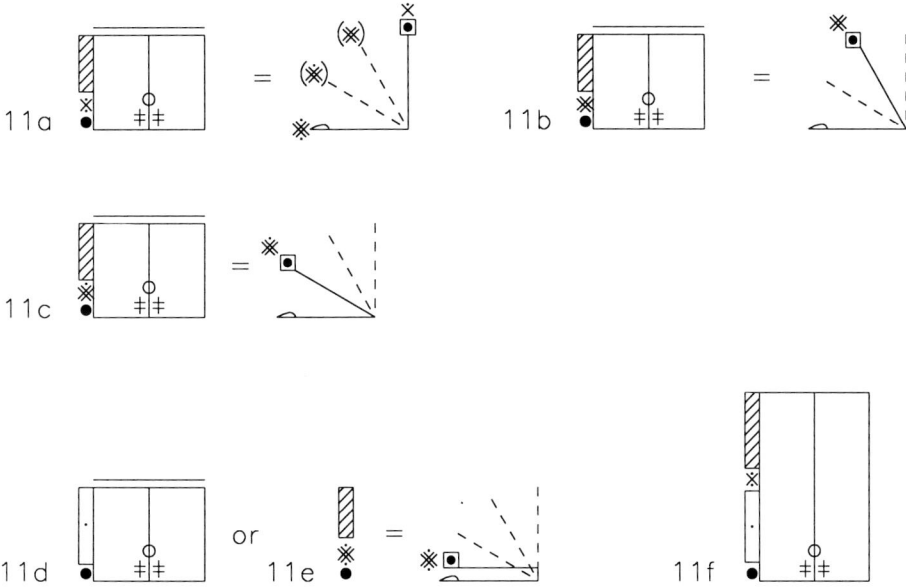

11a   =   11b   =

11c   =

11d   or   11e   =   11f

The 8/8 Scale

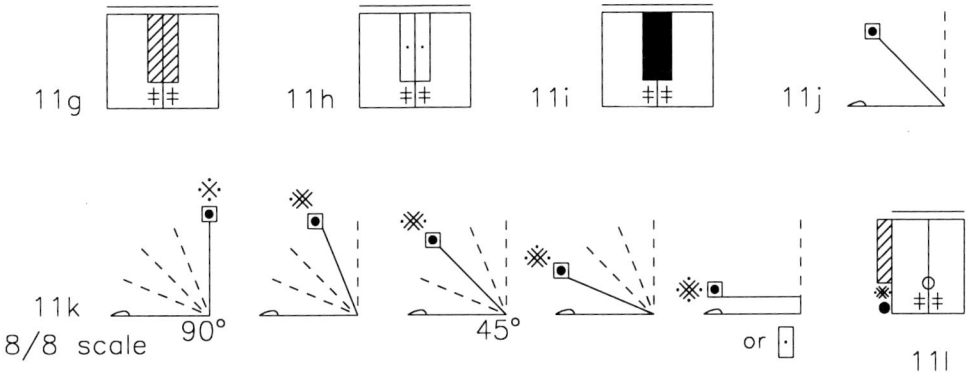

11g   11h   11i   11j

11k
8/8 scale   90°   45°   or   11l

Sitting and Lying

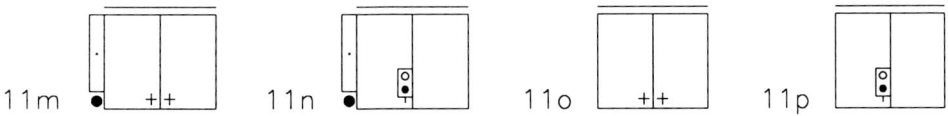

11m   11n   11o   11p

30

12 Level - Validity

12.1. Degrees for low level steps can be indicated by means other than a statement of C of W. Steps which occur after a kneel will be in the indicated level; in **12a** they are normal low steps. Ordinary low level steps occur in **12b** after a lower level start. In **12c** the degree of leg bend is shown to be held; subsequently this is canceled on the third step.

12.2. **Retention of Level.** When a C of W indication is used to indicate level change, it always needs to be specifically canceled.[16] Therefore in **12d** the subsequent steps will remain at the same level (see also **13e**). In **12e** the very small quick jumps are all performed in a low position near the floor, as in a squat (see **8e**); the jumps remain low, the feet only just leaving the ground. The C of W indication is not canceled by a new support indication. In contrast, in **12f** which describes the same movement as **12e** through signs for leg contraction, a retention sign needs to be added in order to retain the low level.

12.3. **Cancellation of Level.** Cancellation of a previous C of W level is as follows: with a place high sign, as in **12g** a back to normal sign, as in **12h** or the cancellation sign of **12i**.[17] In **12j** the last step is still low, hence the standard high level for the C of W is not reached. However, this is not an appropriate application of the back to normal sign.[18] Instead the cancellation sign 'no longer in effect', used in **12i**, is more appropriate. Illustrated in **12k** this shows the last step reverting to standard low level.[19]

12.4. For **12l** the back to normal sign for the C of W is appropriate, because the supports arrive at normal (middle level) standing; but it is not appropriate for **12m** for which the 'away' cancellation is more suitable.

12.5. Starting from a squat, standard low level is achieved as the feet land on count 1 in the series of springs of **12n**. In contrast this cancellation could happen during the first rise into the air, producing a higher spring, as in **12o**.

12.6. The stated middle level C of W, as in **12p**, is not canceled by the high kneel which follows; cancellation must be shown.

Level - Validity

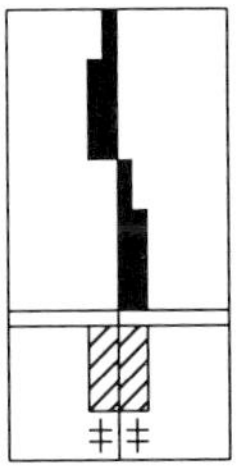

12a

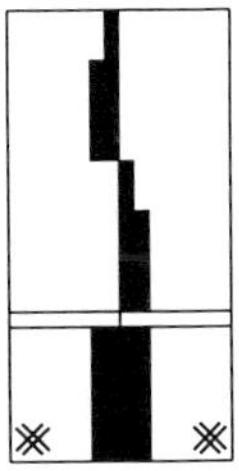

12b

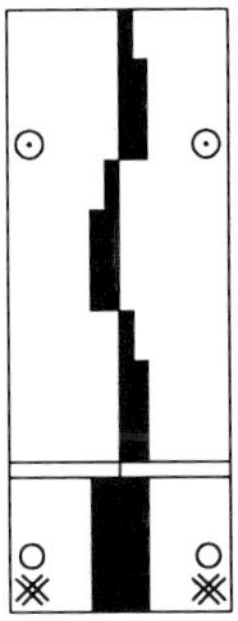

12c

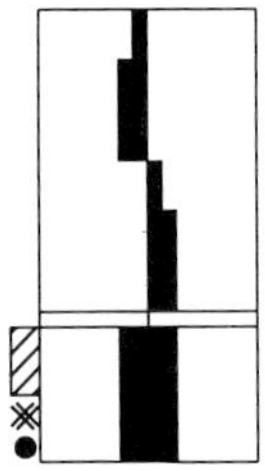

12d

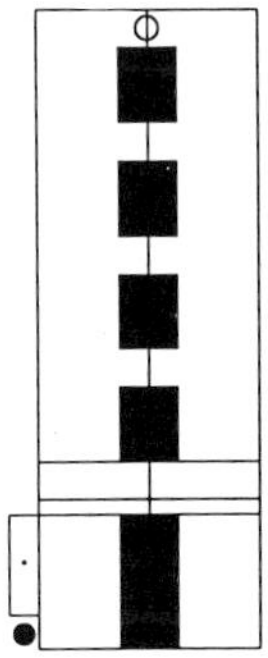

12e

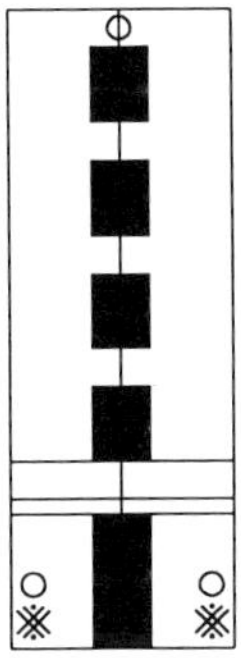

12f

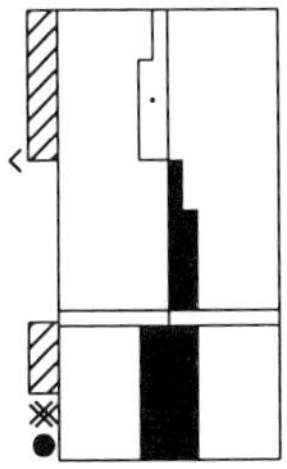

12g

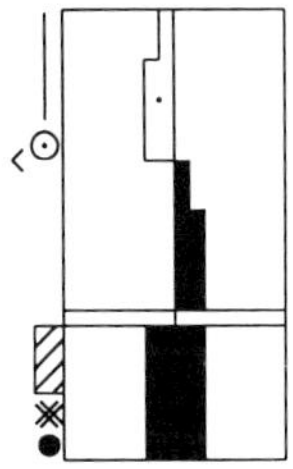

12h

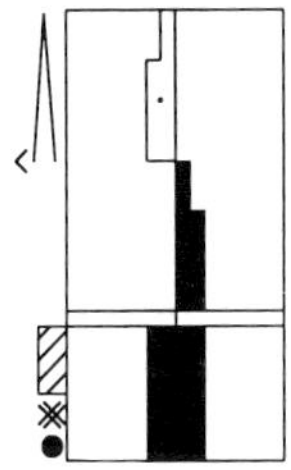

12i

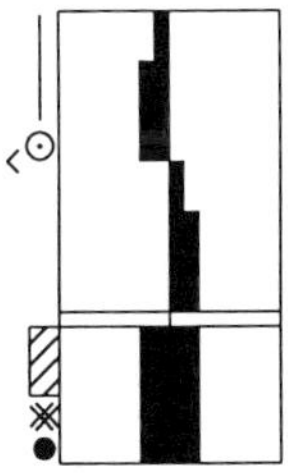

12j

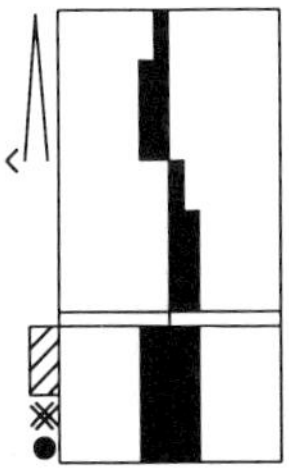

12k

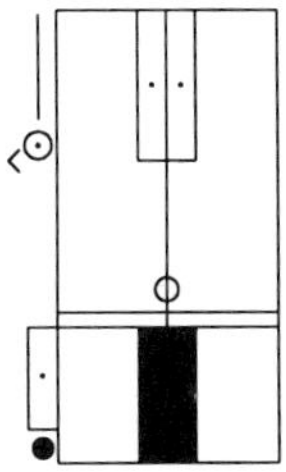

12l

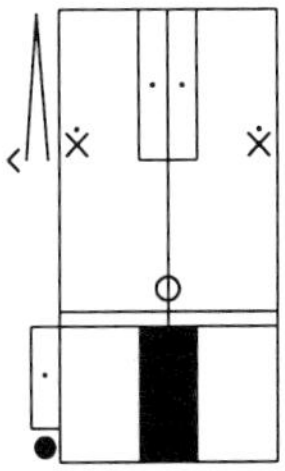

12m

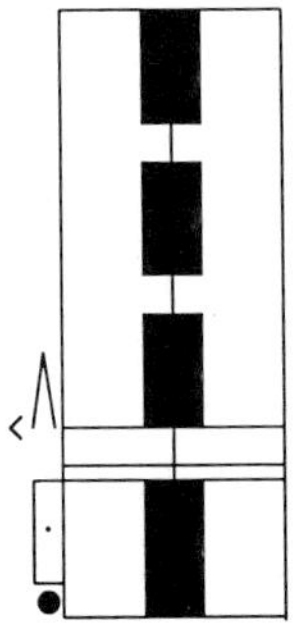

12n

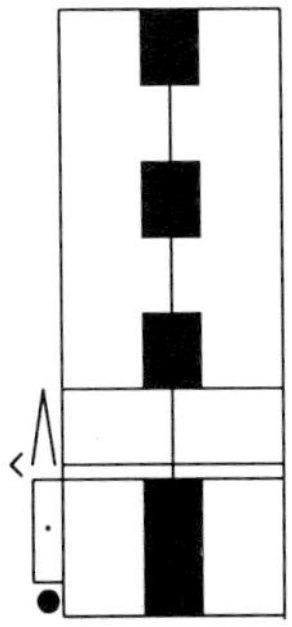

12o

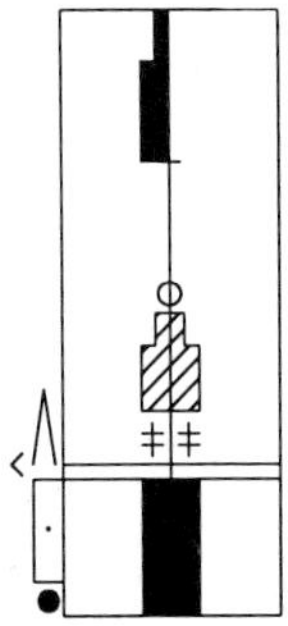

12p

13 Retention Signs for Center of Weight

13.1. The following uses have been established regarding retention symbols for C of W statements. The four retention signs appropriate to C of W indications are: Body Hold **13a**, Space Hold **13b**, Spot Hold **13c**, Standard Retention **13d** (Standard Retention is discussed in 18.25-26). Of these the Body Hold is the most familiar and needs little explanation.

13.2. **Specific Retention of Level.** In **13e**, even though the low C of W level is retained (no cancellation is indicated), it is understood that while the level of these rather low steps is being maintained, they will be performed with natural pliancy, a slight rise and fall resulting from the flexion of the legs and use of the feet. If the C of W is to remain strictly on the same level, i.e. in the same imaginary horizontal plane, this is indicated by placing a hold sign above the C of W symbol. In **13f** the same low level for the C of W is established as in **13e**, but in maintaining the horizontal level, the walking steps must be quite smooth as if on wheels with no rise or fall. The 'body' retention sign here refers to the level of the C of W.

13.3. When no particular level for the C of W has been stated, the retention sign is placed above the C of W sign, **13g**, to show the same strict retention of the established level as in **13f**.

13.4. However, if in examples such as **13g** the natural pliancy normally present in walking and running is to be allowed during the retention of level, the ad lib. sign is added to the hold sign, **13h**. The long low run shown in this example is to be performed with natural pliancy, natural resiliency is allowed while the C of W level is maintained.

13.5. **Retention of Direction in Falling.** A space hold sign is used to retain the direction of falling when turning occurs. Because inertia dictates that once a body is moving in a particular direction it continues on that line, once the body is really falling, the C of W continues in the same direction. In the example of falling shown in **13i**, the person is turning while traveling and falling, thus in relation to that person's front the direction of falling changes, although remaining the same in relation to space. Therefore the space hold sign is used here. The same movement sequence could be written with a Constant Cross direction, as in **13j**. (See also Undeviating Falls, 18.19-22.)

13.6. **Focus on Verticality.** In relation to balance, the awareness of retaining the vertical direction can be indicated with a space hold sign, as in **13k**.[20] Here the first two steps should be consciously vertically in balance, this instruction is canceled on the third step.

Retention Signs for Center of Weight

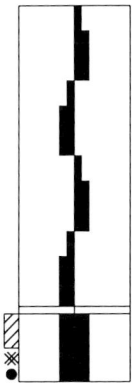
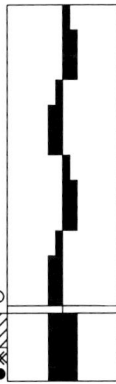
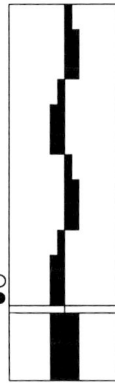
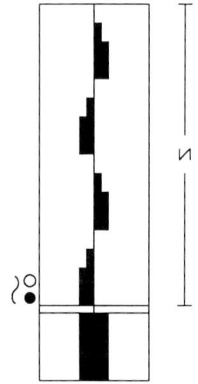

13a   13b   13c   13d

13e   13f   13g   13h

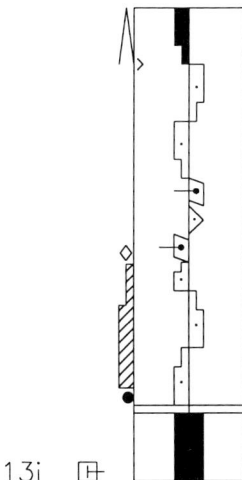
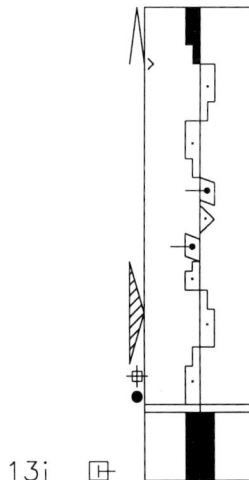
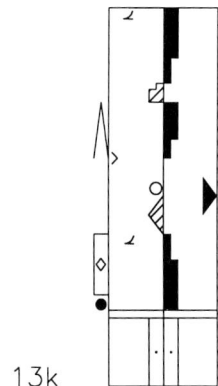

13i ⊞   13j ⊞   13k

13.7. **Retention on the Spot.** If the C of W is to remain at the same spot in space, the sign for retention on the spot ('spot hold') is used. In **13l** the spot hold indicates that the C of W does not shift from side to side during the fast steps. In actual fact weight is not taken totally on each foot, thus the partial supports of **13m** would seem a more truthful description since it indicates that weight is not fully transferred each time. However, **13l** provides the message without the more specific analysis of **13m**. Note that examples of this kind must be performed at sufficient speed for this movement to be possible.

13.8. It is possible to move the feet away briefly from the line of balance, and have the C of W remaining on the same spot. A typical example of this is the Denishawn *pas de basque*,[21] **13n**, in which the steps move sideward while the C of W remains at the same spot, producing a momentary off balance situation. Balance is regained during the low step on the right foot. At this point the retention is canceled; the C of W may move from the spot. Movements of this kind must be performed with a measure of speed, at too slow a pace the C of W retention cannot be maintained. (For cancellation of space holds and of spot holds see 13.12-13.)

13.9. **Retention of Direction - Undeviating Aim.** The centered weight of **13m** can also be performed while traveling. In **13o** the path of the C of W is shown to travel forward on an undeviating path. If the C of W keeps moving in the same horizontal direction without deviating, i.e. if it stays on the same imaginary sagittal line, this is expressed by the retention on the spot sign (spot hold) being placed in the path sign.[22]

13.10. In **13p** high running diagonal steps are shown. Normally, when a person takes such forward diagonal steps, particularly at a fairly slow tempo, the C of W will be displaced laterally, a slight zig-zag path occurs. In **13q** lateral displacement is eliminated by the traveling spot retention for the C of W, written within the direction symbol in the path sign. The C of W remains centered and the whole body smoothly progresses forward.

13.11. Note the difference between the following: **13r** is the simple basic statement of traveling forward; such traveling is of the body-as-a-whole, i.e. traveling of the C of W is understood. Ex. **13s** indicates that the C of W travels forward. Statement of this can be needed while on two, three or four supports. In **13t** while on 'all fours' the C of W makes a path forward, then backward. Note that a body retention sign shows retention of level (i.e. the vertical placement); a space hold (retention in space) is used for directional movements other than on the vertical line, and the spot hold for retention at a spot or for undeviating aim for the path when traveling, as in **13u**.

13.12. **Validity.** *All indications of retention for the C of W have to be specifically canceled.* Cancellation is made by a change to another level, a 'decrease' sign or a return to normal sign, as shown in Section 12. Space holds and spot holds are canceled by one of the signs of **13v**, illustrated in **13n**.

13.13. Cancellation of a body hold for the C of W means that the C of W no longer has to remain on the same level. Cancellation of a space hold means the C of W may now deviate horizontally, i.e. be displaced in a different direction. Cancellation of a spot hold means the C of W may now move from the retained spot. An undeviating aim is canceled at the end of the path.

Retention Signs for Center of Weight (continued)

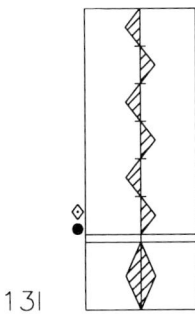

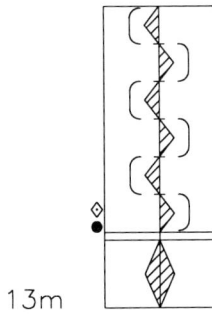

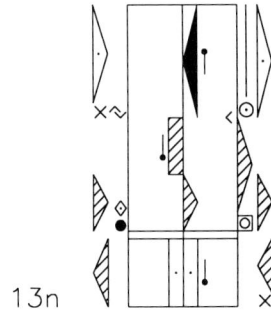

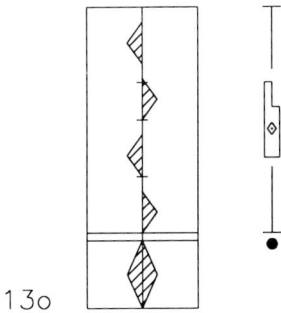

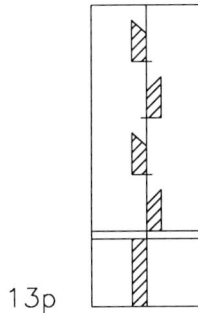

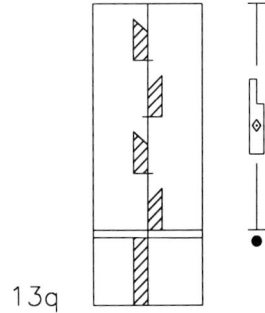

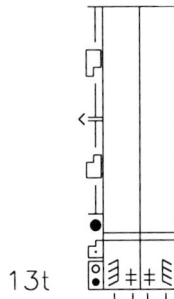

13l	13m	13n
13o	13p	13q
13r	13s	13t	13u	13v

13v: ≈ or ⩰

IV MINOR DISPLACEMENTS

14 Horizontal Weight Shifts

14.1. **Movement Analysis.** Minor horizontal displacements occur when the C of W shifts horizontally in any direction away from its centered vertical line. In most such shifts the C of W usually remains above the base of support; balance is not lost. Such minor horizontal shifts are not to be confused with partial transferences of weight as when completing the weight transference from an open position on two feet to a support on one foot. In this case a new base of support is established and the C of W moves to a point above this new support.

14.2. **Orthography.** Horizontal displacements (shifts) of the C of W are written with middle level pins. In the position of **14a** the weight is shifted forward; in **14b** it is shifted backward.[23] In **14c** the center pin emphasizes that the weight is perfectly centered. The 'centered' pin can also be used to cancel previous shifts. It can also be drawn vertically as in **14d**. Within the range of shifts that are possible without losing balance, these pins do not imply any specific amount.

14.3. The amount of leeway possible in such displacements depends on context and body configuration. In normal standing, as shown, there is more leeway to shift forward than there is backward, because the feet extend forward and can support the weight up to near the end of the toes before falling begins.

14.4. With the feet parallel (pointing forward) a greater degree of sagittal shift is possible while lateral shift is restricted. When the feet are turned out, (pointing sideward) sagittal shifting is restricted, while the lateral range is greater. Supporting on half toe or on *pointe* considerably restricts the possible range of C of W shifting before falling occurs.

14.5. In some positions adjustment of weight placement is needed and occurs naturally to maintain balance. As mentioned earlier, this adjustment is understood and not written (see 4.3). In **14e** the slight backward pelvic shift, illustrated in **14f**, is understood to occur. In this position, keeping the weight forward, often demanded in contemporary dance technique, is written as **14g**, illustrated in **14h**. The written backward shift of the C of W in **14i**, illustrated in **14j**, produces an intentional, more pronounced backward shift than in **14f**.

14.6. In **14k** the weight shift pattern describes a circle. Such adjustments of the C of W are not to be confused with shifts of the pelvis, **14l**. In the latter the pelvis will 'bulge' out of its natural alignment in the body. In **14m** weight is shifted following a figure-8 pattern (as viewed from above). This is written with a design path for the C of W. It is achieved by flexibility in the legs and feet; the parts of the torso must remain in their normal alignment.[24]

Note that the movement of **14m** should not be confused with a design path for the pelvis, **14n**. In the latter, the pelvic area will move out of alignment with the rest of the torso, a familiar action when working with a hula-hoop. (See the Advanced Labanotation issue *Shape, Design, Trace Patterns*.)

Horizontal Weight Shifts

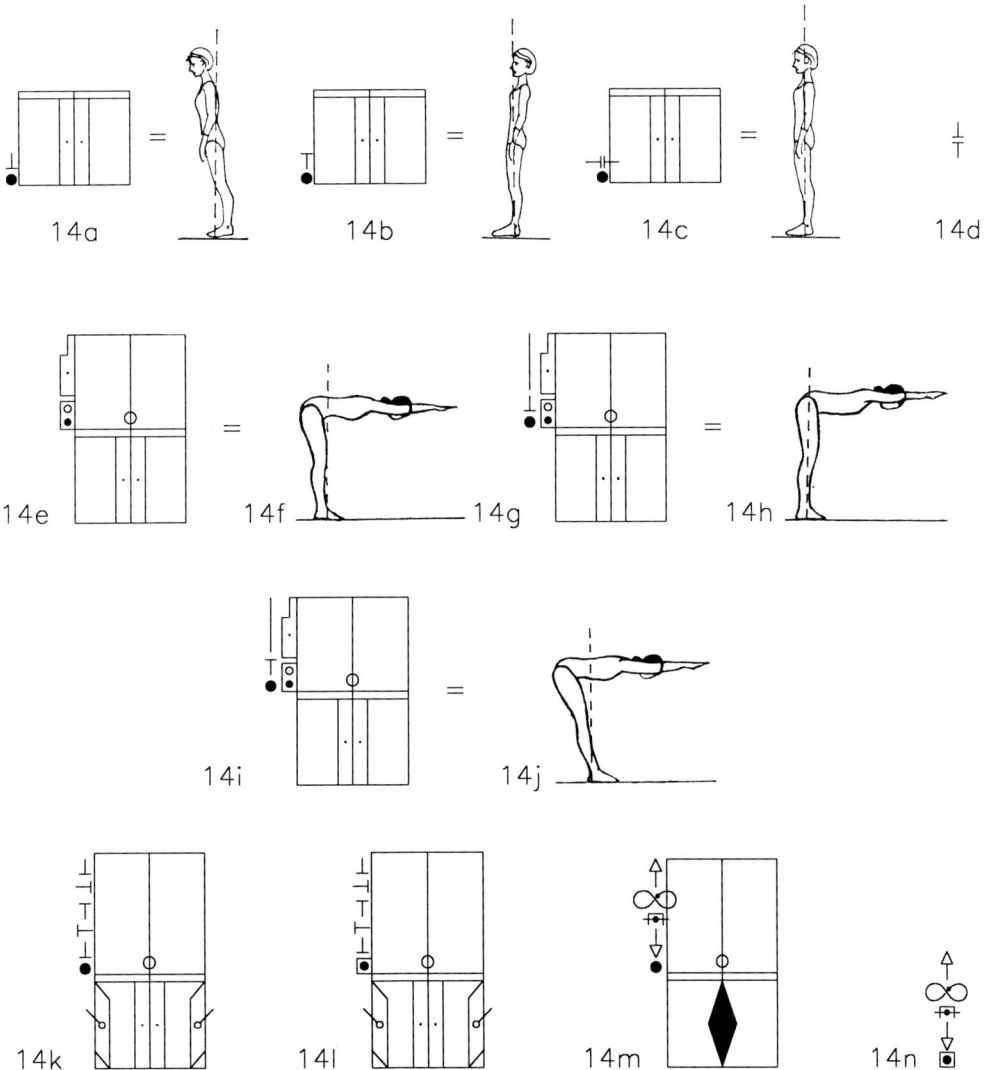

14a   14b   14c   14d

14e   14f   14g   14h

14i   14j

14k   14l   14m   14n

14.7. **Duration.** Indications for weight shifting such as in **14o** are in themselves small and denote quick, although not accented movement. If accented, it would be written as **14p**. A slower movement can be indicated by adding a duration line, **14q**.[25] The weight shift starts where the C of W symbol appears and is completed at the end of the duration line. In this example it overlaps, and is a continuation of, the stepping into *plié* towards the left side. Instead of being centered in 2nd position, the weight is slightly more to the left.

14.8. **Cancellation.** Any displacement of the C of W should be specifically canceled by an indication in the same column (see 12.3-6). The usual options for cancellation exist. The sideward shift of **14q** is canceled in **14r** by a return to normal symbol, in **14s** by the indication for centered weight, in **14t** by the 'away' sign and in **14u** by a new indication for the C of W. In **14v** a forward walk with the weight displaced to the left is followed by a spring forward on both feet. While in the air the weight displacement is canceled using an 'away' indication.[26]

14.9. **Point of Reference.** The point of reference for such displacements indicated by pins is the center point where the weight is centered over the base of support. In **14u** the second indication means that the weight shifts *beyond* the centered position to the other side; it does not mean that, from the position reached after the first shift, the weight returns to where it was at the start. The latter movement is written as **14r**, **14s** or **14t**.

14.10. **Size.** As pointed out earlier, the amount of possible weight shift into any direction depends on the particular context and body shape. As mentioned in 14.2, the pin indications do not imply any specific amount of shift, as long as the C of W does not move beyond the base of support. It is possible to be more specific about the size of a shift by adding measurement signs before the pins. These symbols are a general rather than exact specification.[27]

14.11. Ex. **14w** means a large shift of weight forward; **14x** a very large shift forward; **14y** a small, and **14z** a very small shift forward. These are relative statements in that the greatest distance possible will depend on the size of the base of support at any given moment, hence a large shift in one context may be much smaller than in another. The amount of actual shift also depends on the direction of the shift and the shape and size of the base of support. When on 'all fours' weight shift can be greater. Such shifts are often better written as a path for the C of W, as in **13t**, rather than by using the appropriate displacement pins.

14.12. For a series of shifts the indication of size can be placed in an addition bracket. Reference to space is specified by placing the measurement sign in a diamond. Thus, **14aa** indicates that all shifts are to be very small.[28]

14.13. **System of Reference.** Direction for horizontal C of W displacements is according to Standard Stance, i.e. when the body is twisted, 'forward' for these movements is in the same direction as 'forward' for the untwisted part of the body. In standing this is usually the feet.

Duration

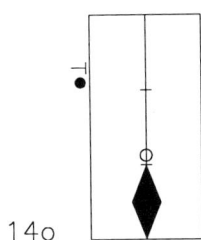

14o

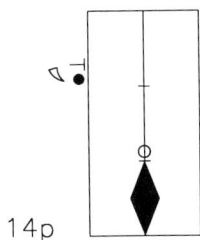

14p

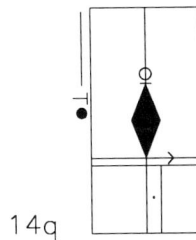

14q

Cancellation

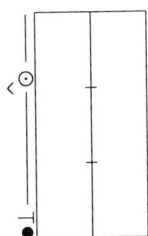

14r

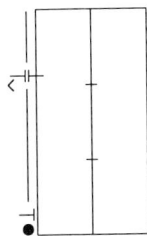

14s

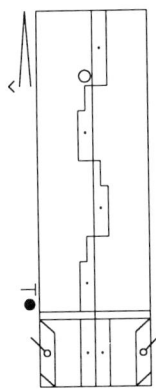

14t

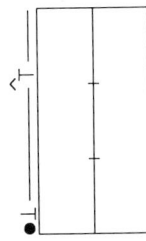

14u

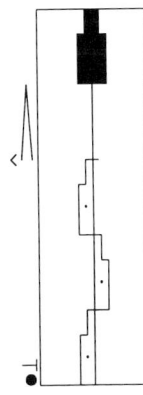

14v

Size

14w   14x   14y   14z   14aa

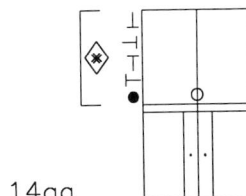

14.14. **Weight Placement in Skating.** As a general rule weight is carried more forward than normal when ice skating. This can be stated in a key at the start of the score, as in **14ab** which shows a typical starting position for skating. Figure Skating is correctly accomplished not on the blade as a whole but on the outer or inner edge, either side of the center groove. Use of these edges is achieved through leaning, slight changes in weight placement of the unit of torso to foot, and not through lateral flexion in the ankle.

14.15. In the skating example of **14ac**, the initial push-off is achieved through the pressure backward on the inside of the left skate which provides the impetus for traveling. At the same time the right supporting leg bends; it then straightens as the whole body travels forward on a clockwise curved path. The C of W shifts to the right at the start of this movement. The free leg then comes into place to be ready for the push-off motion, which starts the counterclockwise curved path. The C of W shifts to the other side as the 'step' (push-off) occurs on the other foot, the path now being counterclockwise.

14.16. For a more compact statement, the traveling can be written in the support columns, the level of the support being shown with flexion or extension signs in the leg gesture columns. In **14ad** weight remains on the right leg and the change to circling the other way is assisted by the change of weight placement. The size of weight shift is shown here, the statement in the bracket placed next to the shift stating spatially very small. Note the left leg gesture with a 'swing' forward as the counterclockwise circling nears its end. Placement of arms and general body configuration can help in achieving correct weight placement.[29]

Weight Placement in Skating

14ab

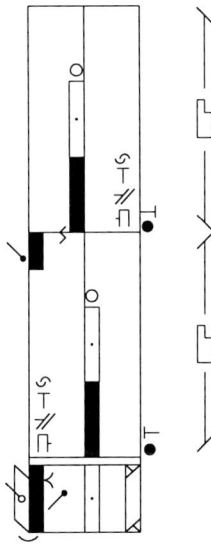

14ac

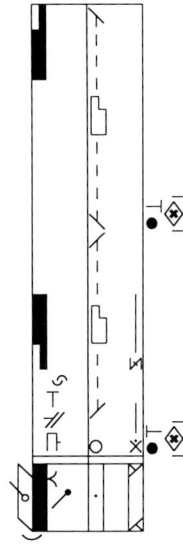

14ad

15 Minor Vertical Displacements

15.1. **Bouncing.** Minor vertical displacements of the C of W are common in many forms of dance, especially in quick repeated up-down movements ('bouncing'). The pin for 'below' denotes a slight 'dip' downward of the C of W and the 'above' pin the same movement upward.[30]

15.2. In **15a** there is a downward 'bounce' at the start of each step. Note the device of the double horizontal stroke to exclude the C of W symbol from the timing of the first pin.[31] In **15b** the downward displacement comes just before the step is taken resulting in an upward movement at the start of the step - quite a different result and expression from the previous example.

15.3. In **15c** a slight lift occurs on each count. A return to center is shown each time in **15d**, an 'away' sign in **15e**.

15.4. The bouncing actions of **15a** and **15b** will mainly take place through relaxed reaction in the ankles, knees and hip joints, but the sense, the feeling, is of the body center being displaced. These actions can also be described through flexion signs for the legs. While in **15c** focus is on lifting and lowering in general, if focus is to be on lifting and lowering of the heels, the sequence can better be described by indicating the specific use of the supporting parts of the feet, as in **15f**. Note that theoretically, a caret should be added before each pin sign to state that the C of W presign is to continue. In a context like this, which is so obvious, the cumbersome repetition of the carets can be omitted.

15.5. **Point of Reference.** The direction expressed by the pins discussed here is *judged from what the level of the C of W would be without modification by pin signs.* In other words, in **15a** the effect of the second pin (the first upward displacement) is not just to cancel out the result of the first pin, but to rise above the level of the C of W in the starting position. If return to the established level is desired, **15d** would be the correct statement. Note use of the cancellation sign in **15e**; this provides a less precise statement than **15d** (as well as a difference in timing). (For validity see Section 12.)

15.6. The C of W in **15a** will end above its expected level. If return to middle level is desired, a cancellation is needed, written by replacing the last pin by a 'centered' sign, as in **15d**, or an 'away' sign, as in **15e**.

15.7. **Duration, Size, Cancellation.** In the same way as for horizontal weight shifts, more specific statement can be made of *duration* (see **14q**) and *size* (see **14w-14z**) of bouncing movements, although this is not often required.

15.8. A temporary displacement can be written in a 'passing state' bow, as in **15g**; the slight lowering occurs and then disappears. Ex. **15h** is a similar statement, but the timing is uneven - a faster lowering and slower recovery.

Minor Vertical Displacements

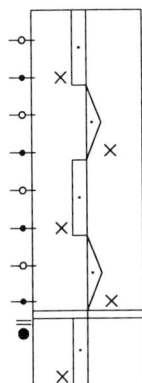

15a

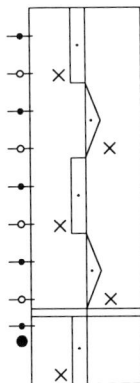

15b

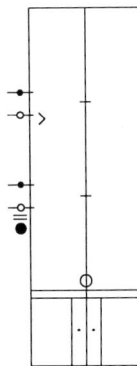

15c

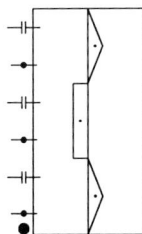

15d

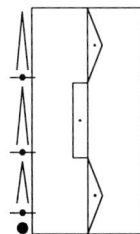

15e

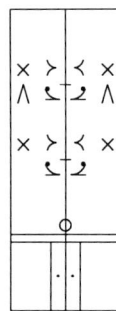

15f

15g

15h

15.9. **Center of Weight Levels in Springing Actions.** During an ordinary spring in which the body is propelled upward, away from the ground, as the legs leave the ground the whole body (including the C of W) moves upward, and then on the landing moves downward to the level of the landing. This is true even for small springs, such as **15i** and **15j**, in which there is a natural upward and downward resilience. In contrast to this, in certain folk dances the small spring may have only a downward displacement or only an upward displacement.[32]

15.10. **'Downward' Spring.** For this type of spring the vertical downward displacement of the C of W is the focus. In such a 'downward' spring, the performer's C of W does not move upward on 'take-off', as is usual with the release of weight from the feet/foot. This type of spring occurs when the C of W is shown to approach downward, as stated in **15k**. In the small spring of **15l**, from the start the C of W action is downward. Because this action is swift, the small double horizontal line is used to separate the C of W sign from the action.

15.11. **'Upward' Spring.** In a comparable way only an upward displacement for the C of W will occur in an upward spring. This displacement is shown in **15m**. Starting with bent legs in **15n**, there is no downward preparation, the small spring takes the C of W directly upward to a position with stretched legs. The sequence of **15o** includes an 'upward' spring followed by a 'downward' spring.

15.12. **Direction of Progression.** This type of displacement for the C of W could also be described as *the direction of progression*. This is indicated by placing an arrow within a direction symbol, as in **15p**. This arrow has the same meaning as when it is used on a floor plan, i.e. the path of the movement in space. By combining this arrow with the 'below' pin, the small downward progression (the downward path) can be expressed, **15q**.[33] The arrow may be placed at either end of an 'above' or 'below' pin, **15r**, it is the pin itself which gives the direction. An upward progression can be stated as **15s**. This usage is less space consuming than the V sign for 'approaching'. Ex. **15t** shows **15o** written with this device. Because this usage of showing the direction of progression (the path) is generally unfamiliar, it should be glossarized.

Center of Weight Levels in Springing Actions

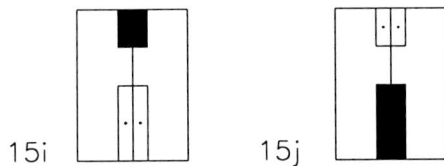

15i　　　　　15j

'Downward' Spring

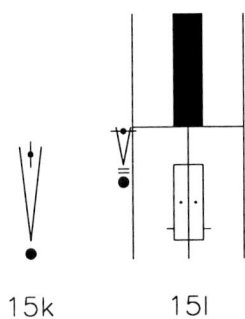

'Upward' Spring

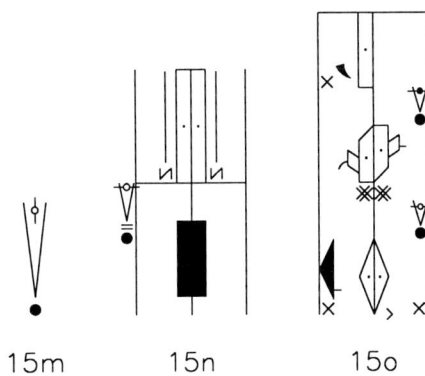

15k　　　15l

15m　　　15n　　　15o

Direction of Progression

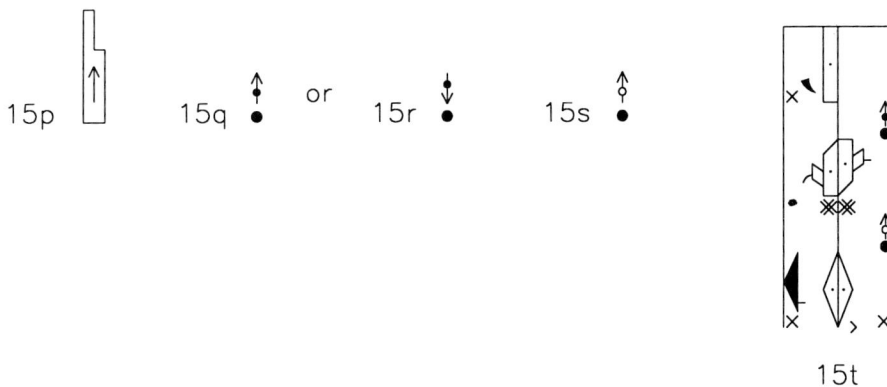

15p　　　15q　or　15r　　　15s

15t

15.13. **'Keep Level' Spring.** Retaining the level of the C of W during small springs is familiar from *terre à terre*[34] footwork, such retention of the vertical level being shown by use of an ordinary hold sign as in **15u**, a long established usage (see 13.3).

15.14. **Release of Weight.** A movement which involves the C of W but is not written in such terms is the lifting action in which weight is released from the support(s) but contact with the floor is not lost. Use of the ordinary release sign, **15v**, or **15w**, means that the feet leave the floor very slightly, contact is lost. The angular release sign, **15x**, derived from the angular horizontal support bow, signifies the release of support, i.e. release of weight.[35] Therefore in **15y** the weight is lifted from the feet while contact with the floor is maintained. A similar action occurs in **15z** where weight is lifted momentarily from the right foot. (See also the <u>Advanced Labanotation</u> issue on floorwork and basic acrobatics.)

'Keep Level' Spring

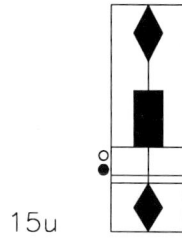

15u

Release of Weight

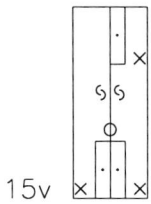

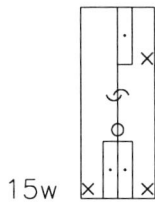

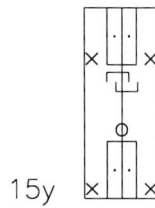

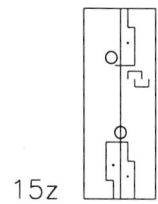

15v   15w   15x ⌐⌐ or ⌐⌐   15y   15z

16 Other Weight Shift Descriptions

16.1. It should be observed that weight placement is an integral feature of Labanotation and is represented by the presence of support and gesture columns. Therefore, shifting the body weight can often be described without the C of W symbol, as discussed in Section 6. We explore here the minor sideward shifts in normal standing, written as **16a**, in which the weight is centered over one foot while the other retains whole foot contact with the floor.

16.2. Ex. **16b** shows that weight is transferred onto the balls of the feet: but without the heels lifting, the whole foot is still contacting the floor. Ex. **16b** can also be written with duration lines in the support column, as in **16c**. These lines indicate the gradual transition to weight on the balls of the feet.

16.3. In **16d**, while in a low 2nd position the right leg has the motion of flexing, while the left leg has the motion of stretching, this movement is then reversed. The result is a weight shift more to the right foot, then to the left. The degree of C of W displacement is not known, nor is the degree of flexion or extension of the legs; the movement focuses on actions (but not destinations) of the legs. In the movement of **16e**, the weight is transferred to the right foot, but the left foot remains with the whole foot touching the floor. This action is a complete transference of weight, i.e. beyond the category of minor weight shifts.

16.4. Degree of weight shared also affects placement of the C of W. In **16f** the left foot bears half of the weight it was previously carrying in the starting position, i.e. a quarter of the body weight. The releasing of only half of its share of weight is expressed by combining the statements of gesture and support. The result is that more weight is shifted to the right. This movement is a less complete version of the weight shift of **16e** (see also 20.2).

16.5. Finer detail of weight distribution can be expressed by using inclusion bows. In **16g** the left foot is shown to retain $3/4$ of its initial share of the weight ($3/8$ of the weight is on the left and $5/8$ on the right foot). The statement is that the left foot frees itself of a small part of its share of weight. The expression used is that the left support includes 'gesture quality'.

16.6. In **16h** weight is almost completely transferred to the right foot but the left retains $1/4$ of its initial share ($1/8$ of the weight is on the left foot).

Other Weight Shift Descriptions

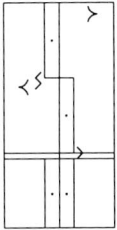

16a

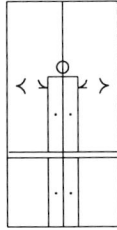

16b

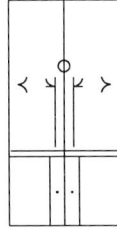

16c

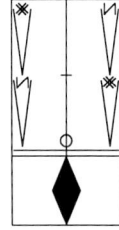

16d

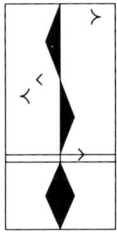

16e

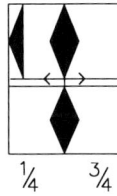

$\frac{1}{4}$ $\frac{3}{4}$

16f

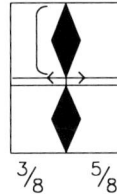

$\frac{3}{8}$ $\frac{5}{8}$

16g

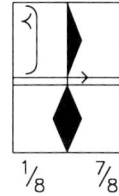

$\frac{1}{8}$ $\frac{7}{8}$

16h

V FALLING

17 Center of Weight 'Leading', Momentary Loss of Balance

17.1. If the C of W (balance) moves beyond the supporting base in the direction of the next transference of weight, momentary loss of balance occurs. Balance is, however, immediately recovered with the next support. The experience is not so much that of falling but of the body weight going ahead, 'leading' the movement. This is written by placing the C of W symbol in a curved vertical bow, **17a**, comparable to the way of writing 'leading with the wrist' etc. (For falling see Section 18.)

17.2. In ordinary walking it is understood that the body is set in motion just before the beginning of a step. In walking forward from standing on both feet, the weight is released from the leg that is about to step to allow it to make a minimal preparatory gesture. The C of W is then displaced into the direction of the step (here forward), even before the heel touches the floor. In **17b** the arrow indicates approximately the moment the right leg moves forward and the body weight starts moving in the direction of the step.

17.3. To indicate that the C of W is to be in motion sooner and to show the timing of this motion, the symbol of **17a** is used. In **17c** the weight begins to move in the direction of the step at the beginning of the bow. The end of the bow slightly overlaps the direction symbol, thus connecting this action to the step. In **17d** the process of C of W moving to the new support is slower; this requires control, the center moving through a forward shift to slight loss of balance.

17.4. A *tombé* is the balletic term for a slight falling onto a new support. It occurs intentionally, precipitating a fall into the new support. This movement, which often occurs from a high support, can also be thought of as 'C of W leading' and can be written as in **17e**.

17.5. Context determines to what extent these movements will be experienced as 'falls' rather than C of W leading. In **17c** loss of balance is hardly noticeable even though the emphasis is on weight displacement. In contrast **17e** is experienced as a slight fall because of the change from high to low level and the comparatively large distance to be covered.

17.6. Observe where loss of balance begins: in **17e** the right leg moves to side low before the body weight is displaced. In **17f** the body weight begins to lead into the long backward step before the right leg gesture has reached its destination.

17.7. The indication of **17a** is self-cancelling: it lasts from the beginning until the end of the bow and has no effect beyond that point.

Center of Weight 'Leading', Momentary Loss of Balance

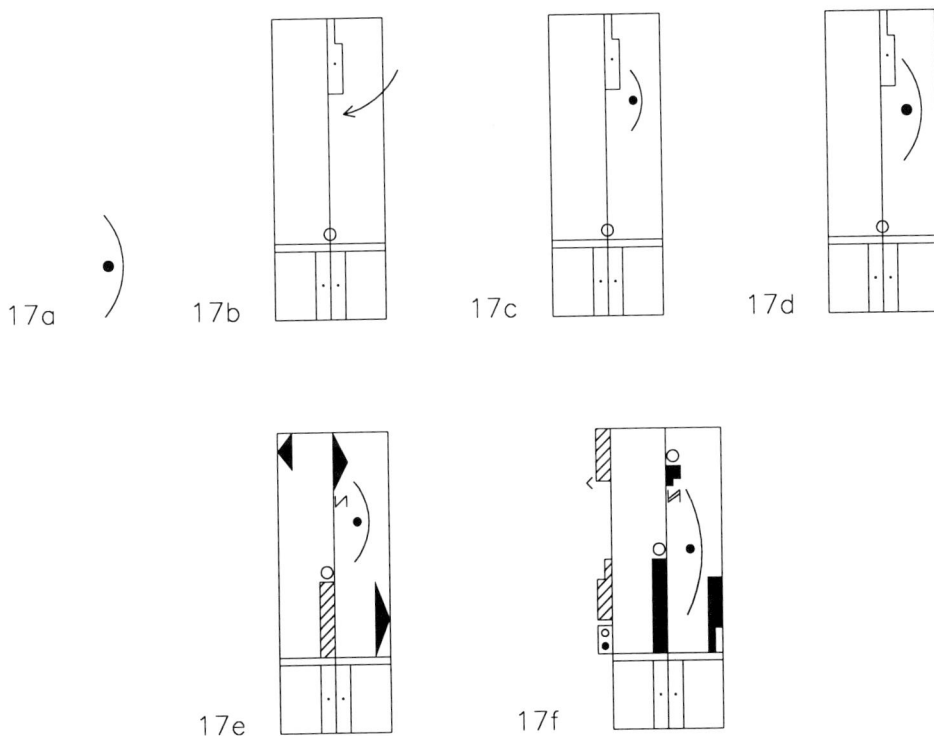

17a   17b   17c   17d

17e   17f

18 Loss of Balance, Falling

18.1. **Orthography.** Falling, a distinct loss of balance, is indicated by *the C of W sign followed by a direction symbol other than a 'place' symbol.* Such directional indications are used only for states of imbalance. A 'place' direction symbol for the C of W indicates that the C of W is over a support and hence is in a state of balance.

18.2. Falling has a distinct quality and a particular intention. Balance is completely lost, there is at least a moment of total surrender to gravity. In all falling movements written with the C of W sign, this is experienced by the performer and clearly noticeable for the observer.[36]

18.3. Direction and level for the C of W in falling is judged in relation to the point(s) of support, middle level being the supporting surface, usually the floor but it could be a chair, table, or a partner's shoulder (see Section 8). From standing, a high level direction for the C of W, forward-high, for example, indicates movement away from the line of balance, but still above the level of support. 'Forward middle' is, therefore, forward of and on the same level as the point(s) of support, i.e. falling forward to the floor or other supporting surface.[37]

18.4. Fig. **18a** shows the eight principal directions for the C of W in the sagittal plane, when supporting on the feet. The dotted line indicates the horizontal level of support, usually the floor.

18.5. Because this section is concerned with situations where support is on a horizontal floor, low level directions for the C of W sign are not being discussed. They apply when writing movement while hanging from the hands, elbows, feet or knees.

18.6. When the body falls to the floor the C of W lowers to middle level. Ex. **18b**, illustrated in **18c**, shows a backward fall onto the hips (buttocks). This simple notation statement has no built-in distance; statement of specific distances will be discussed in 18.13-18.[38]

18.7. To avoid discomfort, falling to the floor is usually partly controlled by counterbalancing and by taking the weight on one body part or another, such as the hands or feet. In the case of falling from kneeling, a high kneel allows for a marked falling action, as in **18d**. In the illustration of **18e** the hands are shown to take weight just before the whole torso supports on the floor. Catching the weight to minimize the effect of the fall is written in **18f**; here the hands take weight only in passing and so the 'taking weight' bow is extended out to the floor, indicated by the letter T (*terra*) in a box. Often this indication of floor is omitted, since it is understood.

Loss of Balance, Falling

Orthography

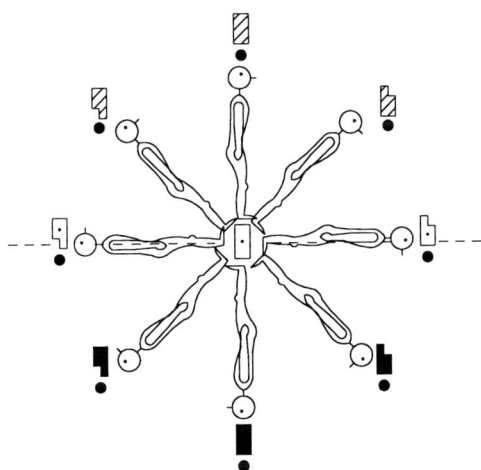

18a

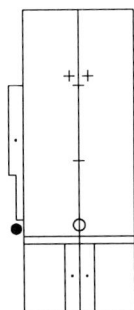

18b

18c

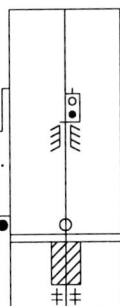

18d

18e

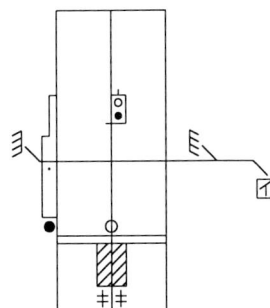

18f

18.8.   In **18g** the forward fall is caught by a lunge on the right foot. The place middle direction for the C of W at the end indicates that the body has regained balance and is as low as possible over the right foot, illustrated in **18h**.

Note that in **18g** 'place middle' is an approximation. It means the C of W is as close to the floor as possible in this configuration. It is, of course, possible to lose balance from here, falling, for example, to the side onto the hip from where no further falling is possible. The same kind of middle level approximation is seen when the 'place middle' symbol is used to write a low crouch or squat.

18.9.   In the more detailed example of **18i**, which starts in a squat, the performer falls into the right diagonal backward direction on count 3 and ends supporting on the corresponding chest surface. This fall occurs smoothly because the right arm helps by extending in the direction of the fall and taking some weight before the weight passes from the right hip (sitting bone) onto the diagonal surface of the pelvis and then the chest. At the end the legs and left arm move into the air. No cancellation is needed for the C of W, as the body-as-a-whole cannot fall any farther. This is true also for **18j**.

18.10.   Ex. **18j** is similar but more difficult to perform. Suddenly, from a squat, the body falls forward onto the knees, the front of the pelvis and the chest. The performer needs to be flexible, push the pelvic area forward and curve the torso backward for a smoother fall.

18.11.   **Other Ways of Writing.** The fact of falling can be written using directional statements with signs for body sections. Ex. **18f** can be written as **18k**, the direction for the unit of knees to chest being stated; similarly, **18g** can be written as **18l**, which shows the unit ankles-to-chest moving to forward high and the unit waist-to-chest returning upright as weight is caught on the right foot. To be the counterpart of **18g**, the degree of knee bend needs to be added to the concluding step. Note that these different descriptions provide a difference in movement idea which is reflected in the manner of performance. Stating the C of W, combined with a direction symbol other than 'place', gives the message that the thrust of the movement is to fall. Use of body sections provides focus on manner of holding the body.

18.12.   **Level of Falling - Degree of Precision.** In falling to the floor the level of falling reaches middle level. As a rule, high level occurs when the weight is 'caught' by a chair, table, or a partner, and when falling as far as the floor is avoided. In these cases the height of the object determines the level of falling, and an exact level is usually not stated.

Loss of Balance, Falling (continued)

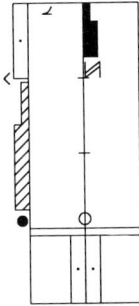

18g

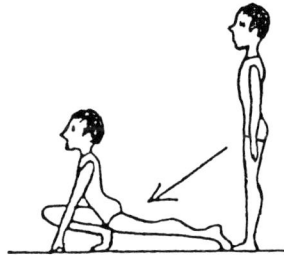

18h

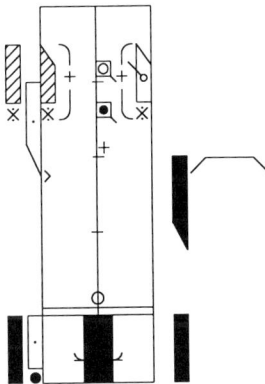

18i

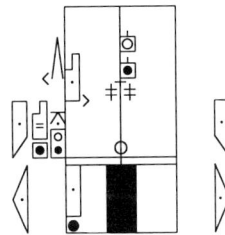

18j

Other Ways of Writing

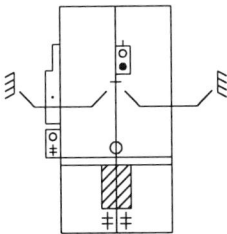

18k

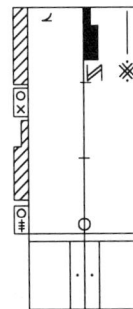

18l

18.13. **Distance of Falling.** In some examples, as in **18b**, distance of
falling is *unspecified*.[39] Specific statement of distance in falling can be made by
using measurement signs as presigns for the C of W sign. The distance stated is
that between the location of the C of W and the starting point(s) of support
('place'). Note that the degree of measurement stated is the same as would be
used to indicate the resulting leg flexion when falling is concluded.

18.14. The chart of **18m** shows the direction symbols and measurement
signs to indicate the destination of the C of W in falling backward from a
balanced standing position. The measurement signs showing distance equate to
the contraction of the legs. Distance may be shown through other means, as in
18l in which the tilt of the unit of ankles-to-chest causes a fall and the distance of
the lunging step provide a clear statement.

18.15. Ex. **18n**, illustrated in **18o**, shows 'falling' to sit, or rather lean,
against the back of a chair; if the chair were not there a complete fall would have
occurred. At the end of the movement, the legs are one degree bent and weight
is partly on the hips supported by the chair. Note the use of horizontal staples at
the start of this example. They indicate that the Inner Subsidiary Column (ISC)
is to be used as an extra support column. (See the Advanced Labanotation issue
on floorwork and basic acrobatics for additional columns.)

18.16. Ex. **18p** describes almost the same movement, with the important
difference that no particular falling occurs. Lowering is controlled by a brief
forward torso tilt, while the pelvis shifts backward. Sitting is shown to be with
the legs two degrees bent. The exact displacement depends here of course on the
height and location of the chair.

18.17. Ex. **18q**, illustrated in **18r**, shows falling into a low comfortable
chair. After landing the legs will be four degrees bent.

18.18. Ex. **18s** is the specific notation of a full length backward fall to the
floor; the hips arrive a full leg-length backward, shown by the neutral sign of
neither bent nor stretched. This fall, known as a 'prat fall', is illustrated in **18t**.
An alternate way of writing a comparable backward fall is given in **18u**, here the
C of W is leading into a backward sit. No distance is indicated in this
description.

Distance of Falling

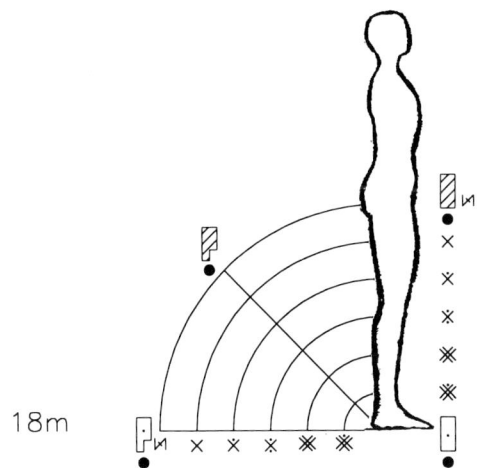

18m

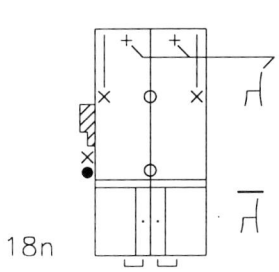

18n

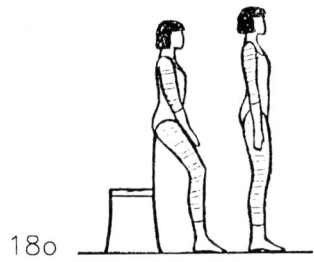

18o

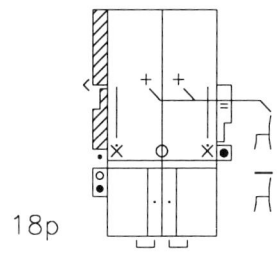

18p

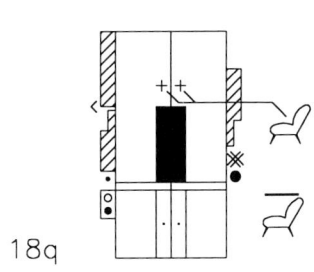

18q

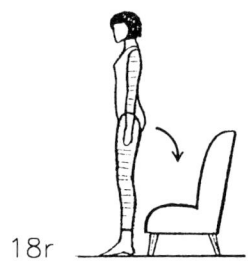

18r

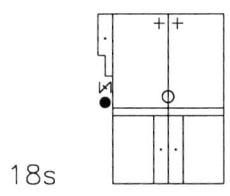

18s

18t

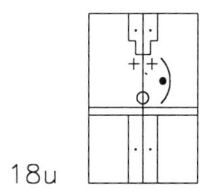

18u

18.19. **Undeviating Falls.** When, in spite of a turn of the body, the direction of falling is undeviated, a space hold is placed within the indication for falling. This use of the space hold corresponds exactly to the standard way of writing undeviating leg and arm gestures during turns. In **18v** the fall starts forward and, following the law of inertia, continues into that spatial direction even though the body has turned. A sideward step catches the weight, and falling is canceled.

18.20. Ex. **18w** is a schematic description of dancer A 'fainting' and being caught by B. The body keeps falling into what was the forward direction before the turn, and, in this example, A ends falling backward. Note the double circle sign for 'each one' used at the start to state that they are facing each other.

18.21. Undeviating falls, as with any other falling indication, can extend over several transferences of weight. If the fall of **18x** is a real, uncontrolled loss of balance, then strictly the turning action would not influence the spatial direction of the fall. However, use of the space hold is a helpful specification. Compare with **13i**.

18.22. In **18y** a movement similar to **18x** is shown as revolving on a straight path, the body keeps falling into the same direction, which is forward at the beginning and backward at the end. The weight is caught by the third backward step. There is a logical relationship between the increased loss of balance and the increased speed of the steps.

18.23. **System of Reference.** If the body is twisted, directions for falling indications are the same as directions for the untwisted part of the body, i.e. the Stance Key is used when standing on the feet. In **18z** the torso is twisted to the left, the steps and the falling action are toward the audience.

18.24. The direction of undeviating falling can also be described by using a Constant Key for the direction. Ex. **13j** is an example of this.

Undeviating Falls

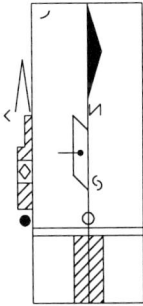

18v

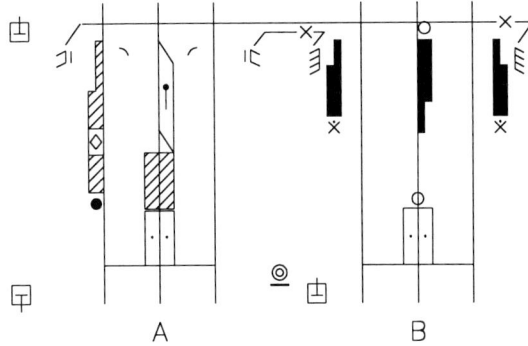

A   B

18w

System of Reference

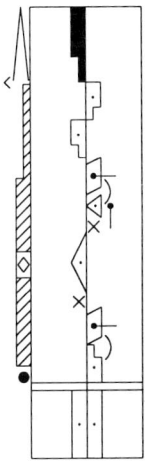

18x

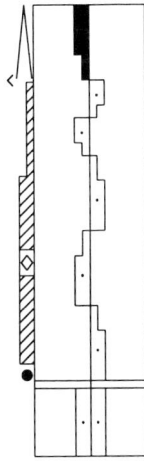

18y

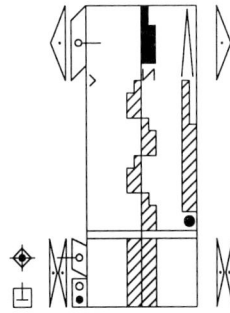

18z

18.25. **Falling on a Curve: the Standard Retention.** If the loss of balance is not too great, it is possible that falling on a curved path may occur instead of on a straight path. This is achieved through pressure from the steps on the floor producing the gradual change of direction. In writing this the C of W must be shown to have a Standard Retention, **18aa**, which means that the direction, forward in the case of **18ab**, is judged from the changing front of the performer, throughout the circular path. This less familiar retention sign is needed because the regular space hold relates to a constant direction.

18.26. To clarify the function and use of the Standard Retention the following progression is presented. In **18ac** the movement pattern is shown as occuring on a straight path, the arm moves forward toward stage right and ends sideward with the performer facing upstage. The left arm directions resulting from the space hold are given in brackets. In **18ad** the performer is traveling on a curved path, performing the same physical pattern as in **18ac**. The original direction, retained through a space hold, will function as if it is a Constant direction, and thus the arm will still be toward stage right. With the performer now facing stage left, having turned an extra quarter turn with the circular path, the right arm would end up backward (as shown in brackets). The Standard Retention is shown in **18ae**, now the arm pattern of **18ac** will occur on the curved path. The ending direction for the left arm is stated in brackets.

Falling on a Curve: the Standard Retention

18aa ◆

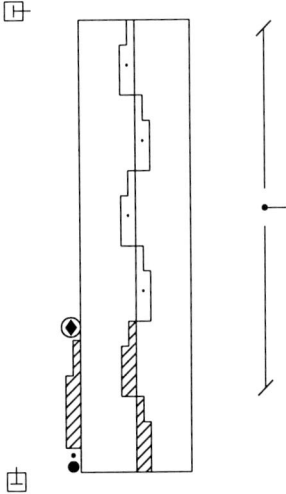

18ab

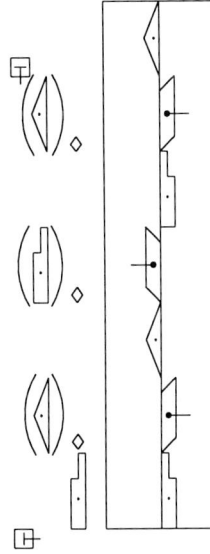

18ac

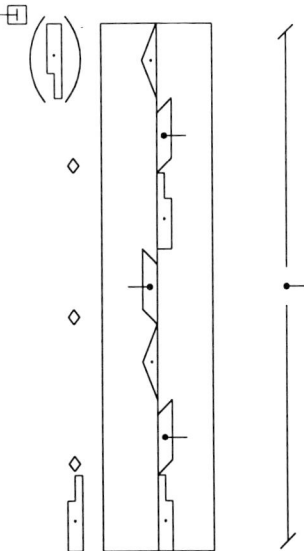

18ad

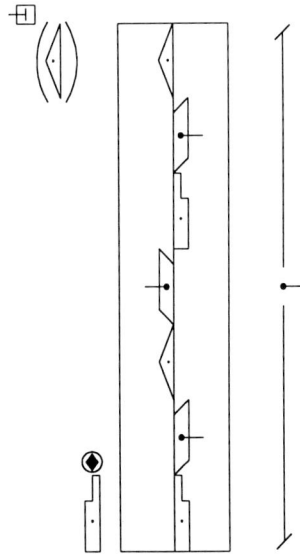

18ae

19 Falling Indications - Validity and Cancellation, Speed and Duration

19.1. **Validity.** *If, in falling, the C of W meets an obstacle which arrests the fall and no further falling is possible, the falling indication is automatically no longer in effect.* Frequently this obstacle is the floor, but it may be an object such as a wall or a partner. The falling momentum may extend to include the immediately following weight transference. In **19a** the C of W is strictly at its lowest point at the moment of sitting, i.e. on the floor, but the falling action is considered to continue until weight is on the stated chest surface, the momentum is lost and no further falling for the body-as-a-whole is possible.

*If further falling would still be possible after arrival at a supporting surface (as in **18g**, repeated here) or if balance is regained before arrival at a supporting object (as in **19b-19e**), falling indications need to be specifically canceled with a cancellation sign.*

19.2. **Cancellation.** This validity rule implies that middle level indications for falling to floor level are self-cancelling. The same applies to high level directions indicating a fall onto an object higher than floor level, which stops the fall (the chair in **18q**).[40] In contrast, high level indications for incomplete falls, i.e. where further falling can occur, need to be specifically canceled.

19.3. A falling indication can be specifically canceled by a 'place' direction for the C of W, a return to normal sign or the 'decrease' cancellation sign (as in cancellation of level using a C of W indication, discussed in Section 12). These are illustrated in the following examples.

19.4. **Speed, Duration.** Loss of balance may be sudden when an anticipated new support is not there to take the weight. It may also be more gradual through muscular control. If a falling indication is comparatively slow, it covers weight shifting leading to falling. In such a progression, speed increases as falling takes over.

19.5. Ex. **19a** is a simplified version of **18i** with the difference that the C of W falling indication extends over three counts. Weight shifting begins on count 1. The exact moment of landing is dictated by placement of the sign for the right hip in the support column.

19.6. In the falling run of **19b** balance is lost quickly and is regained only on the fifth step, when, so to speak, the brake is put on. Before this, each step is still falling. Note the use of the decrease sign to cancel the falling action. Gradual loss of balance backward is shown in **19c**, with balance caught on the fourth step.[41]

19.7. Regaining balance is often rapid; **19d** shows a quick loss and quick regaining of balance. Regaining balance may also be gradual. A slow regaining of balance occurs in **19e**; only on the last step is the weight again centered.

Speed, Duration

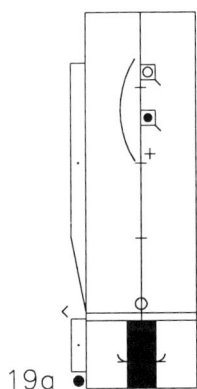

19a

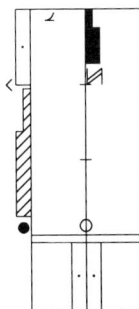

18g

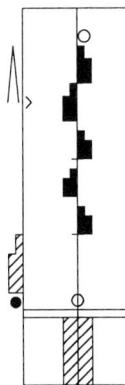

19b

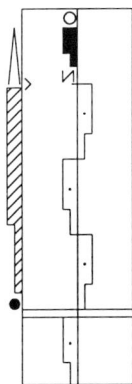

19c

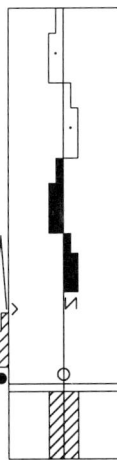

19d

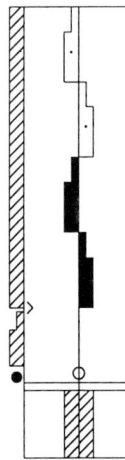

19e

20 Degree of Weight Bearing

20.1. **Analysis of Range.** The transition from contact (touch or grasp), through leaning to degrees of partial weight bearing and then to full weight bearing needs to be explored. Depending on the configuration, a limb may just be touching an object, the weight of the limb may be resting on the object, or part of the central body weight may be placed on that object. How much body weight is supported can vary from slight to an equally shared support and progress to a full single support.

20.2. In investigating this progression we will first review what has been established for the feet, taking the example of distribution of weight in a second position. In the examples, starting with **20a**, the proportion of weight on each foot is indicated. Because such mathematical divisions are physically hard to master, awareness of the quality and feeling of gesture versus support can help.

In **20a** all weight is on the left, the right foot only touches the floor.

In **20b** a slight sense of weight bearing is taken on the right foot.

In **20c** the sense of the right leg is half support, half gesture.

In **20d** weight on the right foot is a little less than on the left, there is still some gesture quality. Precise performance is not easy to achieve and has not usually been required.[42]

In **20e** the right foot shares weight equally with the left foot.

The addition of a C of W shift can augment or diminish what is written. In **20f** for example, slightly more weight would be placed on the right foot than in **20b**.

20.3. **Use of Angular Support Bow.** The angular relationship bow of **20g** provides the information that weight bearing is involved, but not enough weight to put the body part in the support column. The drawing of this bow may vary, as shown in **20h**. The choice depends on what best fits into the score i.e. avoiding adjacent symbols; what must be consistent is that the lines of the bow are always angular. When one end slants upward indicating the part being supported, the other end slants downward to show the supporter, the part or object which is taking the weight.

20.4. A familiar use of this bow occurs when leaning on one arm while sitting on the floor, as in **20i**, written in **20j**. (See the Advanced Labanotation issue on floorwork and basic acrobatics.) In lying down from the position of **20i**, as illustrated in **20k**, the arm often slides out, easing the lowering by taking weight; this is shown in **20l**. This transitory taking of weight is not sufficient for the hand indication to be a major support and hence the hand is not written in the support column.

Analysis of Range

| 20a | 20b | 20c | 20d | 20e | 20f |

Use of Angular Support Bow

20g, 20h

20i, 20k

20j, 20l

20.5. In exploring the range between the hand taking some weight and the hand becoming a major support, we will investigate leaning against a wall with the hands. We will consider in general the change from weight supported on the wall, written in the gesture column, and the greater degree defined by writing the hands in the support columns. The figure of **20m** shows a leaning position in which some weight is taken on the hand, as in **20n**, the supporting bow being linked to the hand gesture column; the person need not fall if the hand support were to be taken away. In **20o** the body configuration requires that a much greater amount of weight be placed on the hands; without their support the body would fall. This position is written in **20p**.

20.6. A familiar example of degrees of weight bearing also occurs in the following stretching exercise at the barre. The dancer begins with weight centered over her left foot, the right leg resting sideward on the barre, **20q**. As the weight travels to the right side the right foot slides along the barre taking more and more weight until it becomes an equal support, as in a very wide 2nd position, **20r**; this is written in **20s**. Note the touching contact for the ankle at the start; the leg will be resting on the barre, but the performer can raise it without having to shift (displace) the central support. Then as the weight travels, the sliding on the barre becomes a weight-bearing slide. At the end the ankle sign is placed in the right support column. Note also the addition of the *sideward angling* for the left leg; this statement gives the finishing configuration for the left leg and hence the extent of the sideward sliding. (For analysis and writing of angling see <u>Advanced Labanotation</u> *Kneeling, Sitting, Lying*.)

20.7. In terms of weight bearing, the positions of **20o** and **20r** are somewhat comparable to a 2nd position on the feet in which weight is equally on both feet. Such a 2nd position with one foot on an object, in this case a box, is illustrated in **20t**, notated in **20u**. To take another example, the position of **20v** with the feet on a low box and the hands on the floor is a form of 4th position in which the hands and feet have approximately equal weight bearing, **20w**. It is important to be clear that no precise weight-bearing measurements are being considered here.

Use of Angular Support Bow (continued)

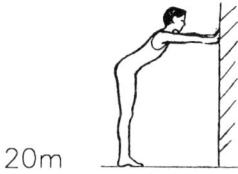

20m

20o

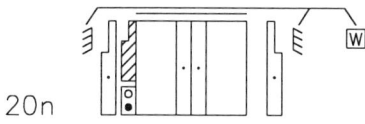

20n

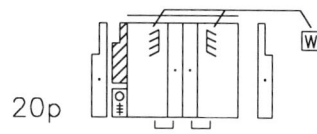

20p

20q

20r

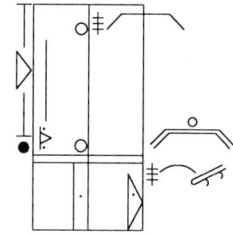

20s

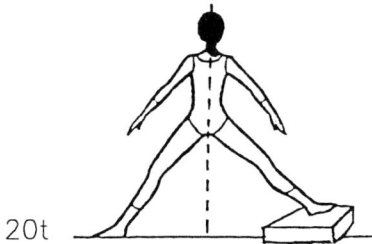

20t

20v

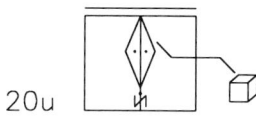

20u

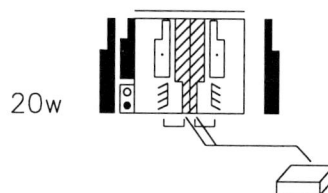

20w

20.8. **Gradations in Weight Placement.** The device of combining the black circle, the C of W sign, with the angular support bow provides indications of increase or decrease in weight placement. The figure of **20x** shows grasping a pole; although the person is leaning forward, if no weight is placed on the pole, the position is written as a touching grasp, **20y**. In **20z** the angular bow is used, therefore the grasp now includes weight bearing, no degree is specified.

20.9. In **20aa** the weight sign is placed closer to the hand, thus more weight of the performer is closer to the body, less on the pole. It is shown in **20ab** to have moved more toward the pole, and in **20ac** even more weight is placed on the pole. Not enough body weight is transferred to the pole to make the hand a major support. When the hand holding the pole becomes a major support the hand support must be written in the support column, **20ad**. Although these indications are becoming more specific, they still provide only general statements and do not represent any precise measurements.[43]

20.10. The above examples have featured one person making use of an inanimate object, such as a pole or a block. It is important to note the difference in weight indication when applied to *two active parties sharing weight*, each of whom has a moveable C of W. A familiar example of sharing weight occurs when partners lean away from each other, as in **20ae**. Here the line of balance falls between their feet. It is assumed that, if they are generally of equal height and weight, each carries an equal amount of weight. The notation of **20af** makes no particular statement about the division of weight. In **20ag**, by centering the weight sign this fact is clearly stated. Shifting more weight to A is shown in **20ah**; in **20ai** more weight is taken by B. Because each person would no doubt fall if the hands were to let go, the hand symbols are placed within the support columns.

20.11. Such shared weight is a common feature in the couple dances of Hungary, where exchange of degree of weight sharing produces a very characteristic style of turning around each other. During this smooth turning, each partner in succession prevents the other from falling.

Gradations in Weight Placement

20x

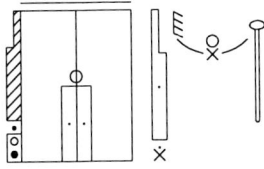

20y

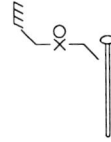

20z

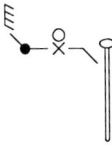

20aa

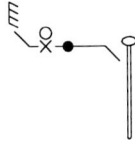

20ab

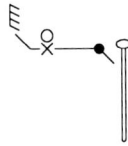

20ac

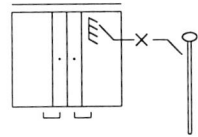

20ad

20ae

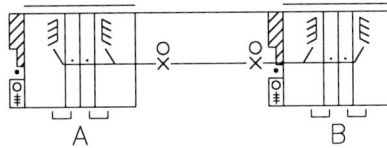

20af

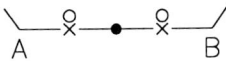

20ag

20ah

20ai

21 Moving into Leaning Situations

21.1. In *leaning* against an object (e.g. a wall) a greater or lesser part of the body weight is transferred onto that object, i.e. the body is no longer entirely supporting its own weight. The degree of movement into a leaning situation may be quite slight, a small shift of weight, or an action closer to falling. Moving into leaning is usually a controlled action.

21.2. The figure of **21a** is standing close to the wall so that only a small backward shift is needed to take advantage of the wall by leaning against it, **21b**; no backward falling need occur. Nor is any falling involved in **21c,** in which the performer starts by standing further away but still fairly close to the wall. Use of a shifting statement here, even of a large one, carries with it the understanding that balance is not lost. In **21d** the torso leans forward, counterbalancing as the weight travels a greater amount backward until the back of the pelvis is leaning against the wall. Here the path of the C of W is greater, but a balanced situation is still maintained; thus this action can be written as in **21e**.

21.3. A slight fall (C of W leading) into a leaning situation is shown in **21f**. The distance between the main support, the feet, and the new supporting surface will dictate how far this slight fall will be. If the distance were greater, then it would be written as **21g**, in which a true falling occurs leading into the double support of being on the feet and on the back against the wall. This action may have been caused by a person being aghast on hearing a shocking statement. A similar sudden falling could be part of choreography in which dancers fling their weight onto partners or objects. While falling onto a wall will cancel the falling action, addition of the cancellation sign in **21g** is an aid to reading.

21.4. The specifications of more or less weight bearing for supporting gestures and for those in the support column, discussed in Section 20, can also be applied here.

Moving into Leaning Situations

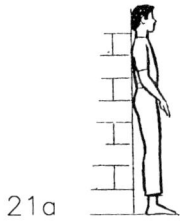

21a

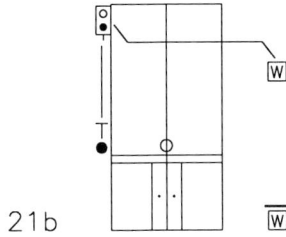

21b

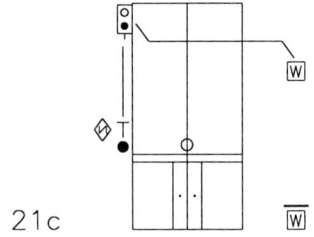

21c

21d

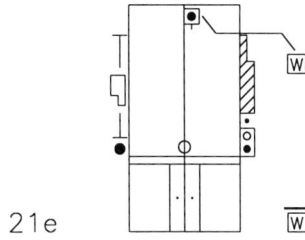

21e

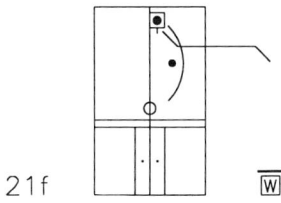

21f

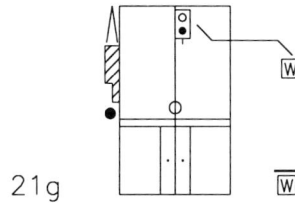

21g

22 Leaning, Mutual Support

22.1. Each person leaning back to back in **22a**, is in a body configuration that would under normal circumstances cause them to fall to the floor. Because of mutual support they do not lose balance; in fact, stability is considerable. The base of support is formed by the four feet, the line of balance, runs through the center between them.

22.2. Because in **22a** the degree of leaning is fairly slight, it can be written as **22b** with indication of a short backward path for the C of W. This statement in a starting position indicates how one gets into that position. A backward falling indication, as in **21f** or **21g**, cannot be used here because no falling occurs. A more precise description can be made with angling for the legs, **22c**. This statement gives the angle between the line of the leg and the floor, in this case one increment backward. With a larger separation between the pairs of feet, as in **22d**, the weight displacement backward is greater, and the degree of weight on each person's back is increased, resulting in the support indication being placed in the support column, **22e**. Note the use of additional support columns. The leg angle in relation to the floor line is now 45° backward, **22f**.

22.3. 'Leaning away from' someone or something, as in **22g**, follows the same rules in relation to balance and stability. Here again, the position is stable when the joint C of W of the two persons is located over the center of the base of support, the four feet. This position is not as secure as that of **22d**, because the base of support between the feet is much narrower (see 3.6) and much weight is outside the base of support in contrast to **22d**, where all weight is inside the base of support. In **22g** the partners have bent arms and are fairly close together, resulting in the angle from ankle to chest being only slightly off the vertical, thus the weight distribution can be written as **22h**. In contrast, in **22i** the body angle for each person is about 30° off the vertical, thus the hands are now major supports, **22j**. Because the unit ankle-to-chest states the directional line, there is no need to state angling in these last two examples.

22.4. The situation of **22k**, written in **22l**, is related to **22d**, but in this example the partners fulfil different roles. The man (A) assumes a particularly stable position to allow the lady (B) to move 'off balance'. B's C of W moves to her left, indicated by the path for the C of W, until a position is reached where, without the support of A, she would fall. The actual amount of control over balance depends, of course, on co-ordination between the performers.

Leaning, Mutual Support

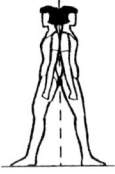

22a

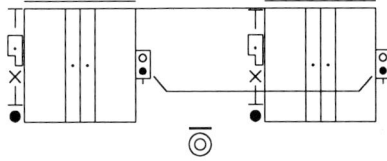

22b

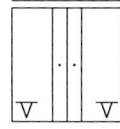

22c

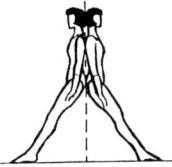

22d

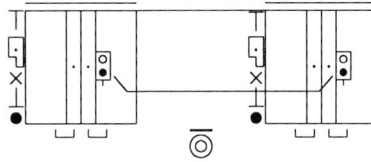

22e

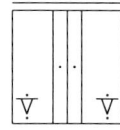

22f

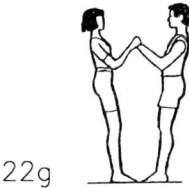

22g

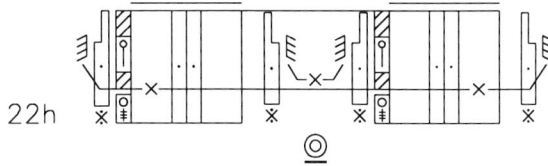

22h

22i

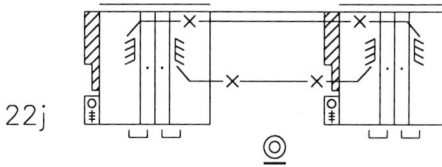

22j

22k

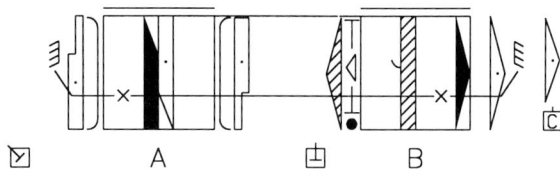

22l

23 Weight of Limbs Supported

23.1. When sitting on the floor with the legs forward, **23a**, the main support is the hips, the legs merely rest on the floor, **23b**. In all such positions it is expected that the person will take advantage of being supported by the floor and allow the floor to take the weight of the limbs (in this case the legs). Contact with the floor is expected, there is no need for contact bows/hooks. With the legs bent, as in **23c**, the part of foot resting on the floor is usually stated, **23d**.

23.2. Similarly, the lower legs resting on the floor during a high kneel, **23e**, help maintain balance. If the lower legs should be lifted slightly, this can be indicated, as in **23f**, illustrated in **23g**. At the end of this example the general sign for contact is used to show. they return to resting on the floor. In **23h** the lower legs are lifted higher, to 45°, illustrated in **23i**.

23.3. In **23j** the lower arms of the person sitting at a table are resting on the table. It is common for people to relax and allow the table to support the weight of the arm. Despite this fact the contact with the table should be written with a round bow, **23k**.

23.4. When the body is leaning forward and the person is leaning on the table, **23l**, an angular bow, **23m**, should be used. Placement of body part in the gesture or in the support column is determined by the degree of leaning, as discussed in the previous sections.

23.5. If the distance between the chair and the table is sufficiently big and the body is leaning more forward, **23n**, the position can result in the lower arm really sharing the central weight of the body, as in **23o**, the sign for the elbow being placed in the support column. When writing the elbow sign one is assuming that the lower arm will be resting on the table. If weight really is on the lower arm, then this part should be stated in the support column, **23p**.

23.6. **Dynamic State of Limb.** Although the limb is expected to relax while resting on the floor, table or other object, the dynamic state of the limb can be expressed directly. In **23q** the lower arm is shown to be relaxed as it touches the table. Heaviness is indicated in **23r** while **23s** states an uplifted quality; the limb will be touching the table but in a 'lifted', 'suspended' state, resisting gravity. Actual pressure downward against the table can be shown, **23t**.

Weight of Limbs Supported

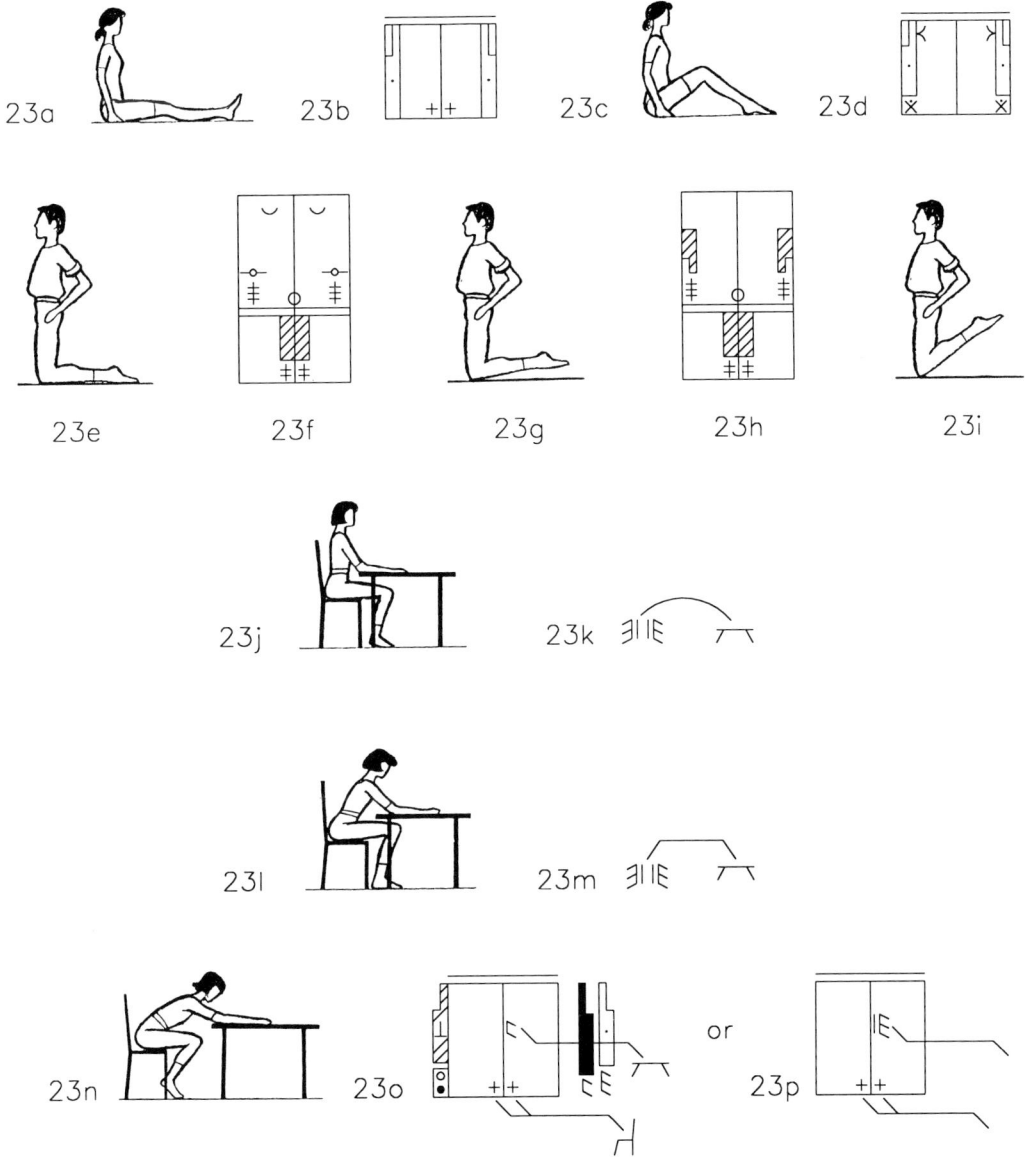

23a   23b   23c   23d

23e   23f   23g   23h   23i

23j   23k

23l   23m

23n   23o   or   23p

Dynamic State of Limb

23q   23r   23s   23t

24 'Falling' Motion of Head, Torso, Limbs

24.1. In this section the term 'limb' can equally be applied to the head and torso as well as to the arms and legs. As a rule, falling refers to loss of balance for the body-as-a-whole and results in an uncontrolled lowering to the floor, the vertical line through the C of W moving beyond the base of support. However, in sitting upright, one has the feeling of falling when the torso tilts too far sideward or backward without control of some kind; the weight of the torso carries it to the floor. One speaks of "falling about with laughter", and indeed in that state of hilarity the torso often "falls about" even when one is sitting on the floor in an otherwise stable situation.

24.2. When an arm is held up, one often speaks of "dropping it" of "letting it fall". Even the head can "fall" forward or backward, as can be seen when a person suddenly falls asleep. Such falling of an individual part occurs when the normal state of tension which keeps it in the designated position is released and the weight of the limb is taken over by the force of gravity. In some forms of dance such dropping, falling actions are intentionally allowed to happen.

24.3. Releasing the normal control is usually a matter of a drop in energy, a letting go, a relaxing of the muscles which are holding the limb up. Therefore such "dropping the arm" might be described as sudden relaxation, or going limp, the dropping down being the result. The question then is one of intent. If the intention is to produce sudden relaxation, limpness, a change in the dynamic state of the limb muscles, then it should be so described. This statement provides a different awareness, a contrasting image to falling, which expresses a positive relationship to gravity. By providing a direct message we give the reader a cue as to the intent of the movement, comparable to the carefully chosen words of the teacher or choreographer.

24.4. **'Falling' for Head.** In **24a** the head starts upright then 'falls' forward, a passive, resultant movement led by the *center of weight for that part.* Because the indication for center of weight leading is localized to the head movement, it is understood to refer only to that part and not to the C of W of the body-as-a-whole. If, in context, there is a question regarding reference to the C of W, the head sign can be stated within the bow, as in **24b**.[44]

24.5. Such falling for the head results from intentional or unintentional relaxation of the neck muscles, either gradually or suddenly. The sign for limp (flop, extreme relaxation) is given in **24c** followed by the resultant forward head tilt. A gradual increase into limpness is shown in **24d**, a sequence often seen when, while seated, a person drops off to sleep. Often the total relaxation forward of the head startles the person into being awake. In a similar way the weight of the head can be shown to take over gradually as the head inclines, **24e**. The head starts to incline forward and the falling action gradually takes over. In **24f** the weight of the head is experienced from the start as it leads into the forward tilt. In **24g** the falling motion for the head ends with an abrupt arrival forward middle.

24.6. The difference should be pointed out between a major C of W movement which may be led by the head, **24h**, and the localized movement of **24b**. In **24i** falling forward into a lunge is shown to be led by the head; no 'falling' action for the head itself takes place.

'Falling' for Head

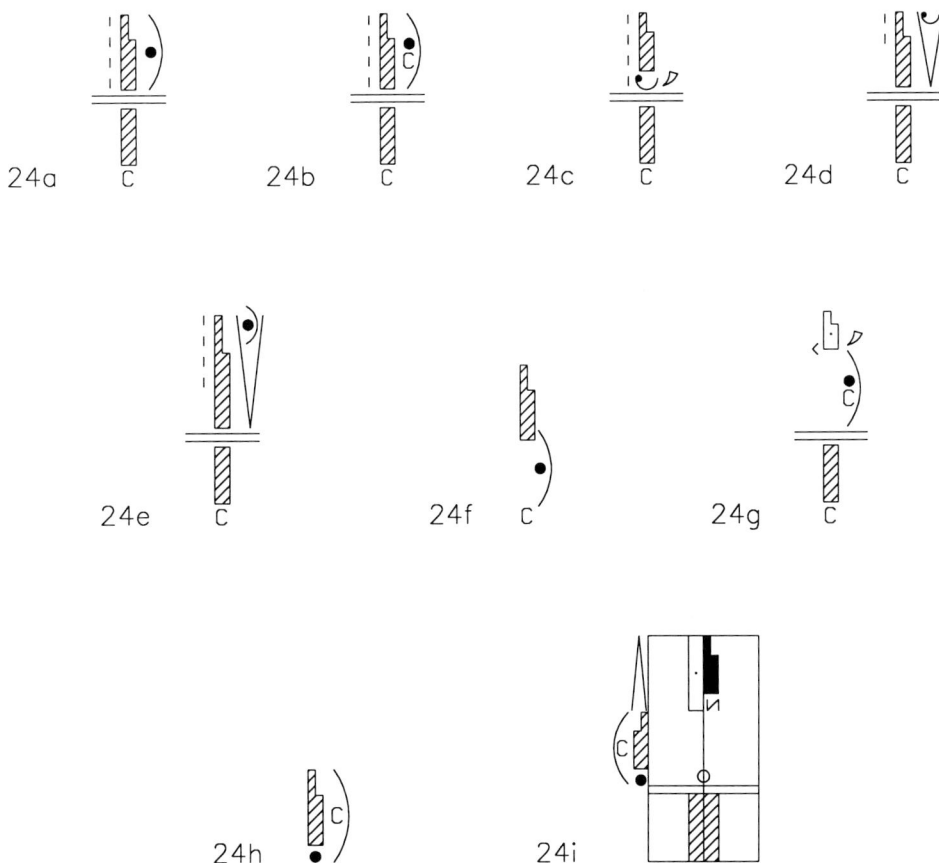

24a   24b   24c   24d

24e   24f   24g

24h   24i

24.7. **'Falling' for Arm.** The following examples feature an arm 'falling'. In **24j**, after being held out to the side, the right arm drops down. The same is described in **24k** but the C of W sign is specified as relating to the arm. The downward movement is resultant, hence the appropriate use of the dotted line.

24.8. Just as one can move slowly into a *tombé*, as in **24l**, so it can be a gradual process in allowing the weight of the arm to take over and cause the arm to fall, **24m**. In **24n** the arm starts up and the falling is via the center point (place).

24.9. **'Falling' for Torso.** While sitting, one can lose balance in the torso resulting in a fall of that part to the floor. In **24o** the torso falls to the side. Here it has been specified that it is the center of weight of the torso; such detail may not usually be needed.

24.10. A slow development into such falling is given in **24p**. In **24q** the movement is described as the result of the increasing drop in energy ending in limpness.

24.11. The same ideas are applicable into other directions and for other parts of the body.

'Falling' for Arm

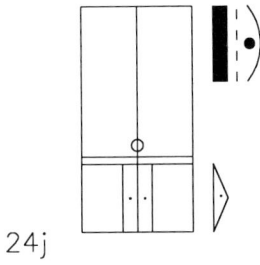

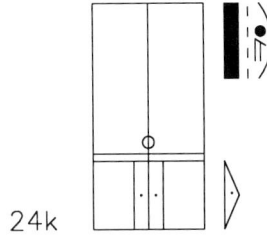

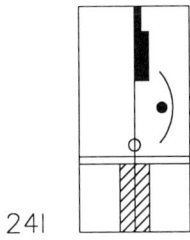

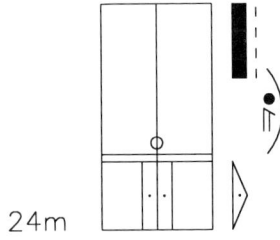

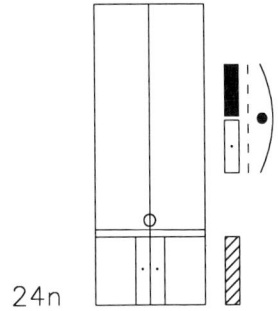

24j

24k

24l

24m

24n

'Falling' for Torso

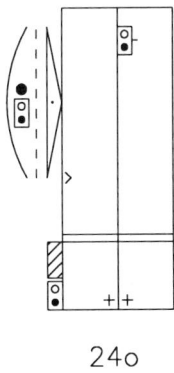

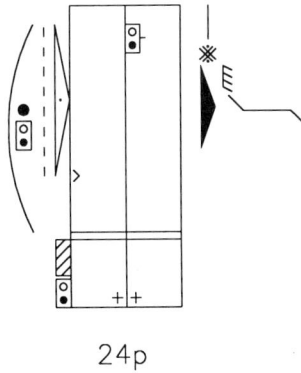

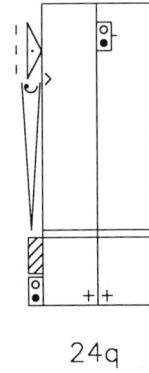

24o

24p

24q

VI READING EXAMPLES[45]

25 Reading Examples - Change of Level

25.1. Ex. **25a** shows a *barre* sequence using *grands pliés* in 1st, 2nd and 5th positions. For classical ballet a full *plié* should be slightly higher than a total squat, i.e. one degree above total lowering on the feet, as shown on count 2 of the first measure. For 2nd position the C of W should lower less than in 1st or 5th: the distance is one degree less than for the *grand plié* in 1st.[46] In each section a *demi-plié* is passed through on the way down and also on the return.[47] The notation shows clearly that because of the quick change into the next position, the rising takes less time than the lowering. In the third measure time is more evenly spread as there is no need to change position. At the end of the example, two other methods of cancellation for the C of W, i) and ii), are given. Note that no C of W level is given for the *demi-plié*, this is because the whole foot should remain on the floor in a *demi-plié*, and the degree of leg flexion in this position varies from person to person depending on the individual flexibility of the ankles.

25.2. In the Humphrey succession of **25b**,[48] after the start in a high parallel 4th position, the upper part of the torso arches backward slightly, then the C of W lowers to a very short distance above the floor. As the *plié* deepens, the torso bends forward sequentially, the arms being carried (indicated by the body hold).

In the second measure, the pelvis thrusting (shifting) forward initiates the wave-like body movement sequentially to incline backward (knees-to-chest as a unit). With an arm swing through down to diagonal backward high and up, the C of W rises, returning to its normal level for a high support on the feet.[49]

During this overall torso movement sequence, which occurs while lowering and rising above the same spot, the body is in balance all the time.

Reading Examples - Change of Level

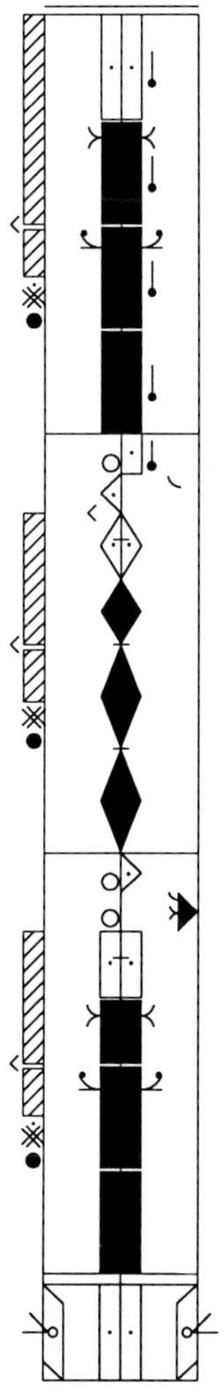

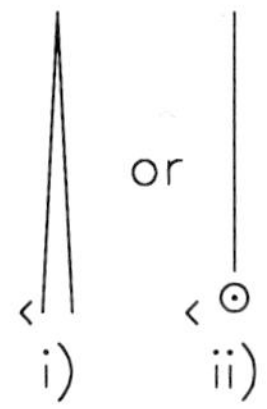

25a

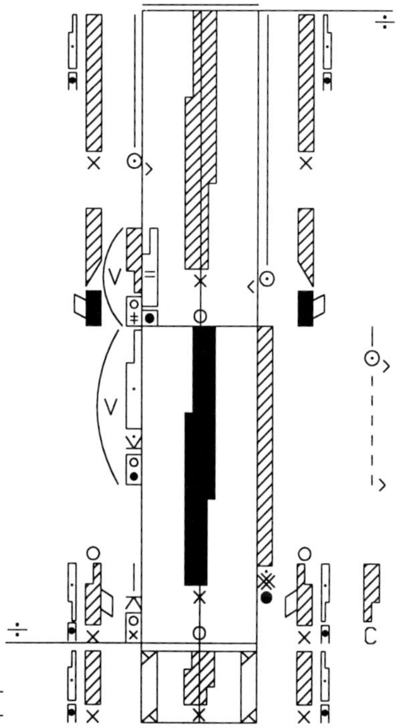

or

i)   ii)

25b 4/4

♩ = 54—56 Largo

25.3.   Ex. **25c** indicates turning, the knees being brought together as the body lowers to kneeling on the left knee.   The gradual bending of the supporting leg is shown by the low level in the turn sign, but an indication for the C of W is added to pinpoint the degree of lowering needed for the kneel.

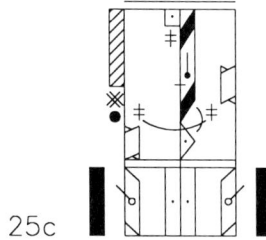

25c

25.4.   Ex. **25d** shows a *plié* in 2nd position with contraction and release similar to that used in a Graham-style modern dance class.[50]   At the start of the contraction the pelvis rotates sagittally while the breastbone shifts slightly backward-upward.[51]   An indication for the C of W is used to describe a deepening of the *plié* on count 2 before weight is transferred to the side and the left leg is straightened.   This same pattern is repeated in measure 2.   In the last measure deepening leads into weight taken completely on the right leg for a turn in *arabesque*.

25.5.   In the very slow *plié* of **25e**[52] the C of W lowers 4 degrees from normal standing level, while the left leg slides out to the side.   Strictly as stated, the *plié* should be as deep as indicated without taking the heel off the ground.   Some performers may have to raise the heel slightly to achieve this level, they may also need to have the left leg gesture include some weight bearing.   Note use of the 'zed' caret linking the left leg gesture to the next support.

Reading Examples - Change of Level (continued)

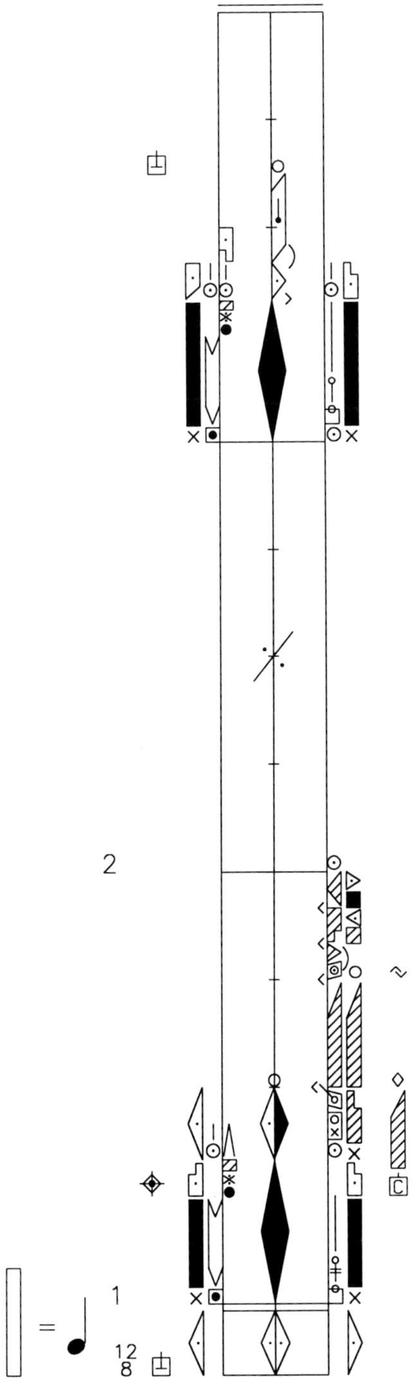

25d

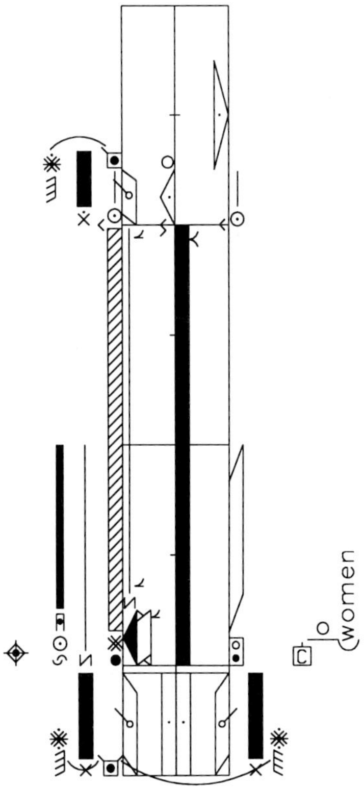

25e

25.6. The starting position of the modern dance *plié* in **25f**[53] is in a small 2nd position with feet parallel, heels off the floor, and body lifted. A further slight lift of the C of W (achieved probably by diminishing ankle flexion) occurs before the complete sink in the narrow 2nd position (a squat). This controlled lowering is followed by an equally slow controlled rising to normal standing. The actions are speeded up as the sequence is repeated. Because carets are used the 'x' for the narrow position need not be repeated.

25.7. Ex. **25g**[54] shows a sequence in which, starting in an *attitude*, the body lowers to sitting in a contracted position while turning and then rises into the same *attitude*, followed by extending into *arabesque*.

At the start the left leg is in a standard *attitude* position, the left arm up, the right arm out to the side. As the turn to the right on the right foot begins, the pelvis 'contracts', the body begins to lower and the left knee crosses behind the right leg before the left foot is placed on the floor. Both legs bend and the C of W lowers to floor level until sitting on both hips close to the feet ('place middle' for C of W) is achieved. From there, turning on both feet to the left with the C of W rising leads into the same attitude, the left arm moving in a sagittal forward overhead circle into the *arabesque* line as the left leg extends into *arabesque*.

Reading Examples - Change of Level (continued)

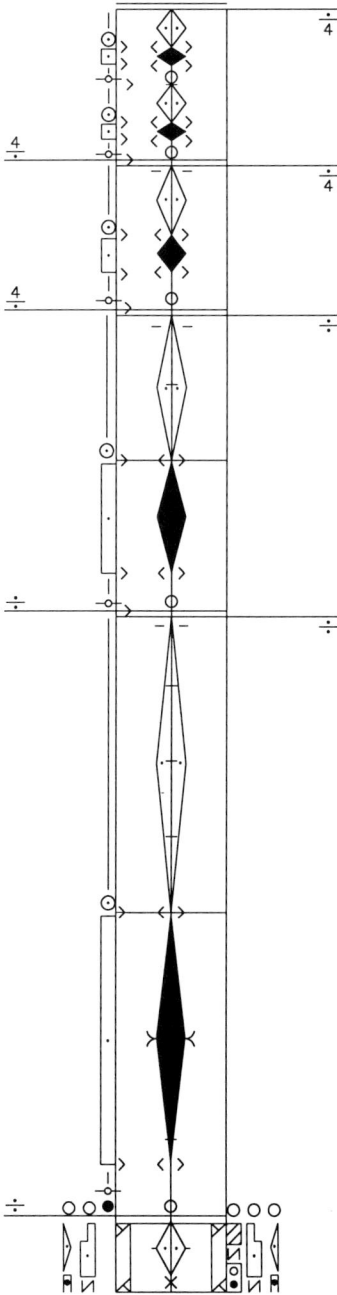

25f

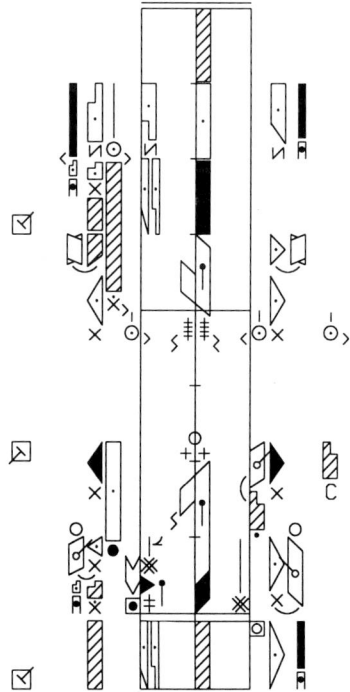

25g

25.8. In the exercise of **25h**, from a slightly opened low kneeling position with the hands taking weight backward of the knees, an arch is produced by shifting the pelvis forward high and raising the level of the C of W. Because the hands and knees stay where they are, it is not possible to raise the C of W very much. While the pelvic shift provides no destination (perhaps as high as the performer can manage), the C of W indication gives a clear level, i.e. destination.

In measure 2, the performer returns to the starting position. Here the C of W lowers to middle level (as in a low kneel), i.e. as close as possible to the level of support.

25.9. In **25i**,[55] starting in a high 4th position with the arms up, the arms come down one by one, each putting the back of the hand on the thigh. At the end of measure 38 the support lowers to middle level. This continues in measure 39 as the C of W moves close to the feet (the point of support), the heel of the right foot leaving the floor. This lowering, the chest bending forward slightly and a twist of the torso to the right leads into a middle level kneel on the right knee. As the torso inclines backward, weight is taken on the right hand sliding backward on the little finger edge; eventually weight is taken onto the right shoulder and hip.

Reading Examples - Change of Level (continued)

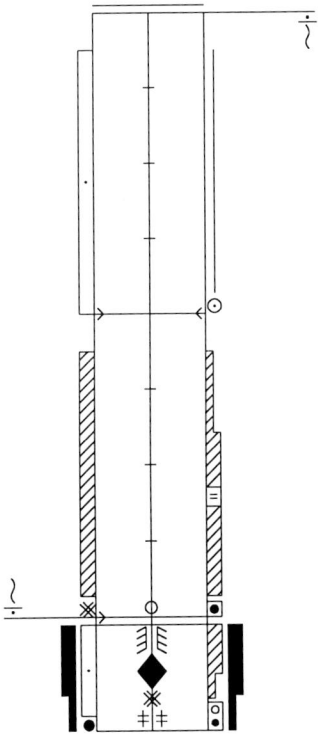

25h

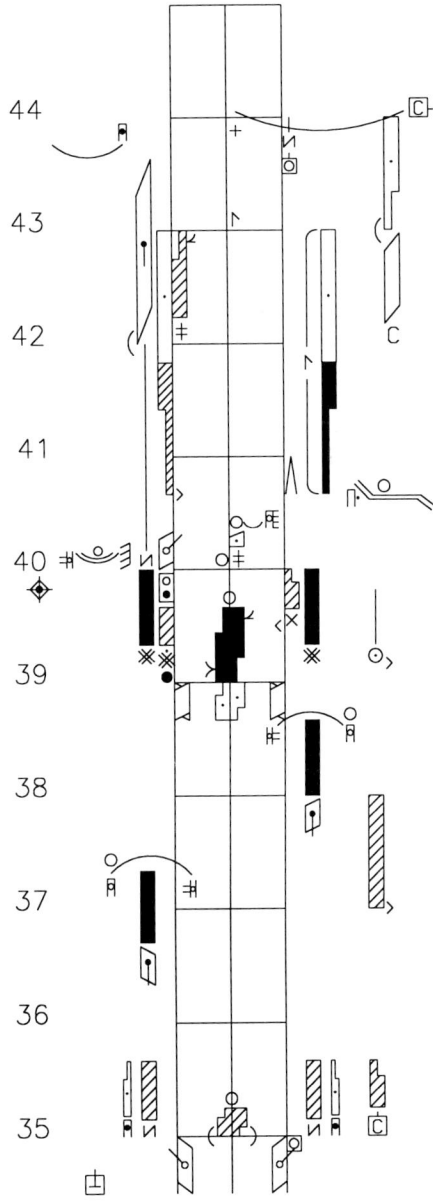

25i

26 Reading Examples - Minor Horizontal Shifts

26.1. At the start of **26a** weight is shifted forward and is maintained there during the forward walks. Weight is centered as the feet close. Such weight placement can express eagerness, an emphasis of the forward direction. For the backward steps weight is shifted backward, as if there is a desire to get away.

26.2. Placement of the weight over to the right, as in **26b**, suggests the kind of displacement from center which occurs when one is carrying a heavy case in the left hand. There should be no tilt of the body, only weight displacement.

26.3. Weight placement in walking can also be applied to running, **26c**. Weight shifted forward helps the easy forward run sequence in measure 1. By placing the weight backward on the following three runs the forward momentum is reduced and the subsequent change of direction prepared for. Weight placement forward while running backward may suggest caution. Weight shift changed to backward in the last measure while running leads to a falling (*tombé*) into a long low step.

Note that in **26a** and **26c** the C of W symbol is repeated. A caret could have been used but the full symbol attracts the eye more easily.

26.4. Ex. **26d** starts with a tango-like walk forward with the weight held back. The transition for the C of W from being shifted backward to shifted forward is smooth as it is centered during the knee bend (*plié*).

In measure 3 weight is held to the left during the low step to the right, but is centered as the legs straighten. This is then repeated to the other side.

Reading Examples - Minor Horizontal Shifts

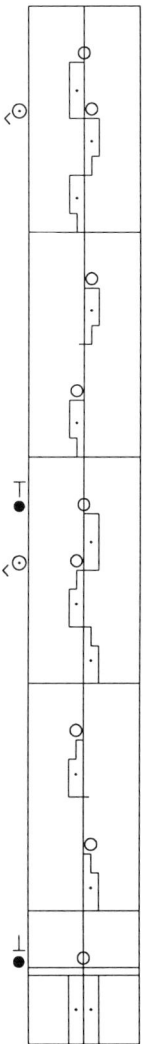

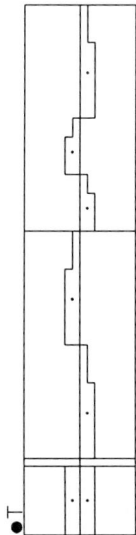

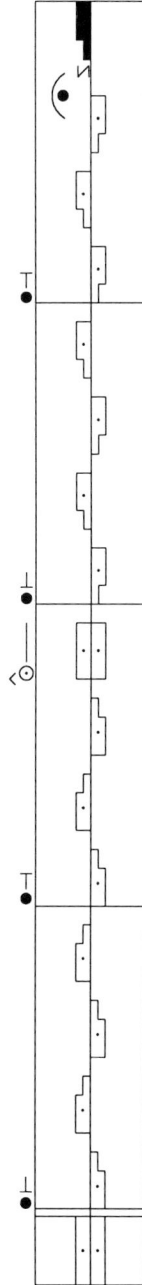

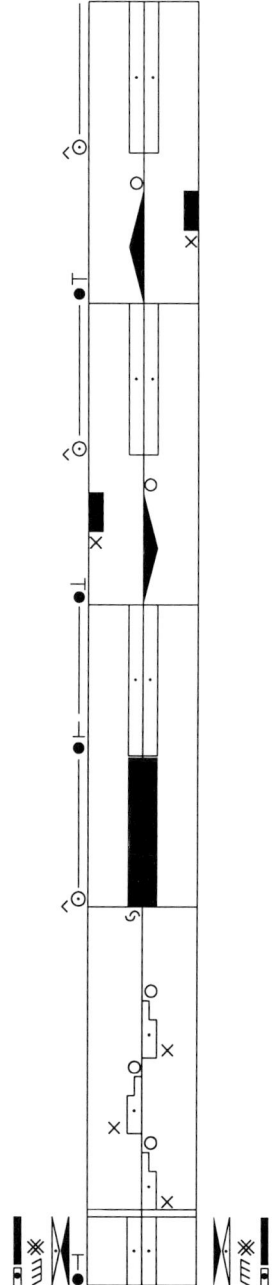

26a 26b 26c 26d

26.5. Ex. **26e**[56] shows the Miller from Léonide Massine's *The Three-
cornered Hat*. After the forward stamping step, the weight (C of W) continues as
a shift into the same direction. This very subtle movement does not lead to any
loss of balance and is canceled on the next step. The Miller is being assertive and
feeling like 'throwing his weight around', one might say.

26.6. Again an excerpt from *The Three-Cornered Hat*, this time featuring
the Miller's Wife, **26f**.[57] The opening position shows her looking into the
distance, shielding her eyes (the thumb-edge near to the forehead). The sense of
still moving forward after the long forward step is indicated by the forward shift
of the C of W during the sliding circular leg gesture. This slight shift does not
cause loss of balance, but adds to the forward projection as the Miller's Wife
looks far ahead into the distance. Note the sweep of the leg gestures, which are
shown to be far from the center through the use of the adjacent wide signs in the
support columns.

26.7. The step from the Baroque period in **26g** features the *demi-coupé*
foot position. The low step forward on the right foot ends with a rise to *demi-
pointe* for a brief balance, heels touching before two continuous steps forward
into a *demi-plié*. At the beginning of the next measure, the right leg rises to
relevé and the left leg slowly gestures forward, keeping very close to the floor
without actually touching it, as shown by the double 'x' in the support column.
The performer 'goes with the leg' and allows the weight to pass almost beyond
the point of support, i.e. the C of W has the sense of 'leading' into the next
forward step. Note use of the 'zed' caret indicating the relationship of the leg
gesture to the step which follows. If C of W leading (the symbol in a curved
bow) were written, as in **26h**, there would be a slight falling action which should
be avoided.

26.8. In lunging to the side in **26i**,[58] a C of W shift sideward
accompanies a chest shift in the same direction. The marked shift of the chest
could lead to a falling action; however control is maintained through muscular
adjustment in the body. The right arm moves sequentially out to the side as if it
results from the sudden chest shift that precedes it.
    Note the change of level for the supporting leg, the sudden stretching which
occurs as the shifts take place. It is important that the C of W displacement is
not performed as a pelvic shift. Release signs in the support column prior to the
sideward steps facilitate reading. However, these signs are technically not
necessary.

26.9. Ex. **26j**[59] is a variation on **26i**. Instead of a chest shift, in this
example the right hip lifts as the right foot releases from the floor. At the same

time the weight is shifted to the right. Hip and weight shifts remain in effect during the lunge. Because of the structure of the pelvis, the lifting of the left hip cancels the previous placement of the right hip.

Reading Examples - Minor Horizontal Shifts (continued)

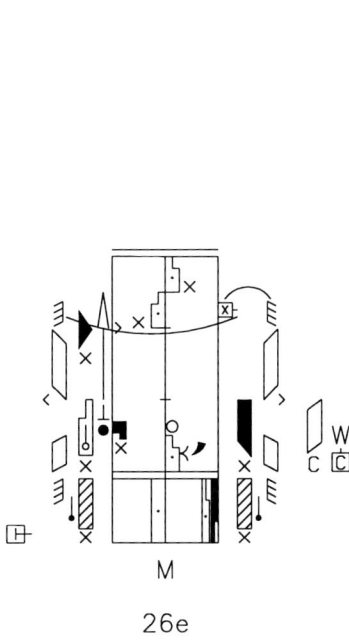

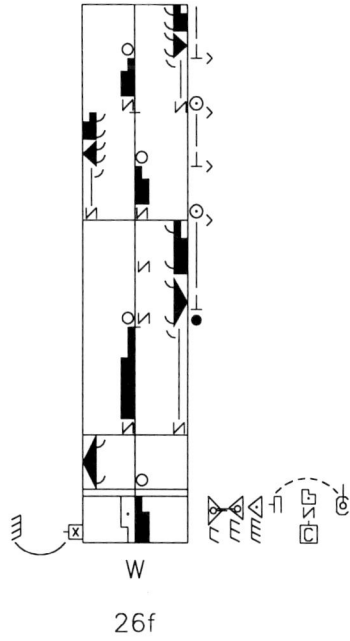

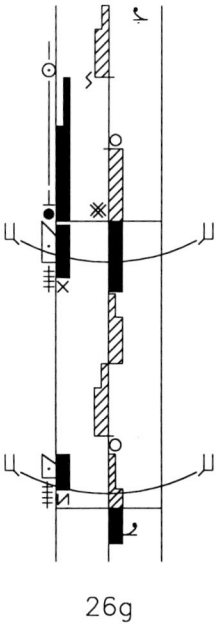

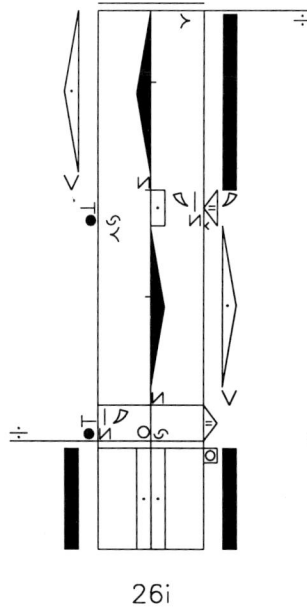

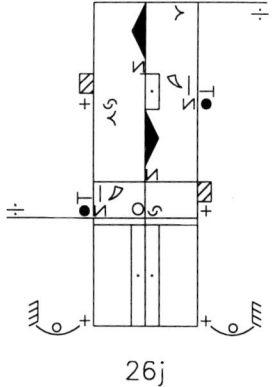

M

26e

W

26f

26g

26h

26i

26j

26.10. Ex. **26k**[60] shows the turn of **25c** in context and written with more detail. After a rhythmic stamping pattern, weight is lowered on the right leg until the left knee takes weight. A step to the right side produces a foot-knee position, the kneeling level having lowered to middle level. There is also a displacement of the C of W to the right. Finally, a pelvis shift to right side high is also added. Such a shift is a major directional displacement within the body but need not in itself cause a displacement of weight.

26.11. In **26l**,[61] when the whole torso tilts forward to middle level, the pelvis is rotated forward around its left-right axis. During the tilt forward, the weight is shifted backwards more than needed to keep balance. This shift and the pelvis rotation disappear on count 4 when the legs bend (*plié*) and the torso bends forward low.

26.12. **Spot Retention.** As the body hinges backwards from the knees during the knee-bend in **26m**, the C of W needs to remain centered over the left foot.[62]

26.13. Starting feet together, with a slight forward tilt of the whole torso, **26n**[63] features steps on the ball of the foot with a bent leg, followed by a heel drop on a stretched leg. With each step the foot moves slightly more out to the side ending in a wide 2nd position.

In spite of stepping to the side there is no displacement of weight because at the start a spot hold is stated for the C of W. Weight can be retained over the same spot only if the steps are fairly rapid. Because the weight is not displaced, 'place' does not move either and step lengths are measured from the same place throughout. Without the spot hold for the C of W, the spatial progression would be of the left foot stepping slightly farther away on each step to the left while the right foot would always step on the same spot, the C of W gradually moving to the left as a result.

Reading Examples - Minor Horizontal Shifts (continued)

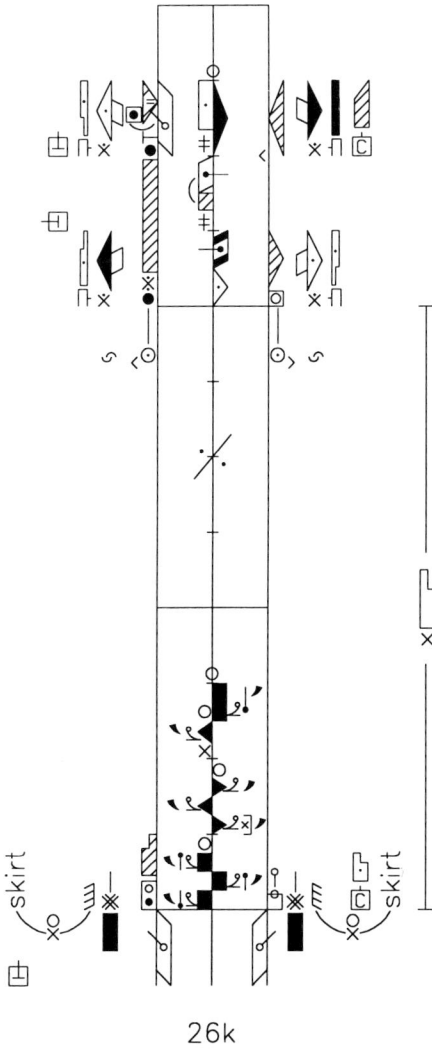

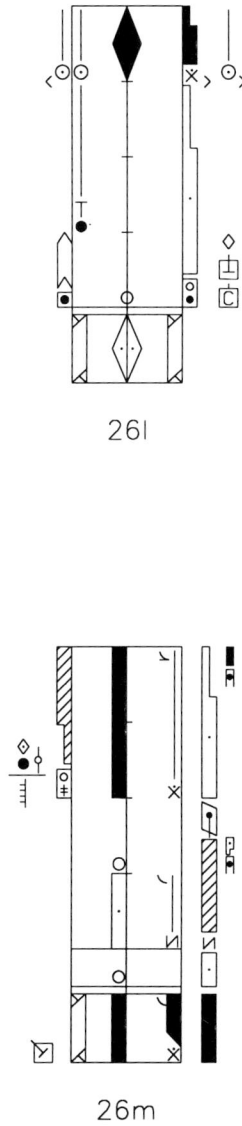

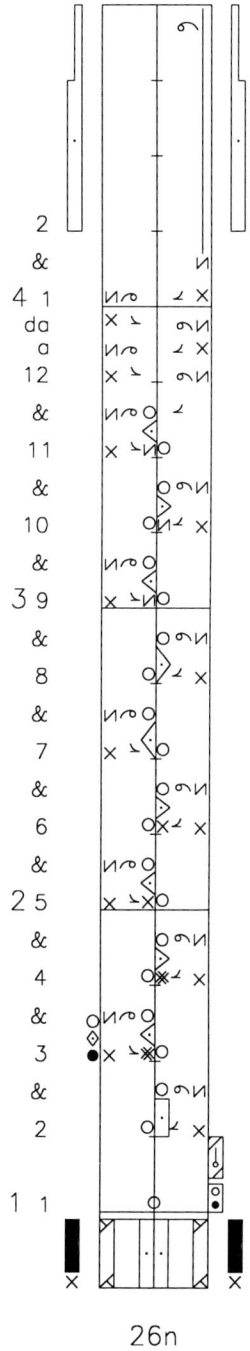

26k

26l

26m

26n

27 Reading Examples - Minor Vertical Displacements

27.1. Ex. **27a**[64] shows minor vertical displacements of the C of W taking place in a deep *plié* in 2nd position. These displacements will actually be achieved through minor flexions in the ankles, knees and hips, but are experienced as a change of level of the C of W. Depending on tempo, they may be either slight lowering and lifting actions, or a bouncing movement. In this example the timing is even and neither the downward nor the upward movement is accented.

27.2. Ex. **27b** is the male's walk from Paul Taylor's *Three Epitaphs*.[65] With parallel feet, the male slides the foot along the floor before putting his weight on it. At the beginning of each of these low, slightly open forward steps, the C of W 'dips'. It then rises slightly, ready to dip again on the next step. The feeling is of 'sitting' slightly into the *plié*. Note the stiff, rigid back and neck and the pompous spread of the chest.

27.3. In **27c**[66] the slumped walk for the females includes the same minor fall and rise of the C of W, i.e. the 'dip' at the start of each step, but the expression is quite different. The body is curved over the front, the lower rim of the pelvis forward (slight backward sagittal rotation), the lungs 'exhaled' and the relaxed head looking slightly upward (hopefully).

27.4. The C of W is slightly lowered in **27d**[67] as the heel is lowered to the floor in order to make the whole foot contact (note use of the heel drop sign). It is understood that the performer actually needs to push the heel toward the floor in order to accomplish this.

27.5. In the well-known bouncing-and-stretching exercise of **27e**, the starting position is a low squat (C of W place middle). The body is bent forward and rests partially on the hands. To start the exercise, a slight upward rise occurs on the upbeat as a preparation for the downward bounce on the beat. After three bounces (it is more common to count the downward bounces than the slight lifts), the legs stretch and the C of W rises to a normal standing middle level support. The torso remains hanging down, the direction - place low rounded - should be the aim although it cannot always be achieved. Stretching indications for the legs are added because it is precisely the stretching that is most important: the legs must end up slightly more stretched than in normal standing.

Reading Examples - Minor Vertical Displacements

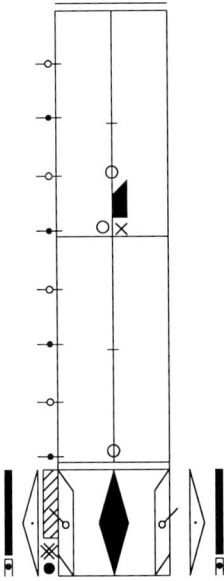

27a

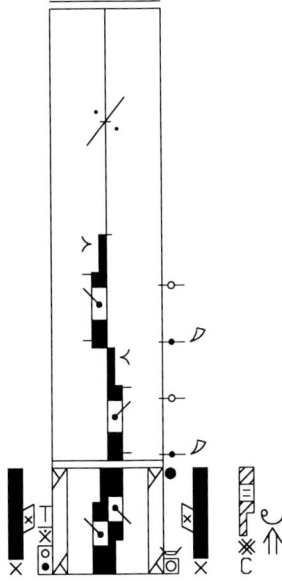

27b

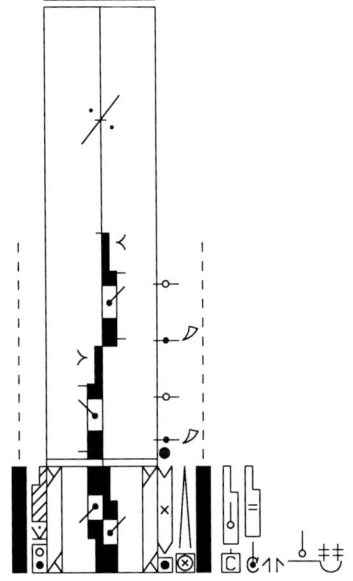

27c

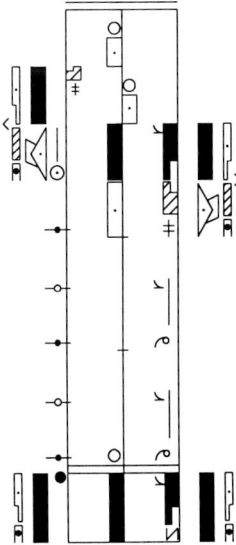

27d

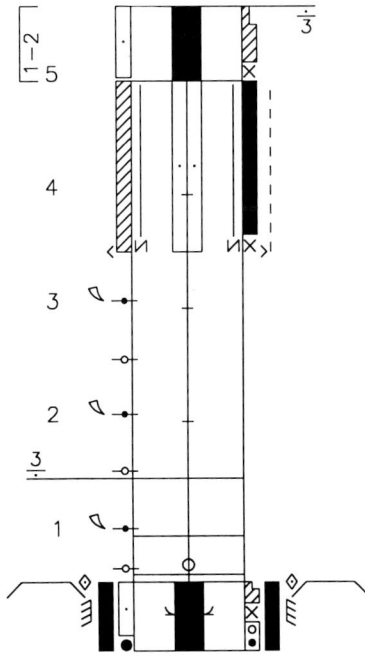

27e

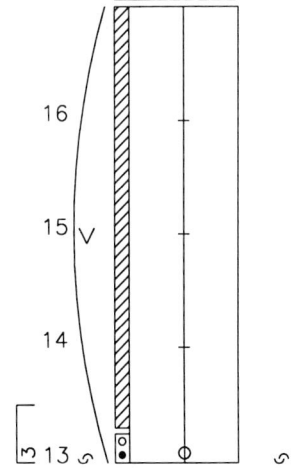

(27e cont.)

27.6.   Three simultaneous up-down actions complement each other in
27f.[68] The C of W movements will take place through slight flexions in the left
leg but are experienced as vertical lowering and rising of the body-as-a-whole.
These movements augment the effect (for the audience) and the feeling (for the
performer) of the lifting and lowering of the right arm, the counter movement of
the head, and the foot releasing and retouching.

27.7.   In order to toll a bell, the right hand pulls on a rope hanging from
the ceiling, **27g**.[69] Rather than using only the arm muscles, the whole body
weight is mobilised. During the fast footwork, the slight lowering of the C of W
accompanies the arm pull.

27.8.   The *barre* exercise of **27h** starts in a narrow 2nd position with
parallel feet; the arms are rather bent as the hands support on the *barre*, the body
inclining forward from ankles to chest in one piece. In the first measure the
movement consists of a slight pushing of the weight forward low. At the end,
the C of W returns to vertical placement over the feet as the hands release weight
(but not contact with the barre). The torso moves to a position a bit below
forward horizontal, the arms are forward, normally stretched and still resting on
the barre. The torso now bounces up and down, while the arms react passively to
allow the torso more freedom to move.

Note that returning the C of W to 'place high' is a clarification to aid the
reader. It can be added even though no previous major vertical lowering was
written in terms of C of W.

27.9.   **Retention of Level.** In measures 12 and 13 of **27i**[70] there is no rise
or fall in the level of the C of W. The body hold sign over the C of W sign
indicates that the body should not rise or lower as would be natural for it in the
sequence of low steps and gestures in this example. This elimination of natural
resilience gives a special character to the performance. Cancellation of this
retention is shown at the end of measure 13 and consists of an 'away' sign; a
return to normal is not appropriate here as normal infers normal (middle) standing
level.

Reading Examples - Minor Vertical Displacements (continued)

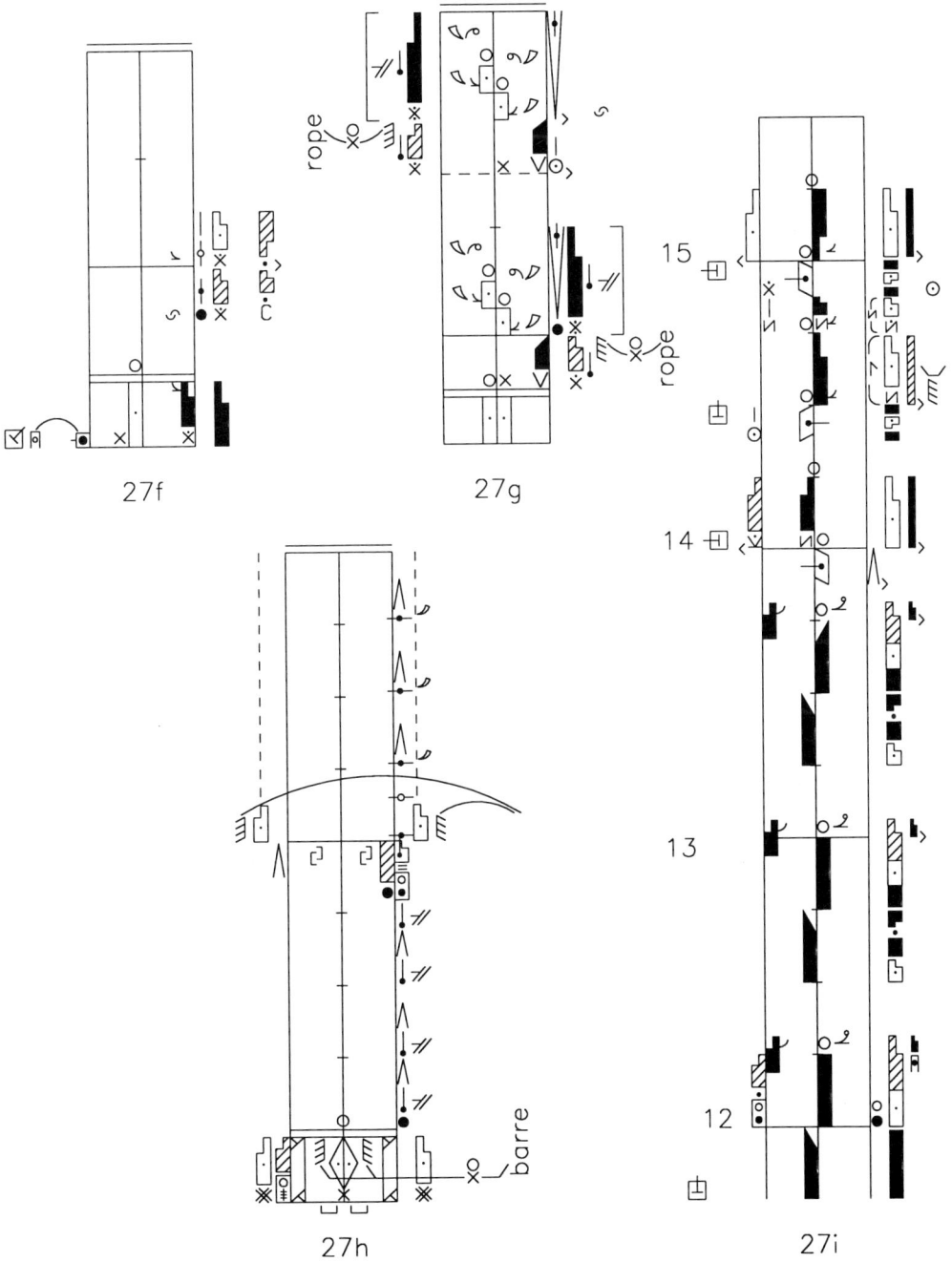

27f

27g

27h

27i

27.10. **Momentarily Lifting the Weight.** The following examples are taken from the Hungarian male dance *Pontozo*.[71] Ex. **27j** starts with the left leg forward, very close to the floor (as shown by the double 'x' sign in the support column). This is followed by a slight spring and the heels clicking together on count 2. Before count 4, as a preparation, the weight is lifted from the left foot while keeping contact with the floor and the right foot is freed from the floor. The small inturned 2nd position on count 4 is a preparation for the small spring clicking the heels together, as before. After the pause weight is lifted from both feet (again while keeping contact with the floor) as a preparation for count 3, when the legs straighten and the heels click on the $^1/_8$th foot. Heels click again on count 4 as they lower to whole foot contact and the knees bend slightly. The heel click written here is an abbreviation, as shown in **27k**; this would be glossarized in a score.

27.11. On count 2 of **27l** a slight spring ends with the right foot landing behind the left, which is just off the floor. At the end of count 3 weight is lifted off the right foot in preparation for the very small inturned 2nd position, which is again the preparation for the heel click on count 1.[72] However, this heel click is achieved through sliding the feet together.[73] Again a lifted heel click on count 3 followed by a small spring into a very small, inturned 2nd position, landing with strong accents, i.e. with sound.

Reading Examples - Momentarily Lifting the Weight

27j

27l

27k

28 Reading Examples - Center of Weight 'Leading'

28.1. Normally, the C of W is set in motion in the preparation for each new step. In **28a**, because the C of W is shown specifically to lead into the next step, a slight falling occurs on each step. In this sequence each step is separated from the next one by a pause for the support, but movement is, in fact, continuous. Apart from the difference in dynamics, the steps in **28a** are different from those in **28b**, in that in **28a** the weight is centered over the foot at the end of count 2 and moves ahead in the next count. In **28b** weight on the right foot is centered later, the action of the legs is continuous.

28.2. In **28c**,[74] after a long sideward crossing step on the left leg, the Miller extends his right leg out to the side before the C of W leads into the long, low step across to the left on count 3 (a *tombé* movement). The feeling and the visual effect of the C of W leading is amplified here by the right leg gesture acting as a temporary counterweight to the other side. Because of the weight of this leg, the C of W can move further out to the left before causing the slight falling movement.

Reading Examples - Center of Weight 'Leading'

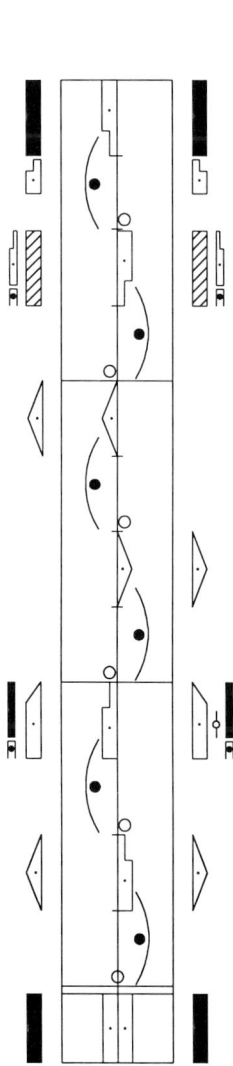

28a

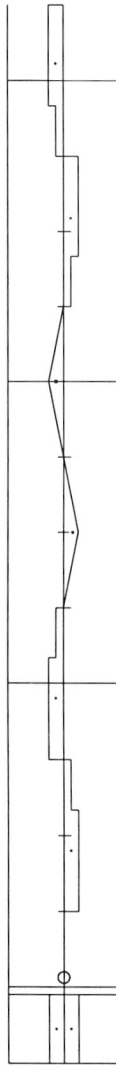

28b

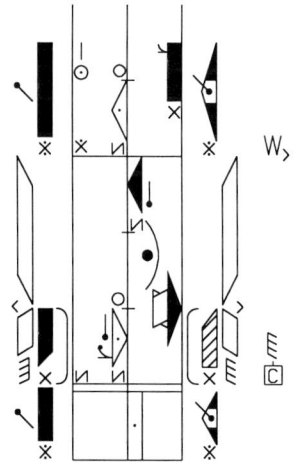

28c

28.3. In **28d**,[75] a variation of **28c**, the foot pattern occurs to the other side, and the body is shown to be continually in motion towards the right side. As before, in the first measure there is no step on count 2, but the C of W leads into the step on count 3. In the second measure the traveling sideward continues through the long steps circling to the right. The body only comes to rest on count 3. Arms and upper torso movements are different here from **28c**; note the hands grasping the waistcoat, represented as 'wt'.

28.4. Ex. **28e**[76] shows a progression on a circular pathway with steps forward on *pointe* into *arabesque*, followed by a *tombé*. The C of W passes beyond the support on the right foot and leads into a slight falling onto the next long low forward step.

28.5. The preliminary steps in the sequence of **28f**[77] lead to a preparation for a high kick (*grand battement*) to the side with the right leg on count 2 of the second measure. On count 3 this leg is brought into a parallel *retiré*, the right foot touching the left knee. From the 3/4 high support the C of W leads forward into a *tombé* on the right foot.

Reading Examples - Center of Weight 'Leading' (continued)

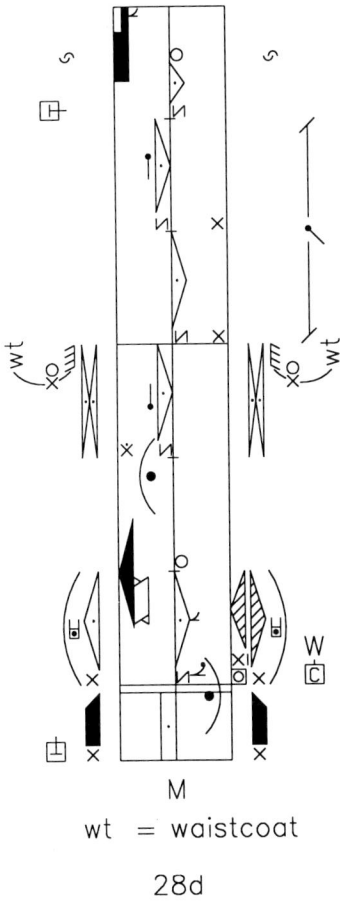

wt = waistcoat

28d

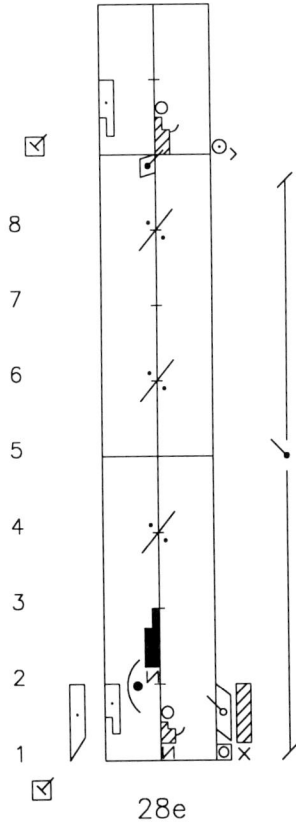

28e

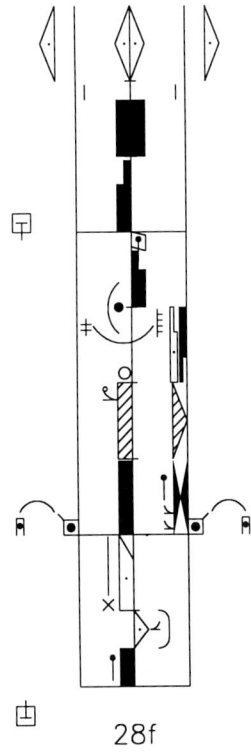

28f

28.6. Ex. **28g**[78] shows the Miller's 'quivering' excitement at seeing the girl. This is followed by an upward body stretch from ankles to head, during which the pelvic area shifts forward out of the body alignment.

In the third measure, the Miller turns to the upstage right corner, swinging the arms across the body in the same direction as the turn. The C of W then leads into the next step, producing a slight falling action. Although the pelvis remains shifted, the loss of balance is not caused by this shifting, but by intentionally displacing the body weight forward of the point of support, thus leading into the direction of the step on the left foot.

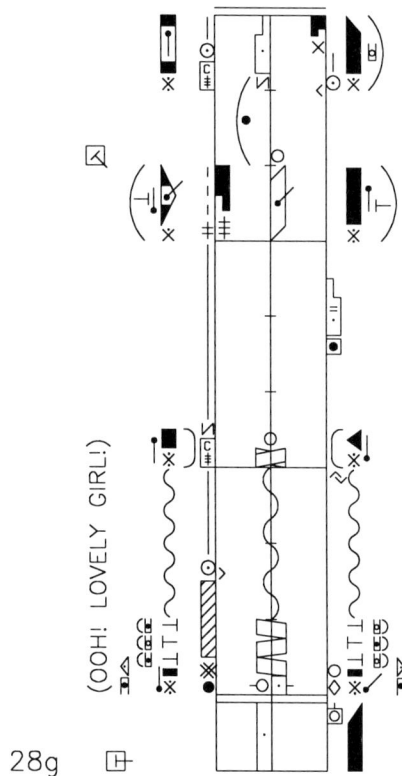

28g

28.7. The crying motif for the Miller's Wife, **28h**,[79] is emphasized by the C of W leading forward from a high support. As she rises over the supporting leg, the working leg performs a Spanish style kick gesture (*développé*). The body gives in to the weight of this leg allowing the natural tendency to fall forward. Note the overlapping sequential forward folds for the torso.

28.8. In measure 2 of **28i**,[80] after a swivel in 4th position, the C of W sign indicates a deep bending on the left leg as the torso tilts forward and twists to the left. This is followed by rising and swiveling to the right. The pelvic shift at the end of measure 4, performed during a diagonally forward low step and retained during the slow rise, is canceled just before the C of W leads into the backward steps circling counterclockwise, led by the left shoulder. Balance is regained on the fourth step as the $^1/_2$ turn whip around causes the performer to face front again. During measures 5 and 6 there is an increasing feeling of pressing and extending.

Reading Examples - Center of Weight 'Leading' (continued)

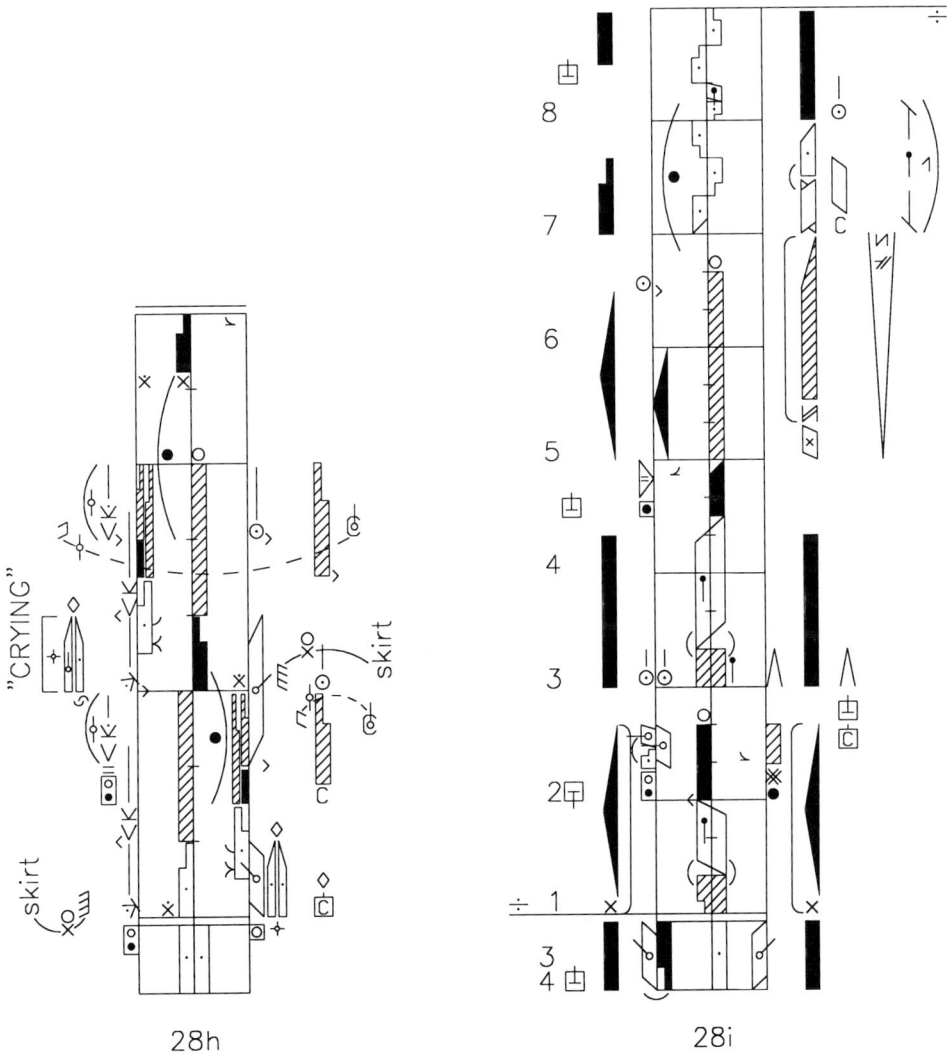

28h

28i

29 Reading Examples - Falling

29.1. **Quick Dance Falls.** The following examples are of sequences which in dance are called 'falls'. Because they are performed rapidly and fluently, there is a sense of falling, but no actual falling occurs, i.e. there is no major loss of balance from standing in which the C of W moves markedly beyond the point of support. Ex. **29a**[81] shows a springing preparation into a backward 'fall', lying backward through a fluent sequence of supports including kneeling and sitting, shown in the support columns. In the process of lowering, the torso assists balance by leaning forward; it then sequentially 'unfolds' backward into lying while the right leg extends forward, the left leg remaining folded under the right leg. The sequence is then basically reversed.

No indications for the changes in level in terms of C of W are given here. After landing from the spring, spatially the weight of the body travels backward in lying down and forward in getting up, during these transitions the weight is always over a point of support.

29.2. The sequence of **29b** is a similar so-called fall to the side and is again written without indication of C of W. There is a relatively quick transition from standing to lying. Because of the speed and the successive use of a number of different supporting body parts, the movement can appear to be a fall, but the performer does not experience any loss of balance. It is not unusual for this kind of 'fall' to be described by showing changes of situation of body sections and supporting parts, rather than by indicating lowering of the C of W.

Reading Examples - Falling

Quick Dance 'Falls'

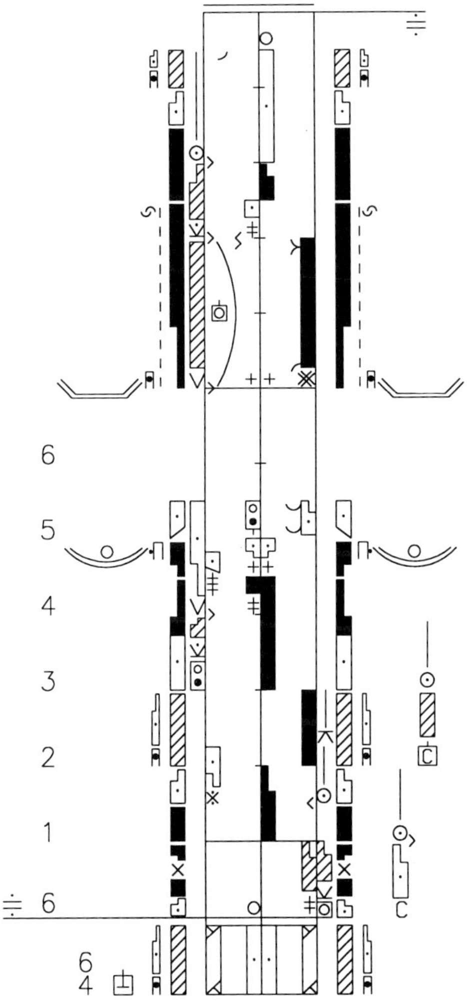

♩ = 152 Allegro

29a

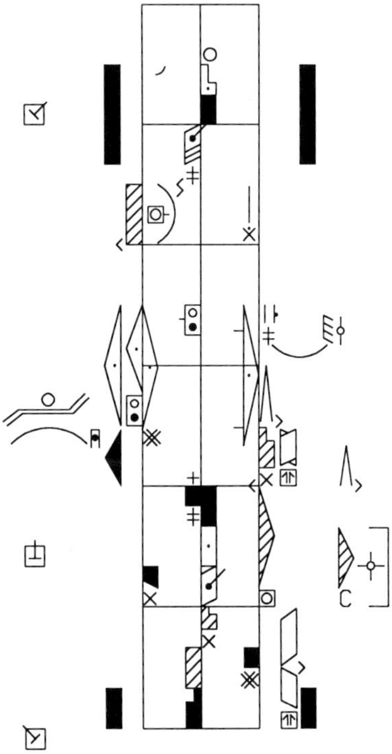

29b

29.3. **Loss of Balance.** During the step on count 1 in **29c**[82] the body tilts to the right side. While maintaining the body shape, the performer moves the center of weight to the left side, causing a definite loss of balance. A full fall is avoided as weight is caught on the left foot by the two subsequent low steps in the same direction. The gravitational pull to the left is exploited in the turn in measure 2. The right arm gesture and the body contraction are also an aid for this turning. The falling motif then occurs in the forward direction, as the torso leans backward.

29.4. For the falling in **29d**[83] one has to have a bit of nerve. During two backward steps, accompanied by a backward torso tilt, the C of W slowly falls backward into sitting on the floor. Immediately the dancer rolls over to the left on knees and hips, around the torso which has a space hold. The rolling ends with turning on the left knee to end facing the original direction. On the step forward which follows, the C of W starts falling into the upstage left direction and continues into this direction while the dancer does a half turn. At the same time the torso, which starts leaning forward, retains that spatial direction and so ends leaning backward. Again the fall, which through the turning, ends as a backward fall, has the dancer ending once more on the hips. During the roll over the hands are used on the floor to assist the rolling. To maintain the correct progression there is an $^1/_8$ circling at the start of the roll.

Reading Examples - Loss of Balance

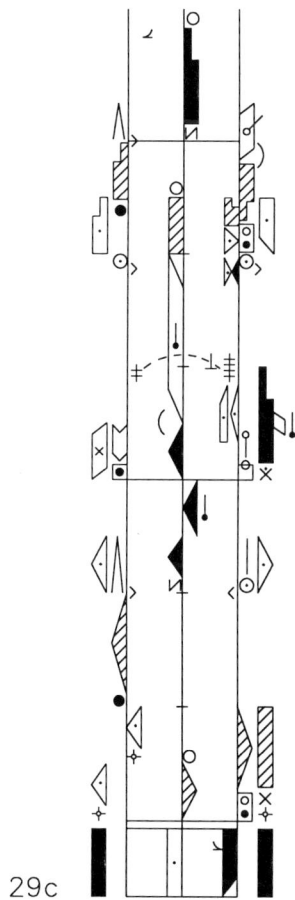

29c

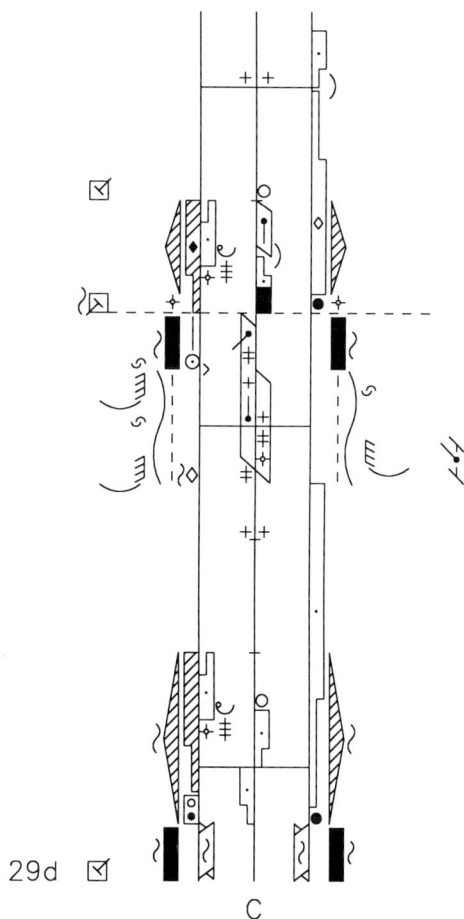

29d

C

29.5. In **29e**[84] on count 1 of the first measure, the pelvic shift is
counterbalanced by the chest tilt. They again counterbalance in count 3 during
which the right leg extends sideward. The body then starts to fall to the side,
this fall being caught by a lunging step on the right leg into a 'sitting' position;
at this moment the hands grasp the skirt, pulling it up so the left leg position,
ankle touching knee, can be seen. After a pause and a quick shaking of the head
(as if shaking off a fly), the body falls to the left and is caught again on a
lunging step, the same position being repeated to the other side.

29.6. The first two measures of the sequence in **29f**[85] both start with the
same movement. Measure 1 begins with a contracting body movement, the right
lower arm under the lifted right leg, momentarily supporting its weight.
Releasing the body contraction, the performer springs forward into a series of
leaps, the free leg extended backward, the torso tilted forward. In measure 2 the
release from the contracted body position leads into a fall forward which ends at
floor level. The weight is caught on the feet in a 4th position squat, again the
body is contracted. The right leg extends backward, the instep touching the floor.
With the C of W remaining close to the floor, there is a quarter turn on the left
foot and the right foot closes into 1st position. The rising of the C of W to
normal (standing) level leads to turning in middle level on the right leg, the torso
tilted far forward (slanting downward) and the left leg extended backward high.

Reading Examples - Loss of Balance (continued)

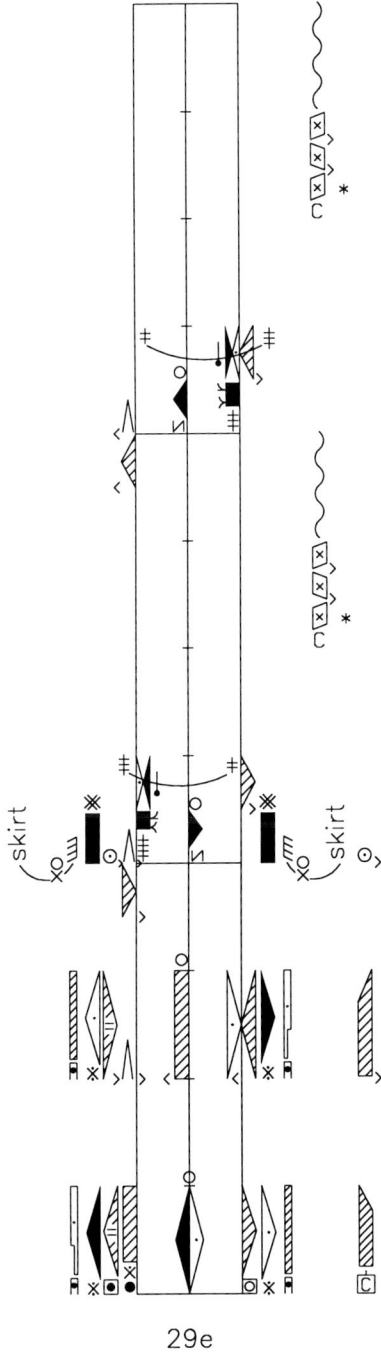

29e

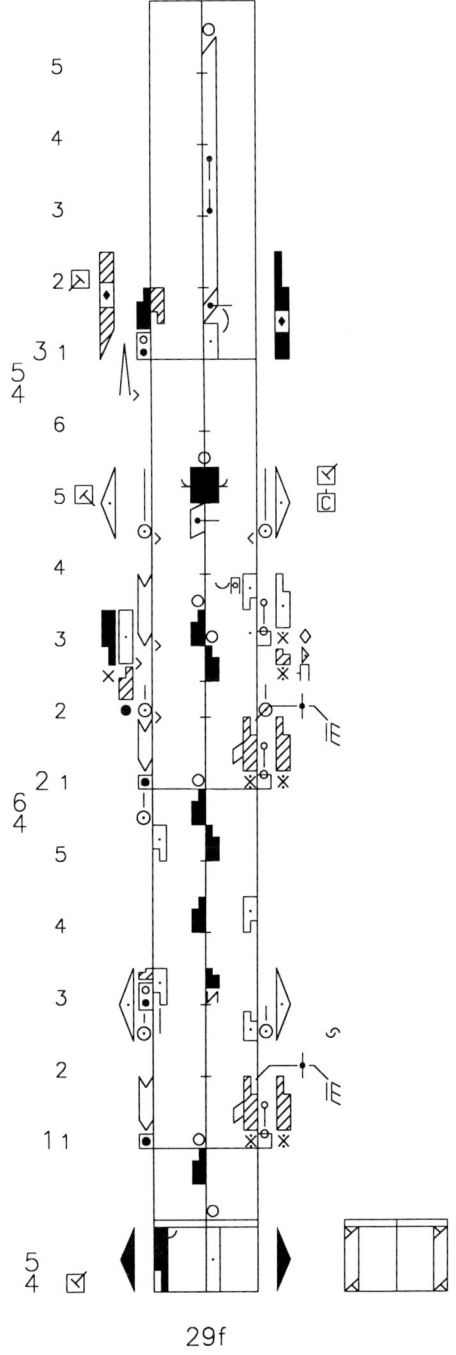

29f

29.7. Great agitation is expressed in **29g**[86] by the Governor as a result of his proximity to the Miller's Wife ('W') and her seductive shoulder movements. As his chest quivers (rapid rotary movements) and the arms gradually cross as though to wrap around his body, the Governor begins to lean forward, rising in the small second position onto half-toe with bent knees. Lifting continues and ends as falling forward, when the Miller's Wife gives his shoulder a shove. His step forward on the left leg does not cancel the falling; this continues and causes faster steps until balance is regained at the end of the second measure when the torso also comes upright.

29.8. Toward the end of the pivot turn on count 1 of **29h**,[87] the C of W falls forward. Falling is caught on the low running steps, but these are still led by the C of W until the final forward step on the left foot. The run is precipitated by the forward loss of balance, giving momentum to the whole action of imitating a bull charging; also note the slight detour to the right. This ends with the Miller's Wife grasping her skirt and placing the back of her hands on her hips. Note the inclusion of the left shoulder and hip as a unit on the last step.

29.9. Starting with feet together, legs parallel and stretched and the body in a typical twisted matador position, the Miller's C of W in **29i**[88] begins to move forward as his right lower leg lifts, his body stretching from the ankle upward, rising onto the low ball of the foot. Balance is regained on the step which follows, as the Miller catches his weight on the ball of the foot and then lowers the heel. Because of context this will only be a slight fall but the weight factor is more emphasised than in C of W leading.

This example illustrates that *direction for the C of W is judged from Stance*, that is 'forward' for the C of W is the same direction as 'forward' for the untwisted part of the body, here the lower body, the pelvis and step direction.

Reading Examples - Loss of Balance (continued)

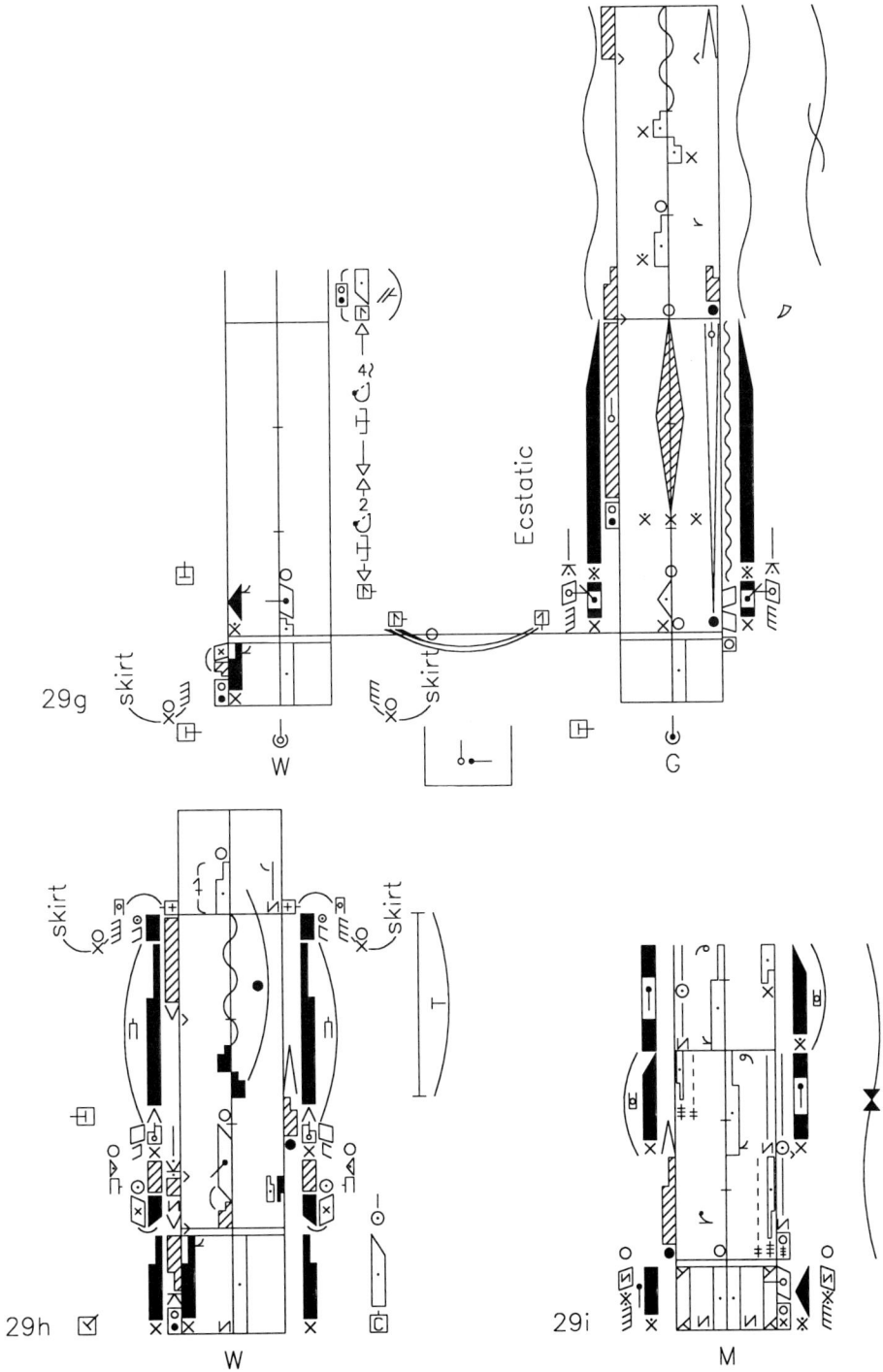

29g

skirt

W

Ecstatic

skirt

skirt

G

29h

skirt

skirt

W

T

29i

M

29.10. In the classroom exercise of **29j**, after rolling onto his back to face stage left, the performer lifts both legs and torso, balancing as a result on the back of the pelvis. As the torso comes upright, weight is taken on the hips and the legs cross. Leading into the next measure, the performer rises into a high 2nd position kneel with legs turned out. On count 2 the torso makes a 'diving' (falling) movement forward, the weight is caught on the hands, arresting further falling, (note cancellation of the falling here). As the arms stretch, the torso rises, arched over the back. It comes upright, contracted over the front, when the kneeling position is regained by pushing from the hands. The sequence ends with a fall backwards onto the back of the pelvis with the legs off the floor and the torso leaning backward as before.

29.11. In the contemporary dance sequence of **29k**[89] the sliding support in measure 4 into a very wide 2nd position (almost a sideward split) automatically lowers the body toward the floor. On count 3 there is an additional falling forward which occurs together with a strong contraction (pelvic rotation and backward high shift in the chest). Weight is partially caught on the right lower arm before landing on the right hip, at which point the falling is canceled. The left lower arm takes partial weight in supporting the upper body.

Performing this sequence requires training. The body contraction after lowering, accentuated by the shape of the lower arms, helps to keep the 'sitting position' before releasing the contraction which, together with a circular leg gesture, leads into rolling to the left and sitting upright.

Reading Examples - Loss of Balance (continued)

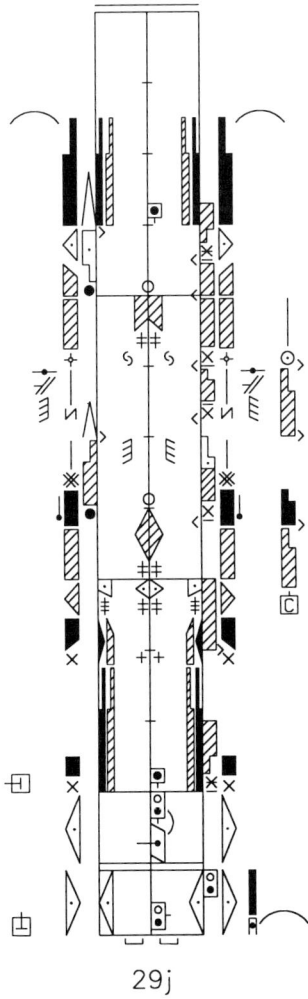

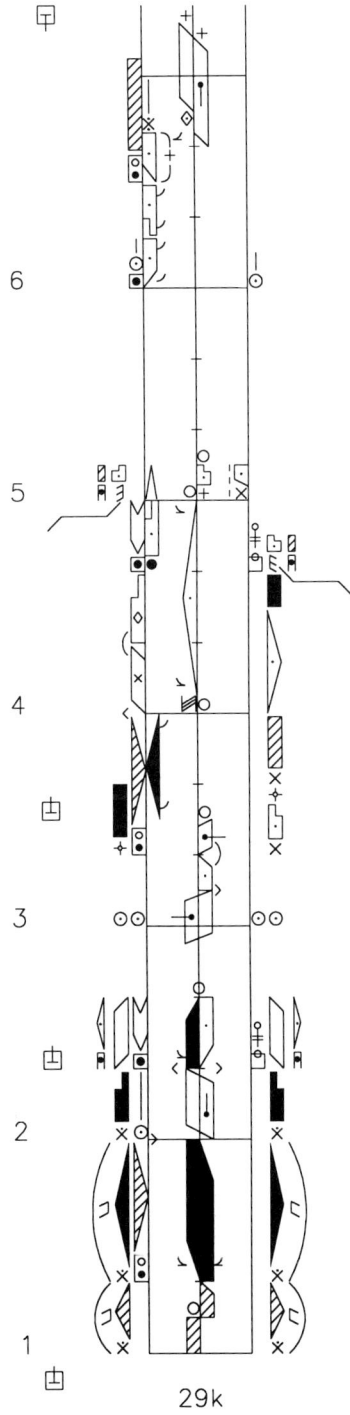

29j

29k

30 Reading Examples - Group Study Featuring Center of Weight

30.1. Ex. **30a**[90] presents a series of common variations in the use of the C of W set in a sequence for a group moving in a circle. In measures 1 and 2 performers sink into a low squat (deep *plié*) and then return to normal standing.

In measure 3 a rise with a forward leg gesture is followed by the C of W leading into a *tombé* forward. A similar rise and *tombé* are repeated backward in measure 4, but the backward step is immediately followed by a quick rebound step forward before stepping back again. During this quick forward step on the right foot the weight remains over the left foot; the body does not travel forward before stepping back again.

Measures 5 and 6 feature falling to the side from a rise on both feet. The falls are caught by a low step in the same direction. On the second fall the C of W is completely lowered in balance, producing a low squat.

In measures 7 and 8, while slowly returning to normal standing, the performers shift the weight from side to side. This is a matter of shifting weight toward alternate feet, and not of shifting the pelvis out of its normal alignment.

Performers now turn to face clockwise and during the next 4 measures travel in that direction, alternating four normal low running steps with four long leaping steps, during which the progression of the C of W is completely horizontal with no rise or fall.

Reading Examples - Group Study Featuring Center of Weight

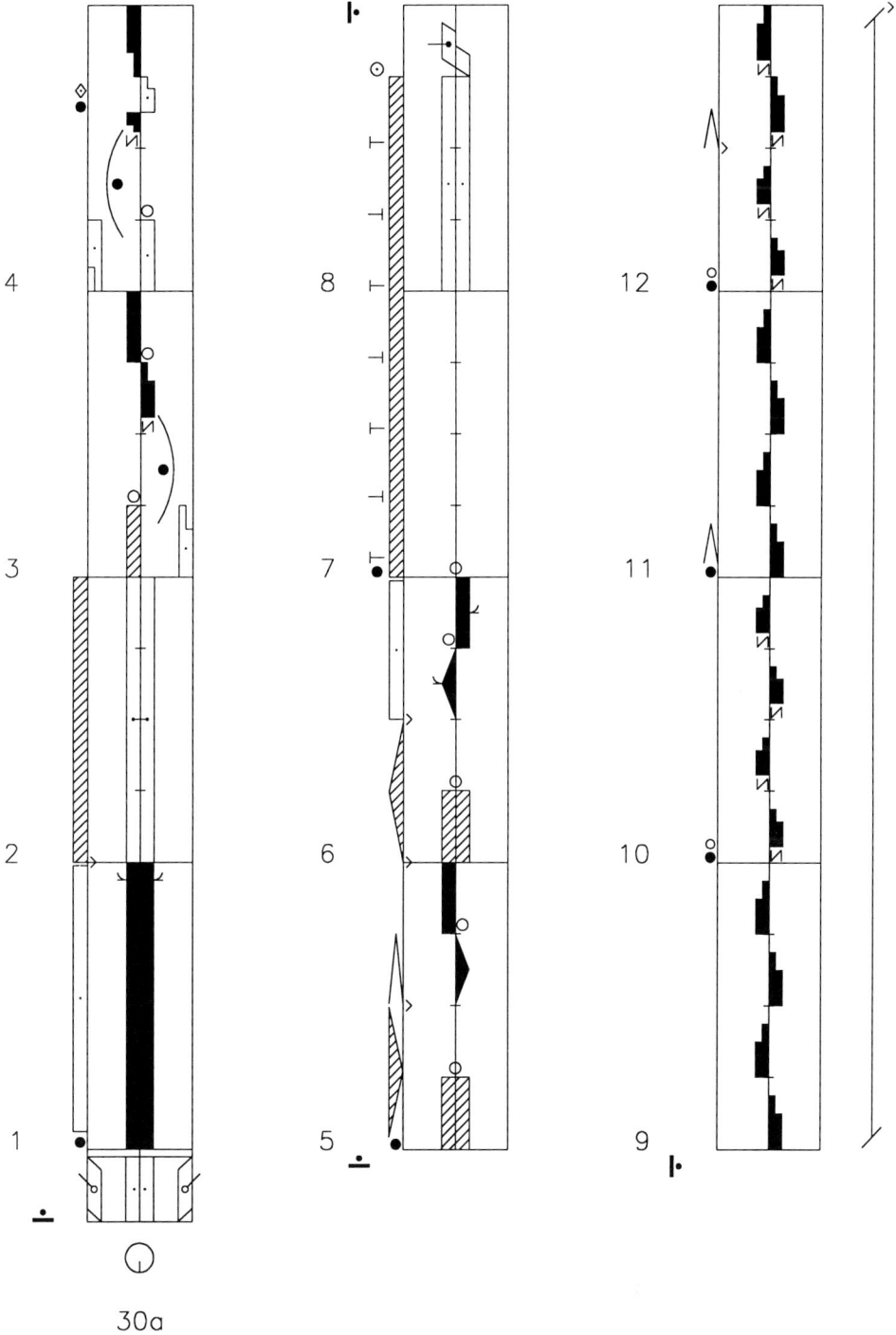

30a

In measures 13-16 the performers continue moving clockwise, taking eight steps to lower gradually into a squat, two steps to rise a little, two more steps to go back to a squat, then rising during four counts to return to normal walking. The smooth changes of level in these measures are indicated through use of the C of W symbol which modifies the indications of level in the support column.

Now the group turns to face inward and performers walk forward to decrease the size of the circle. They take hands, arms bent sideways. Gradually their weight is carried backward, each person supporting the others. Because they are not falling, the C of W indication is of a path backward. The hands stay on the same spot in space, i.e. the arms have to extend a little. Note the indication for 'strong' placed next to the hands. Returning to standing, performers repeat the backward C of W movement, but this time the right leg gestures backwards and, letting go hands and turning to the right, they fall sideward into a very deep lunge. From here, facing outward, rising and walking away from the center, they open up the circle. They then turn to face in and form the larger circle as at the beginning. The study ends with a rise to half toe, then lowering to normal standing.

Reading Examples - Group Study (concluded)

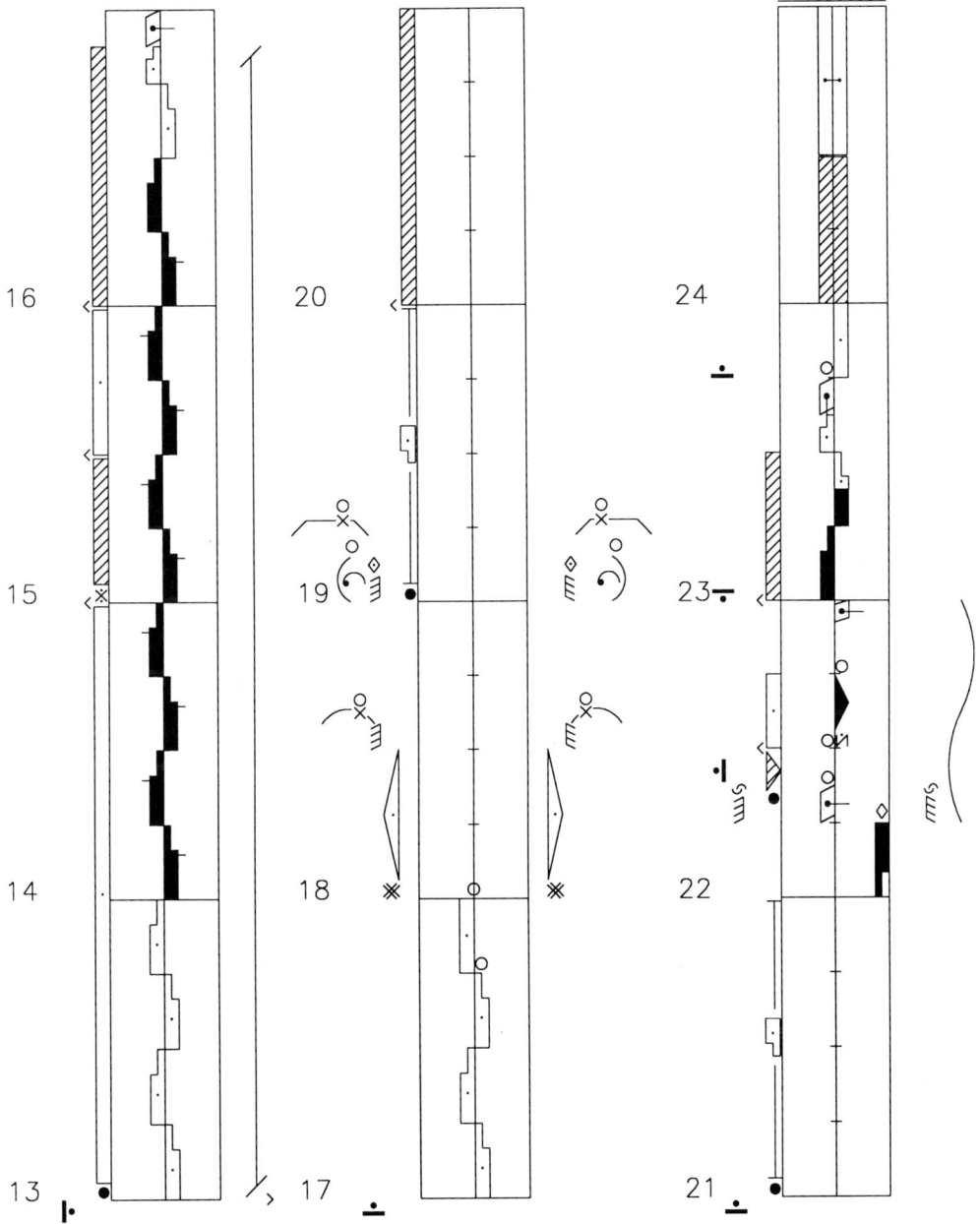

Appendix: Historical Background on Labanotation Textbooks

The authoritative textbook *Labanotation - The System of Analyzing and Recording Movement*, was first published in 1954. The revised and expanded version, published in 1970 (reprinted in 1977) drew attention to a number of topics which were to be dealt with in greater detail in a subsequent publication, referred to as "Part Two". The need for such statements was high-lighted by the reaction of a group in Japan, who, when studying the 1954 Labanotation textbook, assumed that it presented the whole system. Since no handling of long sleeves was included, they decided that the system did not meet their needs. It was therefore important to make clear that much more existed. Labanotation did indeed have the capacity of meeting their needs, and in a wider context it was necessary to draw attention to the fact that the system was applicable across the whole spectrum of human movement.

Detailed information on advanced Labanotation usage has not been generally available. Three volumes on advanced topics were published in 1991 and the present series continues the detailed and more advanced material along the same lines.

Labanotation and *Kinetography Laban, Motif Description* and *Structured Description*

The above terms may need some clarification. The specific subject of this book is *Labanotation*, the name given in the United States to the system of movement notation originated by Rudolf Laban and first published in 1928. Most European notators and dance scholars refer to the system as *Kinetography Laban*. There are some differences between Labanotation and Kinetography in notation usages, and occasionally in symbols and rules, and since 1959 the International Council of Kinetography Laban (ICKL) has provided a successful platform for discussions between practitioners on unification and further applications of the system. Differences are now small so that mutual understanding of scores is ensured. Kinetography rules and usages are catalogued in Albrecht Knust's 1979 Dictionary (see Bibliography).

The aim of the present series of texts is to provide a guide to the *Structured Description* of movement, the fully-fledged notation offering a determinate description of the movement progression by detailing choreographed (or otherwise set) actions. A different and complementary approach is provided by

Motif Description (Motif Writing), which uses symbols to represent movement ideas and concepts and provide a general statement concerning the theme or motivation of a movement.

The term Labanotation is used in this book to refer to the notation system in general and not to mark an opposition with Kinetography or Motif Writing.

Source materials

Advanced Labanotation contains, whenever possible, systematic discussion of other usages and, where appropriate, comments on the history of symbols and rules and the reason for their inclusion in the Labanotation system. The material presented is based on all available textbooks, on earlier writings of Knust and Maria Szentpál, as well as on personal discussions and correspondence with specialists such as Sigurd Leeder, Valerie Preston-Dunlop and members of the Dance Notation Bureau in New York and the Dance Notation Bureau Extension at Ohio State University. Another major source of information are the proceedings of twenty ICKL Conferences.

Much use is made of the comprehensive theoretical account of the system by Knust, summarized in his *Dictionary of Kinetography Laban/Labanotation* (1979), and his earlier publications including his eight-volume encyclopedia of 1946-50 entitled *Handbuch der Kinetographie Laban*. The textbook *Dance Notation. Kinetography Laban* by Szentpál, published in Hungarian between 1969 and 1976 is unfortunately not readily accessible to readers outside Hungary, but Szentpál generously provided an English translation for her many colleagues.

In many cases, writing an advanced text of this kind has meant breaking new ground: the intricacies of analyzing and notating falling for limbs, weight placement in skating, and Center of Weight in springing actions, for instance, were not adequately covered, and some not included at all in the 1979 Knust Dictionary. Some recent developments in the system such as 'DBP' (Direction in relation to the location of Body Part), track pins and symbols for 'design drawing' came too late to be included in Knust's 1979 Dictionary.

The Advanced Labanotation series offers the latest research on the Labanotation system and hence is completely up-to-date as at the date of publication.

Research Involved

A major concern in the research for this book has been the comparison of one rule against another to check applicability in all contexts. Often this has led to discoveries producing new arguments for or against a certain way of writing.

Labanotation is rapidly developing and is accepted as a tool in recording, research and in education. Each of these fields has specific requirements. There is a call for maximum flexibility in the notation system, so that it can provide general and simple statements for particular purposes and at the same time be very precise where such specificity is required. In dance research the need for precision has increased to the point where we are obliged to consider questions about the system that only ten years ago did not seem important, let alone when the fundamentals of the system were devised. In this new text we have tried to take these different needs into account while respecting the system as it has been handed down to us and is now used by people all over the world.

Notes

These annotations are mainly of three kinds. Firstly, they identify other major *rules and usages*. Secondly, they mark symbols and rules that have been *recently introduced* or *not described in other sources*, the origins of these being given. And finally, they give the *references for particular notation excerpts.*

On important or controversial issues, a short discussion of rationale is included. Sometimes, old ways of writing are briefly mentioned.

Research of other usages systematically involved *Táncjelírás, Laban Kinetográfia* by Szentpál and the *Dictionary of Kinetography Laban (Labanotation)* by Knust (see Bibliography). Where needed, other sources were also used.

Numbers in parentheses at the end of each note indicate where the note is in the text. The following abbreviations identify sources, for full bibliographic information see Bibliography.

References

H36-39	Hutchinson 1936-39 notes
H70	Hutchinson 1970
ICKL	International Council of Kinetography Laban
K45-50	Knust 1945-1950
K51	Knust 1951
K58	Knust 1958
K79	Knust 1979
L28	Laban 1928
L30	Laban 1930
L75	Laban 1975
LNTR	*The Labanotator*
PD63	Preston-Dunlop 1963
S76	Szentpál 1969-76
AK	Albrecht Knust
KIN	Kinetography Laban
LN	Labanotation

1. See also H70, pp. 398-413; K45-50, Part H, pp. 1145-1233; K58: 456-479; K79: 509-527; L75, pp. 23, 34, 52, 53, Marriett 1986, pp. 102-104; S76, Part 2, Lesson XVII: 21, 22, figs. 12, 44. (1.1)

2. For details on the scientific fundamentals of the issues discussed here, consult standard textbooks in biomechanics or kinesiology, such as Luttgens and Wells 1982, on which most definitions and much of the basic information in this section are based. (1.3)

3. The term 'center of gravity' has also been used in LN, e.g. in H70. In a dance context the term 'center of weight' is considered more appropriate because dancers tend to think in terms of weight placement, rather than in terms of the location of the center of gravity. (1.3)

4. S76 is the only textbook that does not discuss the subject of C of W extensively. Maria Szentpál wrote while checking the first drafts of this issue: "[I personally cannot] envisage cases or ideas where one would want to 'focus' on a movement of the C of W. [This is related to] the fact that the performer and the perceiver have no neural and muscular sensation of this theoretical point which is not a body part." At that time the term 'Center of Gravity' was used and the idea of a point and its location in the body was the focus of discussion. Since then focus has been on *weight placement* and *balance* both of which are observable and physically understandable functions. (2.7)

5. Friction can be one of sliding friction, as when rubbing something, or it can be static friction, as when pressing against the floor to turn, to leap and so on. If the floor is too slippery, it is difficult to walk; the feet slip, i.e. sliding friction occurs where static friction is needed. (3.9)

6. Historically the sign of a) was used for middle of the body and the sign of b) represented the 'light point' (see L28, pp. 11, 16). In L30, p. 11, the sign of c) meant weight; d) was described as "weight forward (in a horizontal direction)". The sign of b) in L30 was called the 'point of elevation'. In H36-39 c) meant pelvis and also center of gravity. K51 stated that c) meant 'centre of gravity'. K45-50 listed c) as 'the heavy point' contrasting it with the 'light point' of b).

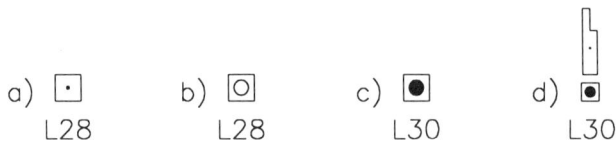

a) ⊡   b) ▣   c) ◉   d) ◉
L28   L28   L30   L30

This use of the sign for both pelvis and center of gravity prevailed until the 1950s. It was understood that the center of gravity was situated near the upper rim of the pelvis. The idea that it could be elsewhere in the body or even outside the body was unheard of. In K58 the pelvis sign was used to mean focal point;

ex. 738f makes the statement that the focal point is the center of the room. However, when the focal point was indicated on a turn sign, only the black circle of e) was used, as in K58: 252d. In the late 1950s the Dance Notation Bureau recognized that identifying C of W with the pelvis was misleading and a separation was needed. AK also recognised this need.

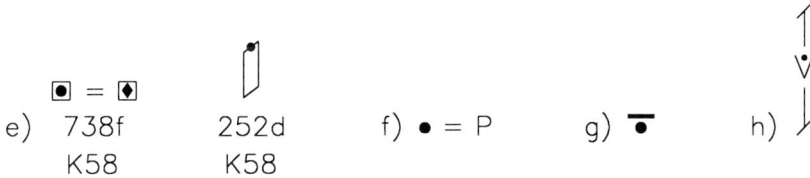

e) 738f   252d   f) ● = P   g) ●   h)
K58   K58

At the 1961 ICKL Conference e) was introduced as the sign for center of gravity to distinguish it from pelvic girdle (ICKL 1961, Technical Report, p. 2). The sign of e) was understood as the focal point (C of W) in the body. Application of this sign to other focal points was known from context, as in f) where the focal point is designated as P; in g) the orientation is to have the focal point behind you while h) states approaching the center of the circle (the understood focal point of the circle). (7.2)

7. Originally the C of W was considered to be at middle level while standing, and to be low when lowered to a sit or squat (H36-39). AK established the present-day levels and designated the point of support as that place from which direction and level for C of W were to be judged (K45-50). His analysis was adopted by LN. (8.4)

8. AK established this analysis of division into body-lengths, K58: 457d. (9.2)

9. This chart (originally published in H70, p. 401, here revised to be more accurate) is based on a rough equation between measurement of distance from the floor and of angle at knee joint. Strictly speaking these are two slightly different scales; however, for LN this difference between leg contractions and C of W indications is negligible.

    For the C of W indications, the measurement signs indicate 6 increments of distance from standing to squatting, the halfway point being shown by the third degree of leg bending (a 90°angle at the knee joint). The C of W at floor level (or as near as possible) is written with the place middle sign, as in a); this has the same meaning as b), the 6/6 degree of distance upward from the reference point, but a) is simpler to write.

a)   b)

    The degrees for level of supports, the comparative degrees between the

C of W levels, and measurement signs in the leg gesture columns, was an issue during early ICKL Conferences. The basic idea of this chart was adopted in 1965 (Technical Report, p. 11, Review no. 3). (10.1)

10. In K58 no low level was written, the legs were understood to bend as a result of the C of W lowering. (10.2)

11. It is true that, when squatting with parallel legs, the C of W appears to move backward of the feet and not straight down, but in fact the backward motion is usually countered by directing the arms and the upper body forward. (10.3)

12. Placement of a foot hook on support symbols is as follows: for a step (a complete transference of weight) the hook is placed at the beginning, the moment when contact with the floor takes place, as in a). In some instances this hook is placed higher up to make reading easier; when only one hook is used, b), this does not change the meaning. Two different hooks placed on a step symbol indicate the change from one part to another, the placement has time significance, c). (See ICKL 1963, Technical Report, item 19 and ICKL 1969, Technical Report, Paper 6, D). When *only a change of level* is taking place for an *already established support,* placement of the hook has time significance. In d) the new supporting part is reached at the end. In e) the support is taken on the balls of the feet while the lowering continues. (10.3)

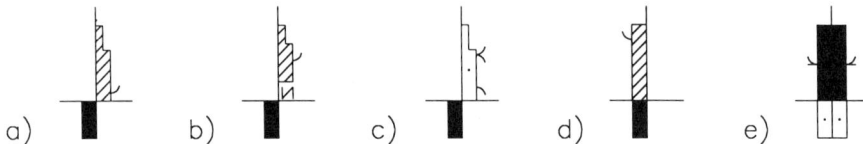

13. Originally high level support symbols for the feet indicated only use of the balls of the feet; it had no link with the level of the body as a whole (see K58: 467a, b). Body level was indicated by the level of the C of W (ICKL 1963, Technical Report, p. 5). Thus, the notation of a) meant a squat on the balls of the feet.

Later this old usage was abandoned and the idea of writing low level supports on the ball of the foot as in **10d** was adopted (see K79: 518h). The old usage shows that level of the C of W was a basic function rather than an alternative way of writing. Ex. a) is now written as b). Note that AK used no hold sign for the supports in a), this followed his logic that you can only have a level for the C of W when you still have a support. With use of a hold sign, the reader does not have to be concerned with this special rule. (10.3)

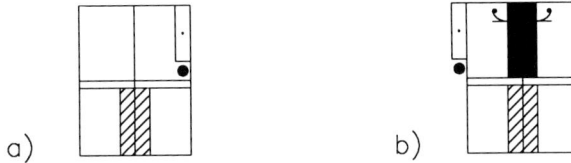

a)   b)

14. 'The direction of the progression' is a term contributed by AK (ICKL 1975, Technical Report, Paper A). The direction stated is judged from the starting point; no destination is given. It is the usual reference for walking, for transference of weight, i.e. directions for supports. The particular use of this term is for gestures which are described in terms of motion rather than the usual statement of destination, i.e. arrival at a destinational point. (10.8)

15. The 8/8 scale was adopted by ICKL in 1999 (Technical Report 1). (11.3)

16. According to an older rule, when a new support on a part of the body other than the feet occurred, as in a), any previously stated level for C of W was automatically cancelled (ICKL 1965, Technical Report, p. 6). An exception to this rule for C of W level occurs for 'all fours' positions (ICKL 1973, Technical Report, p. 4). The present basic rule is that cancellation of C of W level *always needs to be stated*. Therefore, H70: 626c, repeated as a) below, now needs a cancellation symbol. In b), a level change is shown for the C of W when the high kneel takes place; the cancellation is stated with the forward step. In c), the cancellation is shown earlier. For this latter the cancellation sign (the decrease sign) does not mean back to normal, it states that the previous indication is no longer in effect. Cancellation of C of W in falling is dealt with in Section 19. (12.2)

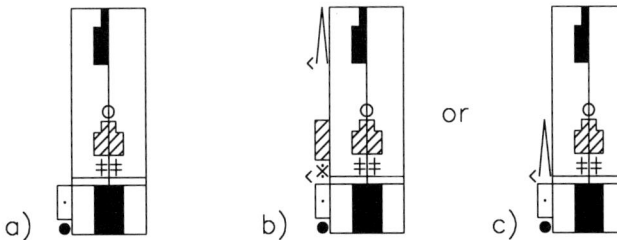

a)   b)   or   c)

17. In KIN the decrease sign is the general cancellation sign for all purposes, except for rotations, twists. In most instances it produces a result equivalent to the LN 'back-to-normal' sign. The back-to-normal sign was never adopted by KIN. In LN the decrease sign does not have the same meaning as back-to-normal, i.e. returning to the normal state for that part of the body; the decrease sign serves for the following statements: "the previous indication is over", "the

result of the previous indication is no longer in effect","forget about it", "the effect of the previous indication has disappeared". An example of this is given in note 16. (12.3)

18. It could be argued that the return to normal sign for the C of W should mean "that level of C of W which is appropriate for an ordinary low support". In this case the return to normal sign would produce no clear cut destination, it would vary because a low level support is not a defined degree of leg bend. (12.3)

19. A shorthand convention adopted by some LN notators is use of a measurement sign above the C of W sign without a direction symbol. Exs. a) and b) indicate a destination of the C of W above the point of support, as stated fully in c). Unless otherwise designated, the C of W is understood to be vertically above the point of support. Therefore b) can be understood as the same usage as in the notation of d), in which the arm is up and then draws closer to the shoulder in that same direction. (12.3)

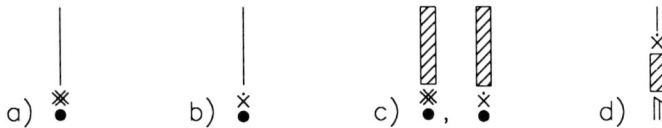

20. This usage of focus on being in balance derives from balance explorations in Motif Description. (13.6)

21. The Denishawn *pas de basque* became a hallmark of the style of modern American dance evolved by Ruth St. Denis and Ted Shawn in the 1920s. For the center of weight to have a spot hold, this off-balance movement had to be performed fairly quickly. (13.8)

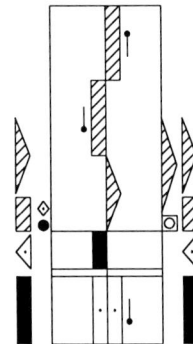

22. ICKL 1967 adopted the possibility to write the movement of **13k** with a straight path sign containing a forward direction symbol which in turn contained a 'spot hold' (Technical Report, p. 5, item 29; see H70: 617c). The idea was of a traveling spot hold. (13.9)

23. In K79 pins for these movements are usually written within increase signs when the movement has duration, as in 526a, 488f, 501f. (See also note 25.) Originally Knust used the 'toward' sign (increase sign) to indicate timing for destinational indications; ex. a) in KIN meant the same as the LN indication of b). When Knust adopted the increase sign to mean 'toward', for him the meaning of a) was changed, he needed a way of stating a destination. Instead of adopting the existing LN usage of b), AK placed the sign for degree of flexion at the end of the duration line, linking them with a bow, c). This has the same meaning as LN b). Note that for b) in LN there is an understood connection between the duration line and the movement indication which precedes it; written fully it could be stated as d), the two indications being connected. (14.2)

24. To indicate size of such movements, measurement signs in a diamond, as in a) and b), can be added. (See also note 28.) (14.6)

25. K79 does not use duration lines, instead the pin is placed within the V (increase) sign meaning 'toward' to provide the duration, as in a). (See also note 23.) (14.7)

26. Theoretically, there can be no C of W indications during jumps, since there is no base of support from which to judge the C of W. However, in **14v**, because a C of W indication was used to indicate the change in the body which is undone during the jump, the cancellation of C of W in this example is easily understood. The meaning here is that the physical modification, necessary to produce the slight shift of the C of W to the left, is canceled. (14.8)

27. The middle level pin sign indicates a horizontal shift without loss of balance. In most cases 'no loss of balance' automatically entails that the movement is quite small. Indeed, the pin carries a meaning of 'smallness'; vertical displacements written with a pin sign are meant to be small.

　　However, in certain 'all fours' positions weight shifting without loss of balance can be considerable. A specific amount of weight shift can be written with the measurement indications described in 14.11. These signs indicate degrees of size within the movement range that is available, always without losing balance.

K79 clearly indicates that the basic meaning of pins in these cases is 'smallness' (526a); for 'on all fours' positions he only addresses slight movements (488f and 479b). (14.10)

28. AK established that 'spatially large' and 'spatially small' are specifically written by placing measurement signs within a diamond, the diamond representing the spatial aspect, as in **14aa**. This indication is placed alongside the movement notation, it does not act as a presign (see K79: 526a). Without the diamond, in KIN the measurement signs would be automatically related to a system of exact distance measurement based on the individual's steplength. (14.12)

29. Placement of the path sign in the support column can be compared with the KIN usage of a hold sign placed inside a step symbol (see K79: 233). The sliding step (transference of weight) of a) continues to slide forward as the leg changes to middle level. The symbol of count 2 shows that weight is retained. In b), the continued sliding is shown with a path sign. It is assumed that sliding is still on the whole foot. (14.16)

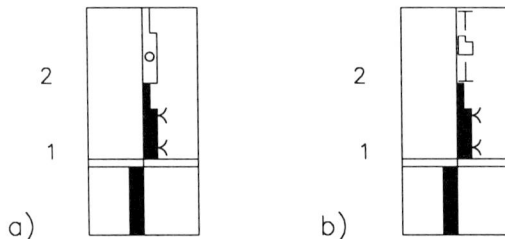

30. Comparable examples are not given in K79. There the minor center of gravity displacements presented, 526a, are slower and therefore written within an increase sign to show the duration. (15.1)

31. These short double lines allow the pre-sign to be omitted from the timing indication and signify the start of action. They are used when space is limited, especially when quick movements need to be shown (see H70: 341). (15.3)

32. This analysis of 'downward' springs and 'upward' springs was contributed by János Fügedi. (See ICKL 1997 paper "An Analysis and Classification of Springs" by János Fügedi. ICKL Technical Report, Appendix D.) (15.9)

33. Application of the arrow for motion to pin signs was first presented in *The Kinetographer* No. 10, June 1976. The arrow within a direction symbol was presented in LNTR No. 67, April 1992, and subsequently in No. 77, October 1994. (15.12)

34. A term in classical ballet, *terre à terre* means 'earth to earth', i.e. springs which stay close to the ground. (15.13)

35. First published in LNTR No. 44, May 1986. In LNTR No. 46, February 1987, Maria Szentpál agrees. (15.15)

36. Jane Marriett writes: "Stating the [C of W] tells the reader that the thrust of the movement is to fall" (Marriett 1986: 460). (18.2)

37. The C of W sign followed by the forward high direction symbol, a), is used for general falling forward, although the C of W usually does not arrive at an angle of 45°. More accurate but not commonly used is the intermediate direction, halfway from place high to forward-high, shown in b); the simpler statement of c) is generally understood to be the same as b). Ex. d) shows this slighter degree of falling in context. In e) a lower level is reached for the landing; after a greater degree of falling than d), the C of W moves further and lower before recovery. (18.3)

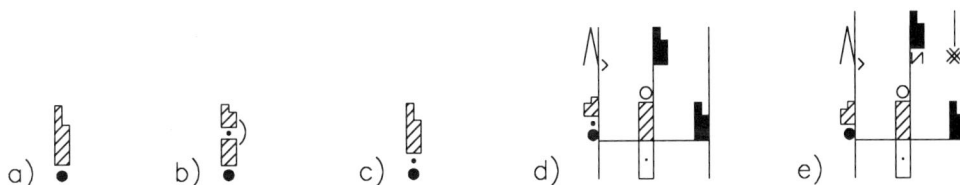

38. K79 uses no hold sign in the support column when the C of W is falling (K79: 523b-d). (18.6)

39. AK's rule for distance in C of W falling to the floor and distance in sitting were both based on the measurement of the length of the legs; if no measurement was stated, the distance would automatically be the length of the legs. The notation of a) is interpreted in KIN as b), sitting a leg-length behind the feet. Because of its simplicity and the desire for unification in usage, this rule was adopted by LN (see H70, pp. 391-392).

The original focus for the Laban system was to describe clear structured movement sequences. As time went by more and more exactness was demanded.

However, in recent years a different need has arisen, that for more general, open statements. In several respects our system did not allow for these. For example "Sit down" may be done as the person chooses. "Sit down backward" is a bit more specific, and "A leg-length distance backward" is clearly defined. The concern now is to provide a *general statement*; the simplest of statements should represent a simple, open instruction.

Therefore, a change has now been made to provide a general statement. When no distance is specified then distance is left open. A comfortable distance in sitting backward, illustrated in c) is now written in LN as a). A specific distance can always be stated, as in d).

This change from the KIN usage has been deemed necessary, because of the particular needs for more open statements in different fields which LN has to serve. (18.13)

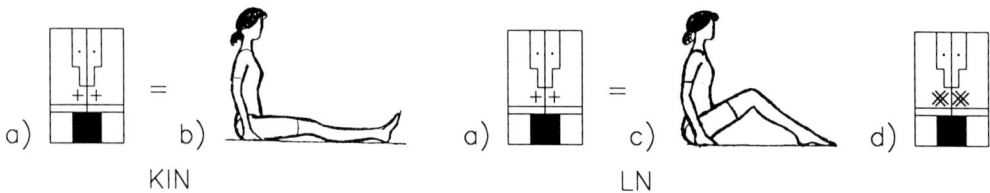

KIN   LN

40. In 1965 the rule was that "C of W indications are canceled by new indications, the decrease sign, the return to normal sign or *by a support on any part other than the feet*" (ICKL 1965, Technical Report, p. 6). This rule was not sufficiently clear, as was found in 1973 when an exception had to be made for C of W level indication in 'all fours' positions (ICKL Technical Report, p. 4). (19.2)

41. Before adoption of this form of cancellation for C of W level, a place high symbol was used. This is incorrect if the supporting level has not returned to middle level. Use of a back-to-normal sign is also questionable if normal level is understood to be a middle level support (one leg-length away from the point of support). For Validity see Section 12. (19.6)

42. Note that the notation of **20c** which uses support and gesture symbols side by side, is seen by many notators as less preferred; the indications of **20b** and **20d** are usually adequate in providing sufficient information. (20.2)

43. A similar shifting of degree of weight can be shown for central (major) supports where the performer has weight equally divided between two supports. For the second position of a), it is assumed that weight is equally divided, no

specific weight statement is made. This position can have an increasing amount of weight placed on the right foot. In b) slightly more weight is being moved toward the box. This amount is increased in c) as the leg bends slightly, and even more in d) for which the right leg is shown to be more bent. The very fact that one leg is bent places weight closer to that side, this is familiar from an ordinary 2nd position standing on the floor. What is significant here is that focus is on the weight placement, this is being featured in the notation; focus is not on a flexed or straight state of the leg. (20.9)

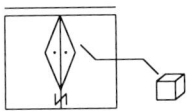
a)

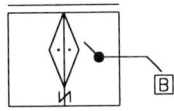
b)

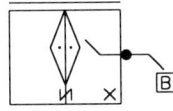
c)

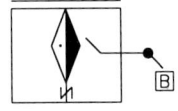
d)

44. Falling of limbs and torso was discussed June 5th, 1986 at the Dance Notation Bureau Advanced Labanotation discussions. (24.4)

45. Reading examples taken from scores are in most cases slightly adapted either for simplification or to comply with more recent developments in the notation system. (Part VI)

46. For finer gradations the 8/8 scale can be used (see note 15). (25.1)

47. As explained in note 12, a single foothook does have time value when it refers only to a change of level in an established support, as in **25a**. (25.1)

48. Notated by Susie Watts Margolin, 1970. Courtesy of Charles H. Woodford. (25.2)

49. To comply with the original score, the back-to-normal cancellation sign is given here; the 'away' cancellation sign would in fact be more appropriate here, because a high level and not the 'normal' middle level support results. (25.2)

50. Part of a classroom combination in Graham technique notated by Diane Gray, 1965. (25.4)

51. The small backward-high shift is shown by the pin being combined with the small equal sign denoting a shifting action, this equal sign being familiar from its use within a direction symbol to specify shifting. (25.4)

52. From *Ritmo Jondo* by Doris Humphrey (1953), notated by Muriel Topaz, Dance Notation Bureau, New York, 1966 ('Of Meeting and Parting', p.43). Courtesy of Charles Woodford. (25.5)

53. *Plié* bounces from Horton technique. (25.6)

54. Modern Dance Technique taught by Norman Walker, ca. 1960. Courtesy of Norman Walker. (25.7)

55. From *Brahms Waltzes* (1961), No. 7 'Luscious Falls' (Opus 39) by Charles Weidman, notated by Anne Wilson, 1964 (measures 35-44). Courtesy of Carol Mezzacappa. (25.9)

56. From *The Three-Cornered Hat* by Léonide Massine (1919), notated by Odette Blum, 1967, completed by Jocelyne Asselbourg, 1973 (The Miller, Part I, 'Start', measure 45). Courtesy of Lorca Massine. (26.5)

57. From *The Three-Cornered Hat* (see note 56) (The Miller's Wife, Part I, 'Start', measures 78-80). (26.6)

58. Jazz isolation exercise, 1968. Courtesy of Maggie Burke Lewis. (26.8)

59. Jazz isolation exercise (see note 58). (26.9)

60. From *There is a Time* by José Limón (1956), notated by Joan Morgan, 1964 ('A Time to Laugh', measures 13-15). Courtesy of José Limón Foundation. (26.10)

61. Jazz technique notated by Billie Mahoney, 1970. Courtesy of Billie Mahoney. (26.11)

62. Jazz technique (see note 61). Without the spot hold, the right foot would always step on the same place because, even when starting from an open position, the direction and distance of a step are always judged from the other foot. (26.12)

63. From *Man with the Golden Arm*, by Jon Gregory at Ballet Arts Studios, New York City (ca. 1954), notated by Billie Mahoney, ca. 1954 (opening sequence, 'Clark Street, The Top'). Courtesy of Billie Mahoney. (26.13)

64. *Plié* bounces from Horton technique. (27.1)

65. From *Three Epitaphs* by Paul Taylor (1956), notated by Muriel Topaz, Dance Notation Bureau, New York, 1971 ('Male Stance and Walk'). Courtesy of Paul Taylor. (27.2)

66. From *Three Epitaphs* ('Girl's Stance and Walk') (see note 64). (27.3)

67. From exercises and jazz combinations taught by Walter Nicks during the "Exploration of Jazz" Program, Dance Notation Bureau, notated by Muriel Topaz and Allan Miles, 1963, copyright Walter Nicks, 1963. (27.4)

68. From *The Three-Cornered Hat* (see note 56) (The Miller's Wife, Part I, 'Start', measure 22). (27.6)

69. From *The Three-Cornered Hat* (see note 56) (The Miller, Part I, 'Start', measure 50). (27.7)

70. Choreographer and notator unknown. (27.9)

71. Exs. **27j** and **27l** are from "An Analysis and Classification of Springs" presented by János Fügedi at the 1997 ICKL conference (Technical Report, Appendix D: JF. Ex.3., JF. Ex.4., p.63). Courtesy of János Fügedi. (27.10)

72. The straight line foothooks with dots underneath, a), indicate that the heels are just off the floor, a lesser degree (i.e. lower) than the eighth foot, b). This barely lifted heel is a degree not commonly needed, but important in Hungarian dances. This special sign is explained in S76, Part 1, Lesson VII. (27.11)

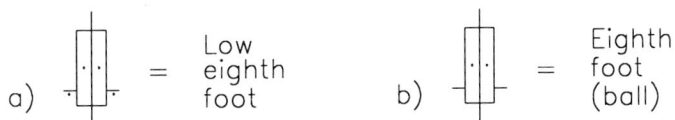

a) = Low eighth foot   b) = Eighth foot (ball)

73. The heel click here is indicated at the right moment, at the start of measure 2. As a convention, the sliding is indicated as starting in measure 2, although of course in reality it happens just before, ending with the click of the heels. The sliding is notated using unit timing, whereas the heel click is shown in exact timing. (Unit timing: a movement, written in the unit of count 1, is understood to occur (arrive) at the start of count 1.) (27.11)

74. From *The Three-Cornered Hat* (see note 56) (The Miller, Part I, 'Start', measures 19-20). (28.2)

75. From *The Three-Cornered Hat* (see note 56) (The Miller, Part I, '3 Men Sacks', measures 44-45). (28.3)

76. From *Concerto Barocco* by George Balanchine (1941), notated by Ann Hutchinson Guest, 1963 (measures 57-58). Courtesy of New York City Ballet. (28.4)

77. Note placement of the C of W leading sign on the left side leading into a step on the right foot; the meaning is the same. (28.5)

78. From *The Three-Cornered Hat* (see note 56) (The Miller, Part I, '3 Men Sacks', measures 10-12). (28.6)

79. From *The Three-Cornered Hat* (see note 56) (The Miller's Wife, Part I, '3 Men Sacks', measures 36-38). (28.7)

80. From *Brahms Waltzes* No. 7 'Luscious Falls' (see note 55). (28.8)

81. 'Back Fall and Recovery from Doris Humphrey's First Series of Falls', notated by Susie Watts Margolin, 1970. Courtesy of Charles Woodford. (29.1)

82. An exercise taught by Mary Hinkson. (29.3)

83. From *Esplanade* by Paul Taylor (1975), notated by Janet Wickline Moekle, 1977, revised 1981 (5th Movement, measure 86). Courtesy of Paul Taylor. (29.4)

84. From *There is a Time* (see note 60) ('A Time to Laugh', measures 16-18). (29.5)

85. A classroom combination in Graham style technique, notated by Diane Gray, 1965. (29.6)

86. From *The Three-Cornered Hat* (see note 56) (The Governor, Part I, 'Grape Duet', measures 19-20). (29.7)

87. From *The Three-Cornered Hat* (see note 56) (The Miller's Wife, Part I, 'Start', measures 17-18). (29.8)

88. From *The Three-Cornered Hat* (see note 56) (The Miller, Part I, 'Start', measures 31-32). (29.9)

89. A classroom combination in Graham style technique, notated by Diane Gray, 1965. (29.11)

90. 'Centre of Gravity Study, for a group of people standing in a circle', by Valerie Preston-Dunlop (1963), has been updated. Courtesy of Valerie Preston-Dunlop. (30.1)

Bibliography

Hutchinson, Ann. Notebooks from the Jooss-Leeder Dance School, 1936-1939.

Hutchinson, Ann. *Labanotation*, Theatre Arts Books, New York, 1970 (1st ed. 1954; 3rd ed. 1977).

Hutchinson Guest, Ann. *Your Move, A New Approach to the Study of Movement and Dance*, Gordon and Breach, London, 1983. (3rd reprinting with corrections in 1995).

Hutchinson Guest, Ann and van Haarst, Rob. Advanced Labanotation, Vol. 1, Part 2, *Shape, Design, Trace Patterns*, Harwood Academic Publishers, New York, 1991.

Hutchinson Guest, Ann and van Haarst, Rob. Advanced Labanotation, Vol. 1, Part 3, *Kneeling, Sitting, Lying*, Harwood Academic Publishers, New York, 1991.

ICKL Proceedings of the Biennial Conferences of the International Council of Kinetography Laban (ICKL), 1959-1999.

Jaffe, Marjorie and Stephanie Cooper. *Get Your Back in Shape*, Thorsons, Northamptonshire, 1984.

The Kinetographer, bulletin, Nos. 1-11 published 1973-76 by the Language of Dance Centre, London.

Knust, Albrecht. *Handbuch der Kinetographie Laban*, unpublished manuscript (8 vol.), written mainly between 1945 and 1950.

Knust, Albrecht. *Handbook of Kinetography Laban*, translated by Valerie Preston, unpublished (1 vol.), 1951.

Knust, Albrecht. *Abriss der Kinetographie Laban*, Das Tanzarchiv, Hamburg, 1956 (Eng. transl. *Handbook of Kinetography Laban*, *ibid.* 1958).

Knust, Albrecht. *A Dictionary of Kinetography Laban (Labanotation)* (2 vol.), MacDonald and Evans, 1979.

Laban, Rudolf von. *Schrifttanz: Methodik, Orthographie, Erläuterungen*, Universal-Edition, Wien, 1928 (Eng. transl. *Script Dancing: Methodics, Orthography, Explanations*, 1930).

Laban, Rudolf. *Laban's Principles of Dance and Movement Notation*, MacDonald & Evans Ltd., London, 1975 (2nd edition annotated and edited by Roderyk Lange).

The Labanotator, bulletin, Nos. 1-25 published 1957-65 by the Dance Notation Bureau, New York; Nos. 26-77 published 1978-1994 by the Language of Dance Centre, London.

Luttgens, K. and K. Wells. *Kinesiology*, 7th ed., Saunders 1982.

Marriett, Jane and Muriel Topaz. *Study Guide for Intermediate Labanotation*, Dance Notation Bureau Press, New York, 1986.

Szentpál, Maria. *Táncjelírás. Laban-kinetográfia*, (Dance Notation. Kinetography Laban), Népmüvelési Propaganda Iroda, Budapest 1969-76 (3 vol., vol. I 2nd. ed., 1st ed. 1964).

Index

In the longer listings, the more relevant references are placed first, separated from the others by a semi-colon (;).

Useful Contact Information

Language of Dance Centre
17 Holland Park
London W11 3TD
United Kingdom
Tel: +44 (0) 20 7229 3780
Fax: +44 (0) 20 7792 1794
email: info@lodc.org
www.lodc.org

Dance Notation Bureau Extension
The Ohio State University
Department of Dance
1813 N. High Street
Columbus OH 43210-1307
USA
Tel: +1 614 292 7977
Fax: +1 614 292 0939
web: http://www.dance.ohio-state.edu
e-mail: marion.8@osu.edu

Language of Dance Center
1972 Swan Pointe Drive
Traverse City
MI 49686
USA
Tel: +1 231 995 0998
Fax: +1 231 995 0998
email: Tinalodc@aol.com

The Labanotation Institute
The University of Surrey
Guildford
Surrey GU2 5XH
United Kingdom
Tel: +44 (0)1483 259 351
Fax: +44 (0)1483 300 803
e-mail: J.Johnson-Jones@Surrey.ac.uk

Dance Notation Bureau
151 West 30th Street, Suite 202
New York NY 10001
USA
Tel: +1 212 564 0985
Fax: +1 212 904 1426
web: http://www.dancenotation.org/
e-mail: notation@mindspring.com

Andy Adamson
Department of Drama and Theatre Arts
University of Birmingham
P.O. Box 363
Birmingham B15 2TT
United Kingdom
e-mail: a.j.adamson@bham.ac.uk

4

Christ's

Law of Love

Written
and Illustrated
by
a Team
of
Daughters of St. Paul

SO-FAE-041

**Based on the most recent
catechetical documents**

St. Paul Catechetical Center

This book belongs to Jamie Lyn
Conant 605 8th street
645-0275

NIHIL OBSTAT:

Rev. John R. Mulvehill, S.T.D.

IMPRIMATUR:

✠ Bernard Cardinal Law, D.D.
Archbishop of Boston

Printed in the U.S.A., by the Daughters of St. Paul
50 St. Paul's Ave., Boston, MA 02130

The Daughters of St. Paul are an international congregation of women religious serving the Church with the communications media.

Excerpts from **The Jerusalem Bible,** copyright © 1966 by Darton, Longman & Todd, Ltd. and Doubleday and Company, Inc. Used by permission of the publisher.

The Ten Commandments, pp. 14, 42, and the eight Beatitudes, p. 84: from the **New American Bible,** © 1970, used herein by permission of the Confraternity of Christian Doctrine, copyright owner.

ISBN 0-8198-0296-4

Daughters of St. Paul

MASSACHUSETTS
50 St. Paul's Ave., Jamaica Plain, Boston, MA 02130 **617-522-8911.**
172 Tremont Street, Boston, MA 02111 **617-426-5464; 617-426-4230.**
NEW YORK
78 Fort Place, Staten Island, NY 10301 **718-447-5071; 718-447-5086.**
59 East 43rd Street, New York, NY 10017 **212-986-7580.**
625 East 187th Street, Bronx, NY 10458 **212-584-0440.**
525 Main Street, Buffalo, NY 14203 **716-847-6044.**
NEW JERSEY
Hudson Mall Route 440 and Communipaw Ave.,
    Jersey City, NJ 07304 **201-433-7740.**
CONNECTICUT
202 Fairfield Ave., Bridgeport, CT 06604 **203-335-9913.**
OHIO
2105 Ontario Street (at Prospect Ave.), Cleveland, OH 44115 **216-621-9427.**
616 Walnut Street, Cincinnati, OH 45202 **513-421-5733; 513-721-5059.**
PENNSYLVANIA
1719 Chestnut Street, Philadelphia, PA 19103 **215-568-2638; 215-864-0991.**
VIRGINIA
1025 King Street, Alexandria, VA 22314 **703-549-3806.**
SOUTH CAROLINA
243 King Street, Charleston, SC 29401 **803-577-0175.**
FLORIDA
2700 Biscayne Blvd., Miami, FL 33137 **305-573-1618.**
LOUISIANA
4403 Veterans Memorial Blvd. Metairie, LA 70006 **504-887-7631; 504-887-0113.**
423 Main Street, Baton Rouge, LA 70802 **504-343-4057; 504-381-9485.**
MISSOURI
1001 Pine Street (at North 10th), St. Louis, MO 63101 **314-621-0346.**
ILLINOIS
172 North Michigan Ave., Chicago, IL 60601 **312-346-4228; 312-346-3240.**
TEXAS
114 Main Plaza, San Antonio, TX 78205 **512-224-8101.**
CALIFORNIA
1570 Fifth Ave. (at Cedar Street), San Diego, CA 92101 **619-232-1442.**
46 Geary Street, San Francisco, CA 94108 **415-781-5180.**
WASHINGTON
2301 Second Ave., Seattle, WA 98121 **206-441-3300.**
HAWAII
1143 Bishop Street, Honolulu, HI 96813 **808-521-2731.**
ALASKA
750 West 5th Ave., Anchorage, AK 99501 **907-272-8183.**
CANADA
3022 Dufferin Street, Toronto 395, Ontario, Canada.

CHRIST'S LAW OF LOVE is the fourth grade text of the ST. PAUL RELIGION SERIES, **which includes the St. Paul** WAY, TRUTH AND LIFE **elementary series and the** DIVINE MASTER **high school series.**

———

The St. Paul Religion Series was produced by a team of Daughters of St. Paul of the American Province in the spirit of Very Rev. James Alberione, S.S.P., S.T.D. The Sisters hold degrees in catechetics, theology, education, philosophy, communications, and art.

THE TEAM OF AUTHORS:
Sr. Concetta Belleggia, M.A.
Sr. M. Catherine Devine, M.A.
Sr. Davina Louise Edwards, M.A.
Sr. M. Anne Heffernan, M.A.
Sr. M. Helen Wallace, M.A.
Sr. M. Mark Wickenhiser, M.A.

EDITORIAL ASSISTANTS:
Sr. Janet Peter Figurant, B.A.
Sr. Christine Robert Rimmele, B.A.
Sr. M. Clement Turcotte, B.S.

ART AND LAYOUT:
Sr. M. Charles Dangrow
Sr. Virginia Helen Dick
Sr. Deborah Thomas Halpin
Sr. Clare Stephen Kralovic
Sr. M. Alphonse Martineau
Sr. Patricia Morrison
Sr. M. Bernardine Sattler, B.A.

Table of Contents

Part I   **God Calls Us to Happiness**

We can reach our goal of happiness because God gives us life, saves us through His Son, and shows us how to live as His children.

Part II   **Jesus Explains the Law of Love**

We love by keeping the commandments, doing acts of mercy and living the beatitudes every day.

Part III   **God Helps Us To Love Him and Others**

As members of the People of God, we receive special help from Him to become holy.

Note to Parents

This year of religion study

should be a very important one for your fourth grader. At this stage of his development, he is rule-conscious and keenly aware that some things are right and others wrong. This is an excellent time to help him deepen his understanding of what God expects of him.

In Christ's Law of Love, the child will learn about the importance of moral guidelines. He will study God's Commandments, the law that God has written in our hearts, the law that was brought to perfection by Jesus Christ Himself. As he learns about the chief works of mercy and the beatitudes, your fourth grader will penetrate the spirit of the law of love. This year he will also learn more about the help that God gives us both through His Church with its sacraments and through the example and intercession of His Mother.

This religion book presents a brief but clear treatment of the sacrament of Penance. If your child is not already receiving this sacrament of mercy, you may

Lesson 1, "We Share a Happy Secret." True happiness comes from loving God and others. We do this when we live by ten rules our wise and loving Father in heaven has given us. **Suggestion:** Build on the groundwork laid in class by holding a table conversation with the children on the importance of rules in life.

Lesson 2, "God Gives the Ten Great Rules." The Ten Commandments keep us "on course," and guide us to our everlasting home. **Suggestion:** Help your fourth grader make a poster on the Ten Commandments as our guide through life. He could keep this in his room as a reminder of the theme of this year's religion program.

Lesson 3, "Our Wonderful God." The Bible, "God's Book," tells us about our loving Father and His goodness to us. **Suggestion:** Give the Bible a place of honor in your home, or if you have already done so, arrange it in a new way. Perhaps each evening, at the children's bedtime, the family might gather before the Bible for prayers—at which time you could check up on the children's knowledge of the basic prayers and their meaning.

Lesson 4, "Our Creator and Father." God, who made all things, made human beings very special. He always acts to save us, through Jesus, His Son. **Suggestion:** Help the children understand their responsibility of help to prepare him for confession by speaking to him of God's love in giving us this sacrament, which draws us always closer to Him. Knowing your child so well, you will be able to suggest particular failings on which to examine himself.

Once your child has received the sacrament, you may wish to suggest that he approach it on a fairly regular basis, perhaps every month or every two weeks. In the encyclical **Mystici Corporis** we read that by the frequent confession of venial sins:

"...genuine self-knowledge is increased, Christian humility grows, bad habits are corrected, spiritual neglect and tepidity are resisted, the conscience is purified, the will is strengthened, a salutary self-control is attained and grace is increased."

Your child will benefit much more from his religion program if you associate yourself closely with it. The eager but restless and often distracted nine-year-old needs more time for deepening his faith than that spent in the classroom. He should re-read the lesson in his text-book, assimilate the material by doing the homework assigned, and translate his learning into action as suggested in the "Response" following each lesson. Your help, your encouragement, and above all your own example of love for God's law are essential.

To help you in your indispensable task of reinforcing the explanation given in class, we offer the following outline of lesson themes, together with suggestions for meaningful home implementation.

using God's gifts of mind and body in good ways, as God expects of them.

Lesson 5, "The Golden Calf."
Because Jesus died and rose to restore the grace lost through man's first sin and all serious personal sins, we should trust that He will always help us overcome our faults. **Suggestion:** Talk with the children about some saints, or outstanding men and women who overcame their defects after struggling and praying a long time.

Lesson 6, "Jesus Brings New Life!"
Jesus came into the world as God-made-man, to be our life and salvation. **Suggestion:** Help your fourth grader make up a prayer of gratitude

to Jesus for coming into the world to be our Savior. Say the prayer together as a family.

Lesson 7, "Our Teacher and Savior."
Jesus taught us how to live to please God. He died and rose so that we might hope to be happy with Him in heaven forever. **Suggestion:** Call your child's attention to the paragraph that begins, "Jesus was so holy and good!" Ask your fourth grader how he can show love for others—older, younger and his own age.

Lesson 8, "Jesus Prepares a Place for Us."
Jesus will reward us according to the way we have lived by His law of love.

Suggestion: Talk to the children about the prizes and awards that are sometimes given for doing something hard. Point out that heaven is the greatest reward, and that while we may not always be rewarded here on earth for the good we have done, God sees everything and will reward us abundantly in heaven.

Lesson 9, "The Real Meaning of Love."

Jesus explained the Ten Commandments and taught that they can be summed up as love of God and love of neighbor. **Suggestion:** Help your child add this thought to the poster on the commandments that he made earlier in the year.

Preparation for Christmas

Jesus came on earth and entered human history to renew the world from within and bring us life and salvation. **Suggestion:** Make sure that your family's preparation for Christmas emphasizes the spiritual aspects of this joyous Christian celebration. Talk about the reason Jesus came and explain the importance of helping Him renew the world by living as His true followers.

Prayers

THE LORD'S PRAYER

Our Father, who art in heaven, hallowed be Thy name; Thy kingdom come; Thy will be done on earth as it is in heaven. Give us this day our daily bread; and forgive us our trespasses as we forgive those who trespass against us; and lead us not into temptation, but deliver us from evil. Amen.

THE HAIL MARY

Hail, Mary, full of grace! the Lord is with you. Blessed are you among women, and blessed is the fruit of your womb, Jesus. Holy Mary, Mother of God, pray for us sinners, now and at the hour of our death. Amen.

GLORY TO THE FATHER

Glory to the Father, and to the Son, and to the Holy Spirit: as it was in the beginning, is now and will be forever. Amen.

THE APOSTLES' CREED

I believe in God, the Father Almighty, Creator of heaven and earth. I believe in Jesus Christ, His only Son, our Lord. He was conceived by the power of the Holy Spirit and born of the Virgin Mary. He suffered under Pontius Pilate, was crucified, died, and was buried. He descended to the dead. On the third day He rose again. He ascended into heaven, and is seated at the right hand of the Father. He will come again to judge the living and the dead. I believe in the Holy Spirit, the holy catholic Church, the communion of saints, the forgiveness of sins, the resurrection of the body, and life everlasting.

6

ACT OF FAITH

O my God, I firmly believe that You are one God in three Divine Persons, Father, Son, and Holy Spirit; I believe that Your Divine Son became man and died for our sins, and that He will come to judge the living and the dead. I believe these and all the truths which the holy Catholic Church teaches, because You have revealed them, who can neither deceive nor be deceived.

ACT OF HOPE

O my God, relying on Your infinite goodness and promises, I hope to obtain pardon of my sins, the help of Your grace, and life everlasting, through the merits of Jesus Christ, my Lord and Redeemer.

ACT OF LOVE

O my God, I love You above all things, with my whole heart and soul, because You are all good and worthy of all love. I love my neighbor as myself for the love of You. I forgive all who have injured me, and I ask pardon of all whom I have injured.

ACT OF CONTRITION

O my God, I am heartily sorry for having offended You, and I detest all my sins, because of Your just punishments, but most of all because they offend You, my God, who are all good and deserving of all my love. I firmly resolve, with the help of Your grace, to sin no more and to avoid the near occasions of sin.

MORNING OFFERING

O Jesus, through the Immaculate heart of Mary, I offer You my prayers, works, joys and sufferings of this day, for all the intentions of Your Sacred Heart, in union with the Holy Sacrifice of the Mass throughout the world, in reparation for my sins, for the intentions of all our associates, and in particular for the intention recommended this month by the Holy Father.

HAIL HOLY QUEEN

Hail, holy Queen, Mother of mercy, our life, our sweetness, and our hope, to you do we cry, poor banished children of Eve; to you do we send up our sighs, mourning and weeping in this valley of tears. Turn then, most gracious advocate, your eyes of mercy toward us; and after this our exile, show unto us the blessed fruit of your womb, Jesus. O clement, O loving, O sweet Virgin Mary.

ANGEL OF GOD

Angel of God, my Guardian dear, to whom His love entrusts me here; ever this day be at my side, to light and guard, to rule and guide. Amen.

GRACE BEFORE MEALS

Bless us, O Lord, and these Your gifts which we are about to receive from Your bounty, through Christ our Lord. Amen.

GRACE AFTER MEALS

We give You thanks for all Your benefits, O almighty God, who lives and reigns forever. Amen.

We Share a Happy Secret

How do we
know when people
are happy?

We can tell by looking at them!
Their eyes shine with joy.
Their mouths curl up in
smiles or grins.

When we look at each other,
we see that **we** are happy today,
aren't we? We are happy to be
together again to start a new school year. We know
that we are going to have many wonderful times.
We are sure that we are going
to learn many new things. That makes us happy.

Happiness is something everybody wants. And
the Person who most wants us
to be happy is God, our Father.

But sometimes people do not do
the right things to be happy. They do what is wrong
and they end up being very unhappy!

Our Father in heaven taught us how to live happily.
The secret of happiness is **love.**
If we love God and others we will be happy.

How do we show love for God and others?
God Himself taught us a simple and very fair way:
He gave us ten rules for loving God and
people. They are called the Ten Commandments.

**If you love me
you will keep my commandments.**
John 14:15

What a privilege it is to know and live by the Ten Commandments!
They are the way to real love and joy. When we keep
these great rules of behavior, we live as God's loving children.

This is the happy secret we share!

9

Will we be rewarded for keeping the Commandments?
Yes, we will, for Jesus said: "Anyone
who obeys these commands
shall be great in
God's kingdom."
see Matthew 5:19

My Response to God

"Response" means
"answer." God calls
me and I answer
Him. God calls me
through the ten
wonderful rules of
behavior He gave.
I answer by keeping
these rules. I answer
by helping others
to keep them. That
makes me happy
and everybody else,
too!

I Speak to God

O Lord,
thank You for Your
Ten Commandments. You gave
them to us because You love us
and You want us to be happy together
now and forever.

10

God Gives the Ten Great Rules

2

Have you ever watched a big jet zooming through the sky far above, and wondered how the pilot could bring that giant plane safely down in an airport thousands of miles away? Maybe you know the answer.

The pilot depends on his radio contact with the airport's control tower. If he did not follow the commands given him over the radio, he would lose his way.

We can say the same thing about everyone on earth. All of us would have lost our way, and would never have reached our destination—heaven—unless God had established contact with us and told us the exact direction to take.

But God, our good Father in heaven, **did** tell us the way to heaven, and if we follow His directions we will live in peace and happiness, just as the pilot feels safe and secure when he follows the directions of the control tower. And we will all reach heaven, just as the pilot will reach that distant airport.

The directions given by God are those great rules called the Ten Commandments.

A great thinker once said that if all the people of the world lived by these **ten wonderful rules,** there would be peace and happiness for everybody.

We would all love God and respect one another, no matter what color a person's skin might be, or what kind of neighborhood he came from,

or what church he went to, or what language he spoke. We would never hurt others or be hurt by them.

If everyone lived by the Ten Commandments, there would be no more violence or war. There would be enough food and work for all. Everyone would have a chance to do something good with his life. No one would be afraid

12

of having his property damaged,
his good name harmed, his belongings stolen.
What a wonderful world it would be
if everyone lived by
the Ten Commandments!

God gave these ten rules to us many, many years ago
through Moses, a very great prophet. A prophet is a man
whom God chooses to be His special messenger.
God called Moses to lead His Chosen People from the
slavery of Egypt into the freedom of the Promised Land.

During their journey to the Promised Land, Moses and
his people, the Hebrews, camped at the foot of Mount Sinai.
While the people waited in the camp, Moses went
up the mountain, and there God gave him the Ten Commandments.
When Moses came down to the camp
carrying two tablets of stone on which the
commandments were written, his face was shining from his
great meeting with God.

Moses had the Hebrews build a large wooden chest, lined
with gold, in which the tablets of the commandments
could be carried while the Chosen People traveled through the
desert. This chest was called the Ark of the Covenant.
The Covenant was the agreement that God and the Hebrews had
made: God promised to guide and protect them as long as they
kept His commandments. And the Hebrews promised that they
would keep the commandments.

How exciting it is to know that we have an agreement with God,
too! If we keep His commandments, if we love Him and all our
brothers, He will make us happy forever!

13

What are the Ten Commandments of God?
1. I, the Lord, am your God.... You shall not have other gods besides Me.
2. You shall not take the name of the Lord your God in vain.
3. Remember to keep holy the Lord's day.
4. Honor your father and your mother.
5. You shall not kill.
6. You shall not commit adultery.
7. You shall not steal.
8. You shall not bear false witness against your neighbor.
9. You shall not covet your neighbor's wife.
10. You shall not covet anything that belongs to your neighbor.

My Response to God

God wants to guide me to the happiness of heaven by means of His commandments. I will study them well and live by them.

I Speak to God

O Lord, I love Your commands.
I will find happiness in them.
see Psalm 119:47

3
Our Wonderful God

We are glad to learn all we can about the rules of happy living. And we are extra glad to learn all we can about the good God who gave them to us.

There is a very special book which tells us about God our Father. It is the most important book in the world. This book is the **Holy Bible.** Everyone calls it "God's Book," or, "the Word of God." Reading this holy Book helps us to be happy, wise and good.

The Holy Bible is also called the **Sacred Scriptures;** it is really not just one book but many, all put together. Reading these holy writings is a way of praying, and a way of coming to know and love God more. No wonder people all over the world show great love and respect for the Holy Bible!

Here are some of the marvelous things that the books of the Bible tell us about God:

GOD is our Father: **You are our Father, O Lord.** see the Book of Isaiah 63:16

GOD is real and living: **He is the ever-living, ever-lasting God.** see the Book of Daniel 6:27

GOD is all-good. He loves us all, even sinners: **The Lord listens when the man in need calls for help. God helps him in all his troubles.** see the Book of Psalms 34:6

GOD can do all things: **Lord, I know that you can do everything.** see the Book of Job 42:2

GOD can see and hear, and know all things: **The Lord sees everywhere. He watches the bad and the good.** see the Book of Proverbs 15:3

GOD always acts to save us: **He said: "I will never let you down, nor will I leave you."** see the Book of Deuteronomy 31:6

GOD gave us Jesus our Savior: **God loved the world so much that He gave His only Son.** see the Gospel of John 3:16

GOD the Holy Spirit lives and acts in us: **The Spirit of truth... stays with you and will be within you.** see the Gospel of John 14:17

How marvelous it is that the three divine Persons of the Trinity — God the Father, God the Son who became Jesus our Savior, and God the Holy Spirit — made us, saved us, and want us with Them forever! They love us!

The more we think about it, the happier we are!

We say, "Thank You, dear God!" and "We love You!" when we pray. What a great privilege it is to be able to talk to God in prayer!

16

It is wonderful when God's people pray to God together.
We do this in our parish church,
we do it in our classrooms, we do it in our
homes. That is why it is good to learn the same great
prayers, like the Sign of the Cross, the Our Father,
the Hail Mary, the Apostles' Creed, an Act of
Contrition, and the Rosary.

But the greatest prayer we can offer together
is the Eucharistic Celebration, which is also called the Mass.

Sometimes we pray by ourselves, saying our own prayers
that we make up. We tell God we love Him and we ask His help,
using our own words.

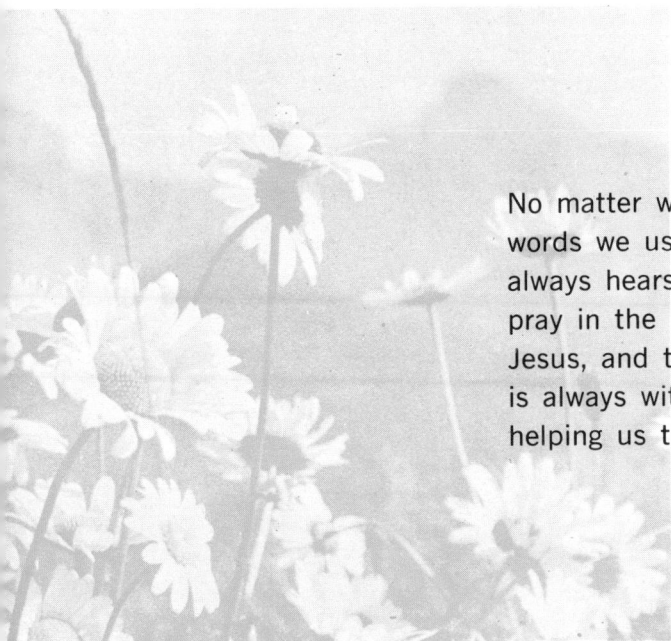

No matter where we are or what
words we use, God our loving Father
always hears our prayers. We
pray in the name of His Son
Jesus, and the Holy Spirit
is always with us,
helping us to pray well.

Is God real and living?
Yes, God is real and living.

**Does God our Father
take care of us?**
Yes, God our Father takes
good care of us. The
Holy Bible says: "Everything
that is good is given to us
by our Father in heaven."

see James 1:17

My Response to God

At Holy Mass I will recite the
Creed with all the People
of God. The Creed tells of my
faith in the Eternal God,
who always was, who
always will be and who
loves me!

I Speak to God

Holy, holy, holy Lord!
The whole universe is
full of your glory.

18

Our Creator and Father

4

Let us read from the "Book of God." First we read that God made all things:

I, the Lord, made all things. I alone spread out the heavens. I alone shaped the earth.

see Isaiah 44:24

Men know how to build houses. But if they decide to build a house, they need cement, bricks, wood — things that are already made. Men **build;** they do not **create.**

To create means to make something out of nothing.

Only God can create, because He is all powerful. He can do anything. And He made the entire universe out of nothing.

In two other books of the Bible we read:

From the earth the Lord created man, and he made him in his own image. He created them male and female.

see Sirach 17:1; Genesis 1:27

God said, "Let Us make man
in Our image and likeness." And He made the
first people, the first human beings,
so special that there was nothing greater than
them on earth!

Each of us, too, is a very wonderful person.

As you know, our body is composed of bones,
muscles, nerves, blood and so on.
Our soul is like God because
it is a spirit. Because we
have a soul, we can
live, think, remember,
and know what is
true, good and
beautiful.

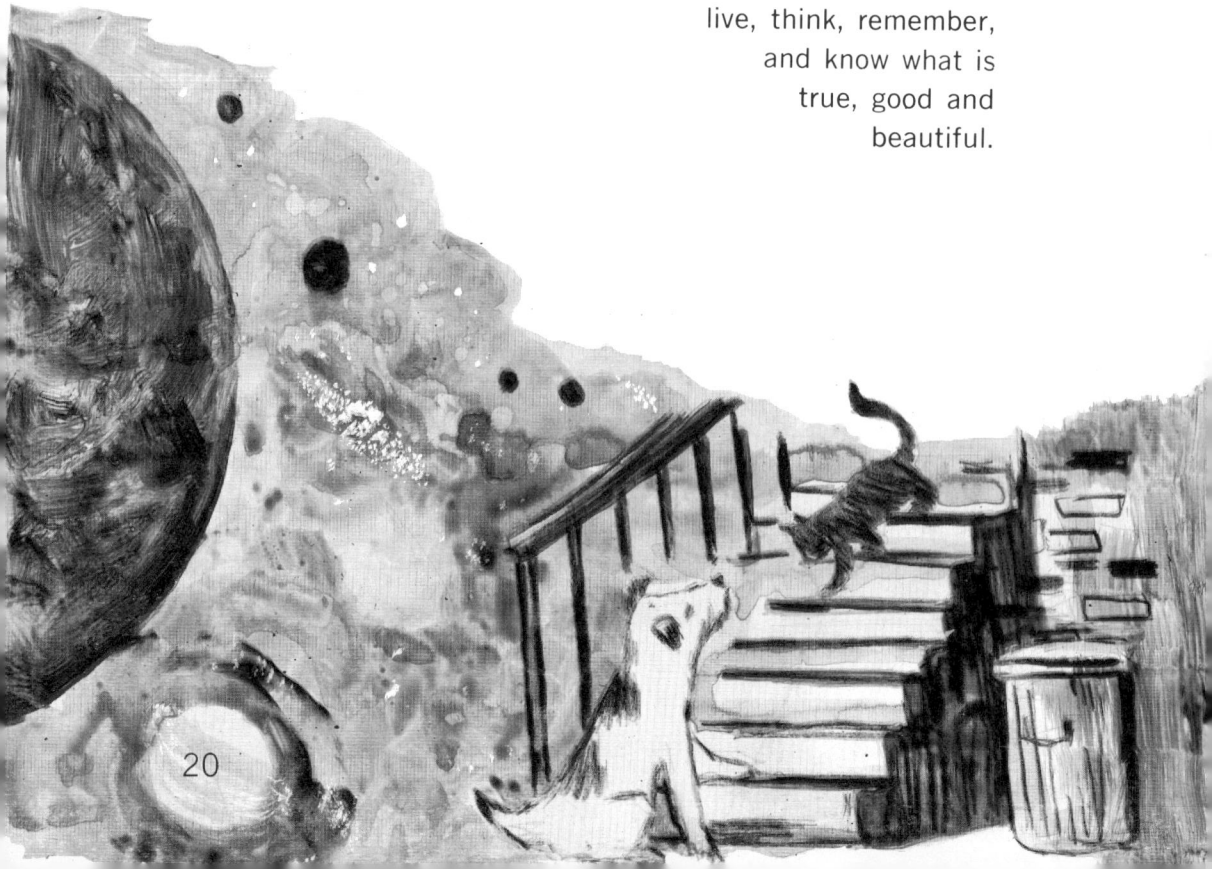

20

Our soul is immortal. "Immortal" means that it will never die. It will live forever and ever.

God created the first people with a wonderful plan of love. He wanted them to go one day with Him to heaven and be happy forever. So He made their souls beautiful with the most precious of gifts— His grace, which is His own life in us.

Before God created the whole world and the first people, He had created the mighty angels.

God made all things, so all things belong to Him!
He is always with us, using His mighty power for our good.
From creation on down through the history of the world—
and right now too—
God always acts to save us
through His Son Jesus.

Did God make all things?
Yes, God made all things.
He Himself said:
"I, the Lord, made all things."
see Isaiah 44:24

Do we belong to the Lord?
Yes,
we do belong
to the Lord. The Holy Bible says:
"God made us. We are his own people."
see Psalm 100:3

My Response to God

I will be thankful to
God for creating me and saving
me through His Son. I will use my
soul and my body to love and serve God.

I Speak to God

We give You thanks, O God,
And we praise the greatness
of Your name!

The Golden Calf

5

We remember that Moses, the great leader of the Chosen People, received the Ten Commandments from God Himself on Mount Sinai. But while Moses was up on the mountain with the Lord, the people below grew tired of waiting for him, because he was gone for forty days. They made a calf out of gold and worshiped it.

Imagine how Moses felt when he saw the people worshiping a piece of metal instead of the God who had done so many good things for them! Taking the golden calf, Moses melted it in the fire and ground it down to powder! It would never again be used by anyone to sin against God!

The people were sorry that they had offended the Lord. And God forgave them.

"My biggest problem in trying to be more like Jesus is ME!" a young girl once said.

Did you ever feel like that?

It would have been a lot easier to be good and holy if the first people on earth had not sinned.

23

The sad story of sin
did not start with the
golden calf. It
started with some of the
angels who became
devils because they
sinned. Then the
first people on earth
turned against God, too.
At that moment they
lost God's life in
them and the special
gifts God had given
them. Because they
lost them, they could not
give them to
us who are their children.

So each of us
is born without the
wonderful life of
God within us. This
sad condition is called
original sin.

Heaven was closed to us
after our first parents sinned. And
the world became quite a sad
place.

But God is all good and all
merciful. He promised right
away that He would
send a Savior to
make up for sin. And, as we
know, God did send the Savior—
His Son Jesus.

Jesus suffered and died to
give us God's own
life again. We received
God's life when we
were baptized.
Yet even after Baptism,
people fail in love of God
by sinning.

There are two kinds of sin.
One kind is called mortal sin. Mortal sin is a very great
disobedience to our loving Father. It drives
the life of God out of a soul.

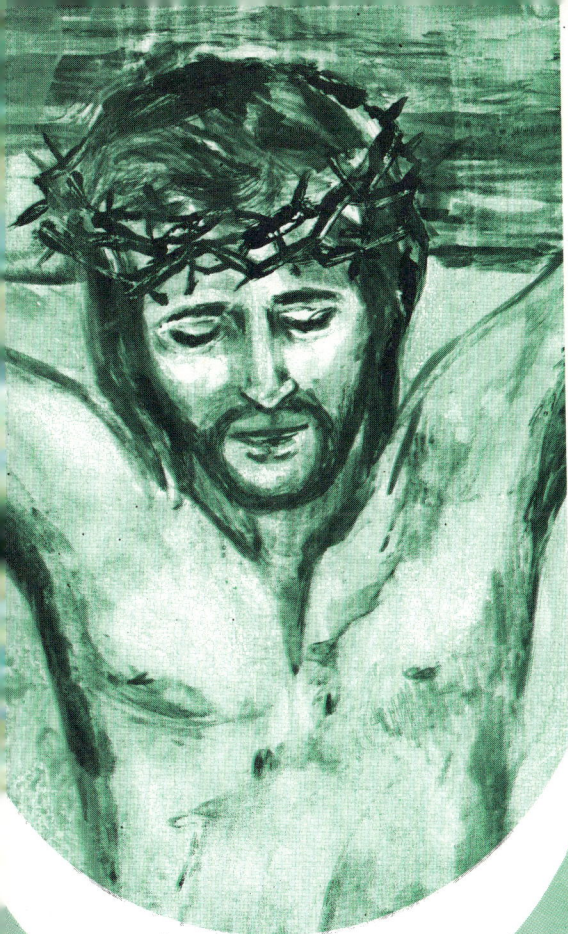

A person commits a mortal sin
—by thinking or wanting or saying
or doing something
which is very wrong;
—which he knows is very wrong;
—which he does anyway, even
though he knows it is very wrong.

Of course, none of **us** wants
to commit a mortal sin.
But do we sometimes do things
which keep us from being really
close friends of God?
These smaller sins are called
venial.

Jesus our Savior never stops
loving His sinful brothers
and sisters. He keeps calling
them back to Himself. He loved
us so much that He died to make
up for our sins and to save us.
The Holy Bible says:

**He was pierced through
for our faults,
crushed for our sins.**
Isaiah 53:5

**Christ died for us
while we were still sinners.**
Romans 5:8

25

When we have sinned,
Jesus will make us His friends
if we are sorry
and promise not to offend Him
again.

Will God always help us avoid sin if we ask His help?
Yes. The Bible says:
"You can trust God not to let you
be tried beyond your strength."
1 Corinthians 10:13

What must we do to avoid sin?
Jesus said:
"You should be awake, and praying."
Mark 14:38

My Response to God

When I feel like doing
something wrong, I will at
once ask Jesus
to help me avoid sin.
And if I do wrong, I will at
once ask Him to forgive me.

I Speak to God

Lord,
we count on You
to help us be
Your loyal friends always.

Jesus Brings New Life!

God sent His Son Jesus because He wanted at any cost to save all men. He wanted very much to bring everyone closer to Him, to make them happy.

27

The Holy Bible says:

> **Yes, God loved the world so much**
> **that he gave his only Son,**
> **so that everyone who believes in him**
> **may not be lost**
> **but may have eternal life.**
> John 3:16

God the Son became one of us to be our life and
salvation. There is no salvation from
anyone else. There never has been, from the very
beginning.

In Jesus, we are all joined together. He makes
us **one** people. He gives each of us the power to do
wonderful things for each other.

Our Lord Jesus came into the world as God-made-man.

The virgin who was to be His Mother was Mary most holy, who
lived in Palestine, in the town of Nazareth. God kept
Mary free from original sin. This wonderful favor is called her
Immaculate Conception. **Immaculate** means "without stain,"
and **Conception** means "coming into life."
God kept Mary free from original sin because she
was to be the Mother of His Son.

28

Mary was living in
Nazareth when
an angel
came from God to ask
her to be the
Mother
of God's Son.
Mary said,
"Yes."

Some months later, Mary and her husband, Joseph, went to
their family city, Bethlehem, to give their names in a census.
When Mary and Joseph reached Bethlehem, they
could find no place to spend the night, because many other
people had also come for the census. Mary and Joseph
were very tired from their long trip, so they went to sleep in a
cold, damp cave where
the animals used to stay when it rained.

All of a sudden, during the night, in that poor, damp cave,
Jesus the Savior was born!
Angels came from heaven to adore Him. Shepherds came too.
They found Him wrapped in swaddling clothes and
lying in a manger, which was the only bed Mary and
Joseph had for Him.

The little baby lying there in the manger was truly God and truly
man. For He had a real human body and a real human soul.
While remaining truly God, the Son of God became a real man. He
was like us in all things except sin. He thought with a
human mind, He acted with a human will, and He loved with a
human heart.

Mary adored Him because He is the Son of the Father in heaven,
having the same divine nature as His Father. Even though
Mary was the wife of Joseph, the child Jesus had no human father.
He has only one Father—the heavenly Father.

The Son of God was named Jesus, which means "Savior." He
came to save all people from their sins. He came
to give us NEW LIFE, God's own life!

**What were the words of the angels
announcing to the shepherds
the birth of our Savior?**
"Today in the town of David a savior has
been born to you; he is Christ the Lord."
Luke 2:11

Is Jesus Christ God and man?
Yes. The Son of God came from the
Father to save us. He was made man by
the Holy Spirit and was born of the
Virgin Mary. He is true God and
true man.

30

My Response to God

Jesus will lead us back to our
heavenly Father. At Mass, with great joy
and thanksgiving, I will say the prayer,

"Glory to God
in the highest!"

I Speak to God

O God, thank You
for sending
Your only Son
to save us.

31

7 Our Teacher and Savior

Jesus is the Teacher of all men. He taught us in two ways: by what He did and by what He said.

When He was still a little boy, He helped His mother with the duties of the house. He worked hard with St. Joseph, too.

When Jesus began to teach what people should do to lead good lives and to please our Father in heaven, everyone said, "He really is the Master." **Master** means great teacher.

But we know that Jesus is more than a great teacher. He is God. At a wedding party He first used His mighty power when His mother asked Him to: He changed water into delicious wine!

Jesus showed Himself to be God by forgiving sins. To a paralyzed man He said, "Your sins are forgiven." And to show that He could forgive sins, He worked a miracle. He made the sick man well!

Jesus' greatest miracles were the raising of the dead. Lazarus, one of His dear friends, had been dead four days and was lying in a tomb. Jesus called out, "Lazarus, come out!" All the people were greatly amazed when the dead man got up and came out of the tomb! Lazarus was the third person Jesus had raised from the dead.

By these mighty acts of power Jesus proved that He is God.

32

It is because He is God that Jesus is the only true "Master"—
the greatest teacher who ever lived. Once, when Jesus
was on a mountain with Peter, James and John,
the heavenly Father spoke these words about Jesus:

This is my Son, the Beloved.
Listen to him.
Mark 9:7

Jesus was so holy
and good! His
goodness made Him a
Friend to the poor, the
sick and the sinners. He loved
children, teenagers, grown-ups
and old people. With all of them
He was gentle and kind, and He
helped them all.

But although Jesus was so loving,
He Himself was not received with
love by some of the leaders of the
people. They were jealous of
Him and condemned Him
to death. Jesus knew
beforehand that He was to
be betrayed and killed.

33

With His death, He would save us from our sins. Jesus **chose** to die for us. He said,

I lay my life down freely; no one takes it from me.
see John 10:18

After being betrayed by Judas the traitor, our Savior was arrested, falsely accused, whipped, crowned with sharp thorns, and condemned to die on a cross. Jesus' tremendous sufferings show us what a terrible thing sin is.

Jesus Christ died for all men. Yes, He suffered and died to reopen heaven to each one of us. Each of us can repeat the words of the Bible for himself:

The Son of God loved me and sacrificed himself for me.
see Galatians 2:20

After Jesus had died,
some of His friends
took His body down from the cross
and laid it in a new grave.
Jesus' body
remained in the grave
from Friday evening
until early Sunday morning.
Then when the holy women
came on Sunday morning
to anoint His body,
they found an angel
who said to them,

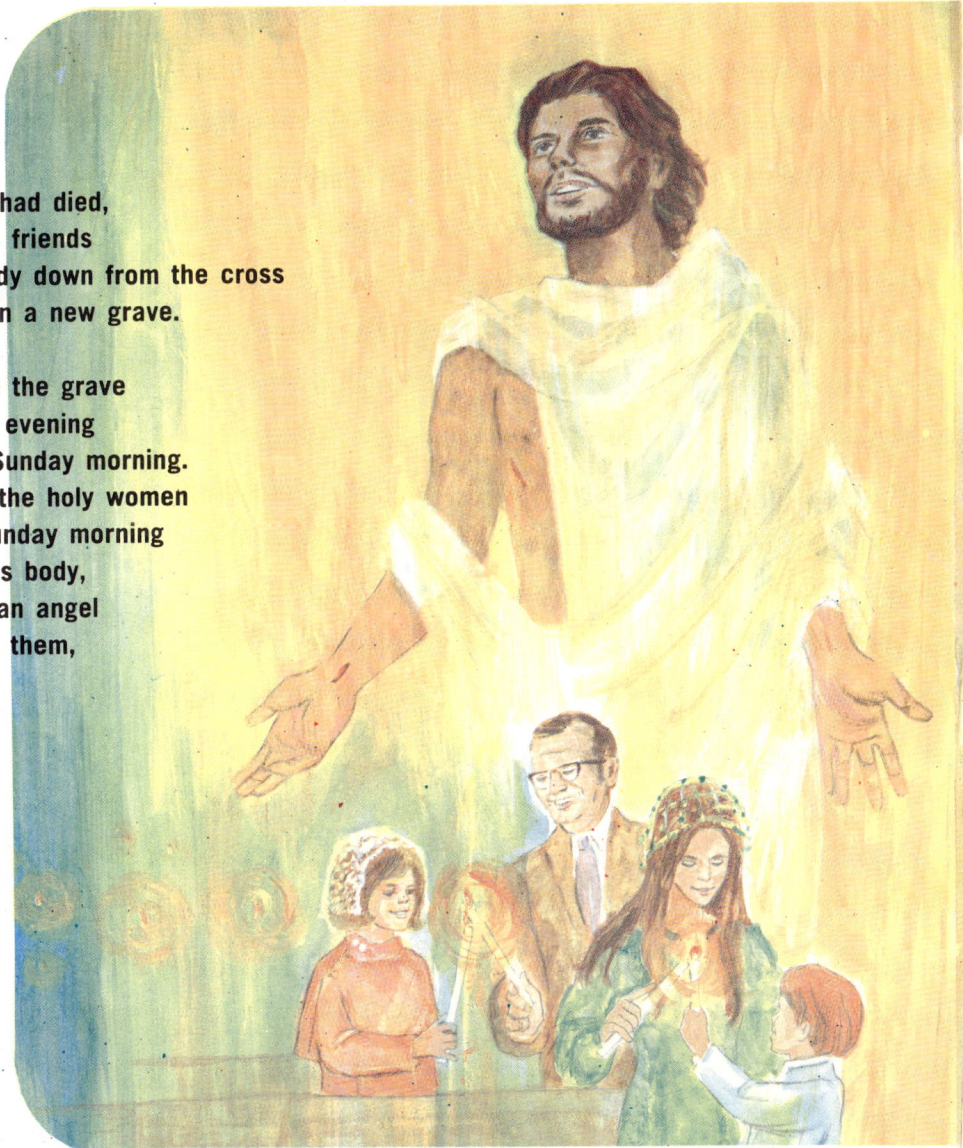

There is no need for you to
be afraid. I know you are
looking for Jesus, who was crucified.
He is not here,
for he has risen,
as he said he would.
Matthew 28:5-6

Jesus had risen from the dead!
How brightly shone God's mighty power
in that amazing event!

Jesus had come into the world as God-made-man
to be our Savior. By His death and resurrection
He saved us from slavery to sin and to the devil.

What a glorious Savior we have! Because of Him
we have God's life in us. Because of Him we can hope to
be happy forever in heaven after we die.

**In the risen Jesus we live, we die,
and we shall live again!**

How fortunate we are to believe in Jesus Christ!
Believing in Jesus means believing everything Jesus taught us in the
Gospel. It means trying to live as He did, loving God our Father
and all our brothers. It means growing closer to Him, especially
through the Mass and the wonderful sacraments He gave us.

How do we know that Jesus is God?
We know that Jesus is God because He proved it by the
miracles He worked. And He said: "Believe in the work I do
[miracles]; then you will know for sure that the Father is
in me and I in the Father."
John 10:38

What does it mean to believe in Jesus?
To believe in Jesus means to believe all that He taught,
to love God and people as He did, and to grow closer to Him,
especially through the Mass and the sacraments.

**My Response
to God**
I will often tell
Jesus, my Savior, "I believe in You
and I love You."

**I Speak to
God**

**O Jesus,
I believe in You!
I hope in You! I love You
with all my heart!**

36

8 Jesus Prepares a Place For Us

In the Eucharistic
celebration we proclaim
with all the People of God:

Christ has died;

Christ is risen;

Christ will come again.

What do we mean when we say: "Christ will come again"?

After His glorious resurrection, Jesus went back to heaven,
to the glory of His Father.
He went to prepare a place for us in that
wonderful home of true and everlasting
happiness.

If during our life we keep Christ's law of love, we
will live with Him in heaven for ever and ever.

When we die, we will immediately be judged by Jesus
on the way we lived.

People are punished in hell who committed mortal sin and died without
being sorry. Even though Jesus suffered and died to save
them, they chose to sin seriously. They gave up
God's friendship and His life in them. In hell
they suffer greatly and their suffering will never end.

People are rewarded in heaven who died
with God's life of grace in them and made up for their sins.

There is also purgatory, where those who have
to make up for their sins go
until they have been purified. From purgatory souls go
to heaven.

In heaven we shall be with Jesus, our Leader and King. We
shall see Him as He is, face to face. We shall be happy with
Him in His glory. In heaven there will
be no more suffering,
no more sickness, no more troubles or death. In
heaven we shall enjoy forever everything we want.

The Holy Bible says:

For those
who love him,
God
has prepared
things
that no eye
has ever seen and
no ear
ever heard.
see 1 Corinthians 2:9

At the end of the world, there will be another judgment, for all the people who ever lived. That is when "Christ will come again." By the power of God, the body of every person who has ever lived on earth will rise from the dead and be united again to its soul. Then Jesus will judge each of us again, in the presence of everybody. Imagine what that will be like!

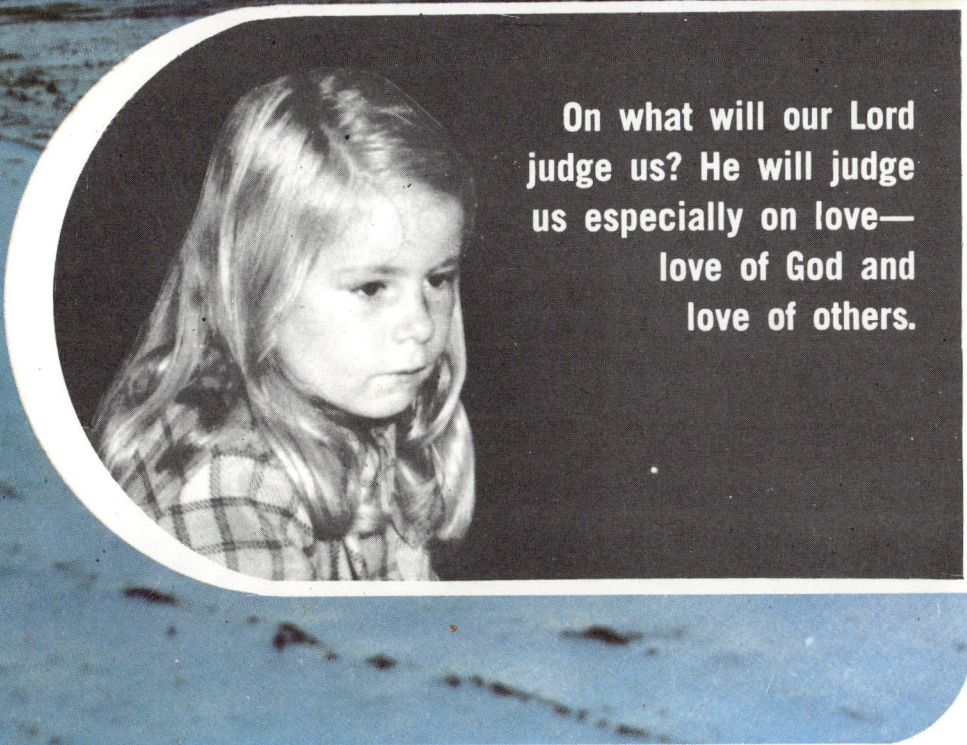

On what will our Lord judge us? He will judge us especially on love— love of God and love of others.

That is why our religion study is especially important this year. If we study, we will learn well about Jesus' law of love. And if we **live by** this law, we shall grow more and more like the Lord Jesus every day. And that will make us and everybody around us happy!

Will everyone be judged immediately after death?
Yes, everyone will be judged by Jesus immediately
after death and rewarded in heaven
or punished in purgatory or hell. This is called
the particular judgment.

**At the general judgment, after all men have risen from the
dead, what will Jesus say to the people who lived
good lives?**
Jesus will take the good people into heaven, saying:
"Come, you whom my Father has blessed,
take for your heritage the kingdom prepared for you since
the foundation of the world."
Matthew 25:34

My Response to God

Now that I am starting to really study Jesus' law of love,
the Ten Commandments, I will pray and try to do
whatever God expects of me.

I Speak to God

Lord Jesus,
keep us free from all evils
and from sin
so that we will live our lives
in the joyful hope
of Your coming.

9

The Real Meaning of Love

Great crowds of people used to follow Jesus because He cured their sicknesses and taught them how to live. One day when He saw the crowds, Jesus went up a mountain and sat down to teach. He had some very important things to say.

The people all knew the Ten Commandments that God had given them through Moses. Now, Jesus was far greater than Moses. Jesus was the Son of God. What did Jesus say about God's law, which we call the Ten Commandments? Jesus said:

Do not think I have come to destroy the law. I have come to complete it.

see Matthew 5:17

And then He began to explain the Ten Commandments in a new way. He made each of them more complete, more perfect.

Jesus explained the commandments very carefully, because they are so important for us. He said that to enter heaven it is not enough just to **say** we love God. We have to **show** we love Him by obeying Him—by keeping His commandments.

41

In the first three
commandments we are
taught how to love God.
These are the first three:

In the other seven commandments we are
taught to love our neighbor. These are
the other seven:

1 I, the Lord, am
your God.... You
shall not have
other gods
besides Me.

2 You shall not
take the name
of the Lord your
God in vain.

3 Remember to
keep holy
the Lord's
day.

4 Honor your
father
and your
mother.

5 You
shall
not
kill.

6 You shall
not
commit
adultery.

7 You
shall
not
steal.

8 You shall not
bear false
witness against
your neighbor.

9 You shall not
covet your
neighbor's
wife.

10 You shall not
covet anything
that belongs to
your neighbor.

**You
must love
the Lord your
God with all your
heart, with all your soul,
and with all your mind. This is the
greatest and the first commandment. The second
resembles it: You must love your neighbor as yourself.**

Matthew 22:37-39

To help us understand what He meant by loving our neighbor Jesus told us this story of the Good Samaritan

While he was traveling to Jericho, a Samaritan saw a poor Hebrew, beaten and robbed, lying at the side of the road. Now the Samaritans and the Hebrews were enemies, but this good Samaritan felt sorry for the Hebrew, so he stopped to take care of him. After bandaging up his wounds, the Samaritan put the half-dead Hebrew on his own donkey and took him to an inn. He told the inn-keeper to take care of him and promised to pay him for doing so.

This wonderful example of love is what Jesus wishes us to imitate. We—people from all over the world—are all children of God. We are all brothers and sisters, no matter what color a person's skin is, or what country his parents or grandparents came from or what church he goes to. "To love our neighbor" means "to love everyone," because everyone is our neighbor.

It is not always easy to keep the Ten Commandments. What can we do when we find it hard? In the Sermon on the Mount, Jesus told us to pray. If we pray, Jesus said, God will help us to want to be good and really to **be** good. Then we will be true followers of Jesus.

43

How do we show Jesus that we love Him?

Jesus said, "If you love me you will keep my commandments."
John 14:15

Which are the three commandments about love of God?

(See the list on page 42.)

Which are the seven commandments about love of neighbor?

(See the list on page 42.)

My Response to God

I will live up
to Jesus' command to love God
and my neighbor by worshiping God
at Mass, by not hurting anyone with
words or actions, and
by being fair, kind and helpful
to everyone.

I Speak to God

O my God,
I love You
above all things,
and my neighbor
as myself.

44

Lesson 10, "The First Commandment of God."

God deserves our love and the highest honor. We are to pray to Him, believe everything He has taught us, and act according to our belief. **Suggestion:** Your fourth grader has recently studied the Apostles' Creed. This would be a good opportunity to re-inforce the class experience by questioning him about the meaning of the Creed.

Lesson 11, "The Second and Third Commandments of God."

Through the second and third commandments, God teaches us to honor His name, His friends and His day. **Suggestion:** Gather the family before the enthroned Bible to recite the Divine Praises (one member reading a line, the others repeating it) or Psalm 113 (formerly 112), verses 1-5, repeating verse 2 after each line.

The Divine Praises
Blessed be God.
Blessed be His holy name.
Blessed be Jesus Christ, true God and true man.
Blessed be the name of Jesus.
Blessed be His most Sacred Heart.
Blessed be His most precious blood.
Blessed be Jesus in the most holy Sacrament of the Altar.
Blessed be the Holy Spirit, the Paraclete.
Blessed be the great Mother of God, Mary most holy.
Blessed be her holy and Immaculate Conception.
Blessed be her glorious Assumption.
Blessed be the name of Mary, Virgin and Mother.
Blessed be St. Joseph, her most chaste spouse.
Blessed be God in His angels and in His saints.

Psalm 113:1-5
You servants of Yahweh, praise,
praise the name of Yahweh!
Blessed be the name of Yahweh,
henceforth and for ever!
From east to west,
praised be the name of Yahweh!
High over all nations, Yahweh!
His glory transcends the heavens!
Who is like Yahweh our God?—
enthroned so high, he needs to stoop
to see the sky and earth!

Lesson 12, "The Fourth Commandment of God."

We are to respect, love and obey our parents and teachers and the other leaders whom God has placed over us to take care of us. **Suggestion:** Patriotism, too, comes under the fourth commandment. If possible, take the children to visit a local historical monument or museum, or watch a patriotic film or program. Explain to them why it is important to respect just laws and those who enforce them.

Lesson 13, "The Fifth Commandment of God."

Brotherly love shows that we are followers of Jesus and makes us happy. **Suggestion:** Help the children make a large "mural" of magazine photos on the theme: "Love one another."

Lesson 14, "The Sixth and Ninth Commandments of God."

God wants us to use our gifts of body in the right way. **Suggestion:** While continuing to check on the TV programs the children watch and the boys and girls they go around with, you may also want to check on the content of local magazine racks which cater to children.

Lesson 15, "The Seventh and Tenth Commandments of God."

Through the seventh and tenth commandments God teaches us to respect the property of others and not to be greedy. **Suggestion:** Help the children deepen their appreciation of what they have by learning how to take good care of their things: mending, cleaning, repairing, putting in order, storing properly, etc.

Lesson 16, "The Eighth Commandment of God."

Our heavenly Father wants us to speak kindly and truthfully. **Suggestion:** Through a "round-table" discussion, stress the harm often done by untruthfulness or name-calling.

Lesson 17, "Actions That Show Our Love."

The Holy Spirit prompts us to be like Jesus in performing good deeds or works of mercy. Jesus looks upon whatever we do for others as done for Him. **Suggestion:** Decide with your family upon some particular work of mercy you can perform together this week.

Lesson 18, "Eight Wonderful Blessings."

Living by the eight beatitudes, we grow closer and closer to Jesus and are happy. **Suggestion:** Since the spirit of the beatitudes is a spirit of seeking God and putting Him first, encourage the children to show their love for Him by making a special sacrifice this week.

page for parents

10 The First Commandment of God

God is our Creator and Father. We
have nothing of our own. God made us. He gave us all we have.
He is always so good
to us. The Holy Bible says:
**Everything that is good
is given to us by our Father in heaven.**
see James 1:17

As grateful children we respond to God's love for us by
loving Him above all
things. We worship Him alone. We give Him
the highest honor. In this way we keep the first commandment.

The **first** commandment of God is:
**I, the Lord, am your God....
You shall not have other gods besides me.**

This commandment is about worshiping God. To
worship God means to pray to Him and to believe all He has said.

Prayer is the
greatest privilege we have
on earth. To pray
means to speak
to God, and let God
speak
to us.

More than four hundred
times in the Holy Bible,
God urges us
to pray. Many times
it would be impossible
to love God and others
if we didn't pray.

We pray in the morning
when we get up, and at night
before we go to bed.

We can pray
anywhere because God
is always in our heart.
Of course, it is easier to pray in church
than on the street.
. The church is God's house and
our Lord is there
present in the Holy Eucharist, ready
to listen to us
any time.

We pray to tell God
we love Him and want to obey Him. We
pray to thank God for
all His blessings. We pray to ask
pardon for our sins. We pray
for what we
need and for what
others need. We pray especially
in times of trouble and temptation.

The Mass is the best prayer of all,
the most powerful
and most pleasing to God.
In the Mass Jesus Himself prays
with us and for us to His
heavenly Father.

By the first commandment, God asks us to trust Him.
We would not keep God's first commandment
if we were superstitious and trusted
in "good luck" charms or other
foolish things instead of Him.

To keep the first commandment of God, we must study our Faith
as well as we can in our
religion classes. The more we know God,
the stronger our faith grows!

Our faith in God is shown by good actions.
As true followers of Jesus,
we should try to act and speak as Jesus did, to show
our belief and give good example.

The Second Vatican Council
says, "Children also have their own apostolic work
to do. According to their
ability they are true
living witnesses of Christ among their
companions."

How do we worship God our Father?
We worship God our Father
by praying to Him, by believing all He
has said, and by acting according to our belief. In
this way, we
keep the first commandment.

My Response to God

I will say my morning and night prayers
well, and will stop in church
to pray when I can. I
will study my religion well, too.

I Speak to God

The Lord is
my light and my
salvation;
I will sing
and praise the Lord.
see Psalm 27:1-6

11 The Second and Third Commandments of God

In the Holy Bible we read about the great prophet, Samuel. He had a very special name, for "Samuel" means "the name of God." And how great God's name is!

The **second** commandment of God is:

You shall not take the name of the Lord your God in vain.

God's name is holy. Jesus taught us a beautiful prayer—the Our Father. In it Jesus told us to say:

"Hallowed be Thy name," which means, "May Your name be blessed, O Lord, and praised."

To keep the second commandment of
God, we must speak about
God and about His
special friends
in heaven and on earth with respect.

Some people use God's name and the
holy name of Jesus "in vain," which means
"in fun or in anger." This is wrong.

Some people have the bad habit of cursing.
To curse means to call down evil
on anything or anyone. To wish a serious
evil on another person, and really mean
it, is a mortal sin. Let us
obey our heavenly Father.
He teaches us in the Bible:

Bless, and never curse.

see Romans 12:14

By the second commandment we are also
commanded to show respect for holy things and places.

The **third** commandment of God is:

Remember to keep holy the Lord's day.

In this commandment God tells us
to worship our heavenly Father on every Sunday and holyday
of obligation by participating in the Mass.
The Mass is the prayer of the new People of God. In it we join
Jesus our Leader to praise and thank our
heavenly Father and to ask Him
for blessings.

Adults and children seven years of age or over are
obliged to go to Mass on Sundays and holydays.
(The Sunday and holyday Mass can also be celebrated on
the evening before.)

Of course, it is no sin at all to miss
Sunday Mass if it is very hard for
a person to get to Mass either because he lives
very far from the church, or because
he is sick, or because he has to take care of
someone who is sick.

On the Lord's day, we must not
be late for Mass if we can help it.

The third commandment of God forbids God's people to do
unnecessary work or shopping or business activity
on Sunday.

Sometimes work is necessary, and then it is allowed. For
example, a farmer may have to do some
of his work on Sunday when it
looks as though bad weather is coming. Firemen, policemen
and nurses are also allowed to work on Sunday. God
forbids only **unnecessary** work and business.

Some activities **not** forbidden on Sunday are reading,
writing, typewriting, studying, drawing,
playing music, traveling, hunting, fishing, swimming,
skiing, skating.

Sunday is the day set aside for the special worship of God
and it is called the day of rest. It is a joyful day.

What does God tell us in the second commandment?
In the second commandment God tells us
that we must speak about Him and
about His special friends
in heaven and on earth with respect.

**What does God tell us
in the third commandment?**

In the third commandment God tells
us that we must worship Him on
Sunday by participating
in the Mass.

My Response to God

I will always show respect for God's name and
for His day. God established
Sunday for our good.
I will make sure to keep
it holy.

I Speak
to God

Sing praise to God,
all you lands.... Give
thanks to him; bless his
name. Yes, the Lord is
good.

see Psalm 100:1-5

12

The Fourth Commandment of God

Where are these children showing their love of God and others? At home! God wants us to have great love for our own home and family and especially for our parents.

The **fourth** commandment of God is:

Honor your father and your mother.

Jesus, our Leader and Brother, showed us how to love and obey our parents. When He came down from heaven, He chose to be born and brought up in a family, just like any other child. Although He was the Son of God, He respected, loved and obeyed His mother, Mary, and His foster-father, Joseph.

Fathers and mothers try to imitate God's own love for His children. They make all kinds of sacrifices for the good of their children.

Children show their love for their parents by respecting, obeying and helping them.

The Holy Bible says:
Children, be obedient to your parents in the Lord — that is your duty.
Ephesians 6:1

54

Sometimes parents have to punish their children. But good children are grateful to them even then. They know that their parents punish them for their own good. The Holy Bible says:

A man who corrects his son, loves him.
see Proverbs 13:24

When your father or mother scolds you or punishes you, say to yourself:

"They are doing this because they are good parents who really care about me."

There are other people whom God placed over us to take care of us. They are our teachers, and the leaders of our Church and of our country. We respect, love and obey them, too. The Holy Bible says:

Obey the authorities over you. All authority comes from God.
see Romans 13:1

What does God tell us in the fourth commandment?
In the fourth commandment God tells us:

"Children, be obedient to your parents in the Lord — that is your duty."
Ephesians 6:1

55

Are there other people whom we should obey?
Yes. God placed over us our teachers, our leaders in
the Church and in the country to care for us. We must
respect, love and obey them, too.

**Do parents, teachers and other leaders receive their
authority from God?**
Yes, they do. The Holy Bible says:
"All authority comes from God."
see Romans 13:1

I Speak to God

O Lord Jesus Christ, help my family
to be as happy and
loving as Your holy family was.

My Response to God

I will obey my parents,
teachers and leaders.
I will always speak
respectfully to them and about
them.

The Fifth Commandment of God

13

There are so many things
we cannot do alone. What
would we do without
our family and friends?
What fun would a boy or girl
have if left all alone?
It takes more than one person to make a family, and
it takes more than one family to make a
neighborhood where friends play.

But here is something to think about: it takes more than just
people together to make a **happy** family, a happy neighborhood,
or a happy class. It takes people **plus love!**

To make happy communities, God gave us a
commandment: to take good care of our own body and soul
and of our neighbor's.

57

The **fifth** commandment of God is:

You shall not kill.

In the fifth commandment, God forbids:
— murder, which means taking somebody else's life;
— suicide, which means taking our own life;
— fighting, anger, and hatred;
— revenge, or "getting even," which means hurting someone
  because they hurt us;
— drunkenness;
— taking drugs which can be very harmful to body and
  mind, even for life;
— giving bad example, which means leading someone else to do wrong;
— refusing to do what we can to help somebody who
  really needs help.

In the fifth commandment, God tells us to take care of ourselves
and of our neighbor. To take care of ourselves means
to take care of our health and to grow
in the life of Jesus, doing the right thing always. To take
care of our neighbor means being kind to others, being patient,
doing things for others, helping people who are suffering and sad,
working with others happily and forgiving those who hurt us.

When Jesus explained this commandment, He said,

Treat others as you would like them to treat you....
Grant pardon, and you will be pardoned.
Luke 6:31, 37

Let us always try to make our home, our school, our neighborhood a
happier and nicer place by our goodness to everybody.

What does God tell us in the fifth commandment?
In the fifth commandment God tells us that we must love one
another, because we are all children of God and
brothers among ourselves.

What did Jesus say about brotherly love?
Jesus said: "By this love you have for one another, everyone
will know that you are my disciples."
John 13:35

58

My Response to God

From now on,
for love of God, I will
be kind to
those boys and girls with
whom I have not been too friendly.

I Speak to God

**Jesus, meek
and humble of heart,
make my heart
like Yours.**

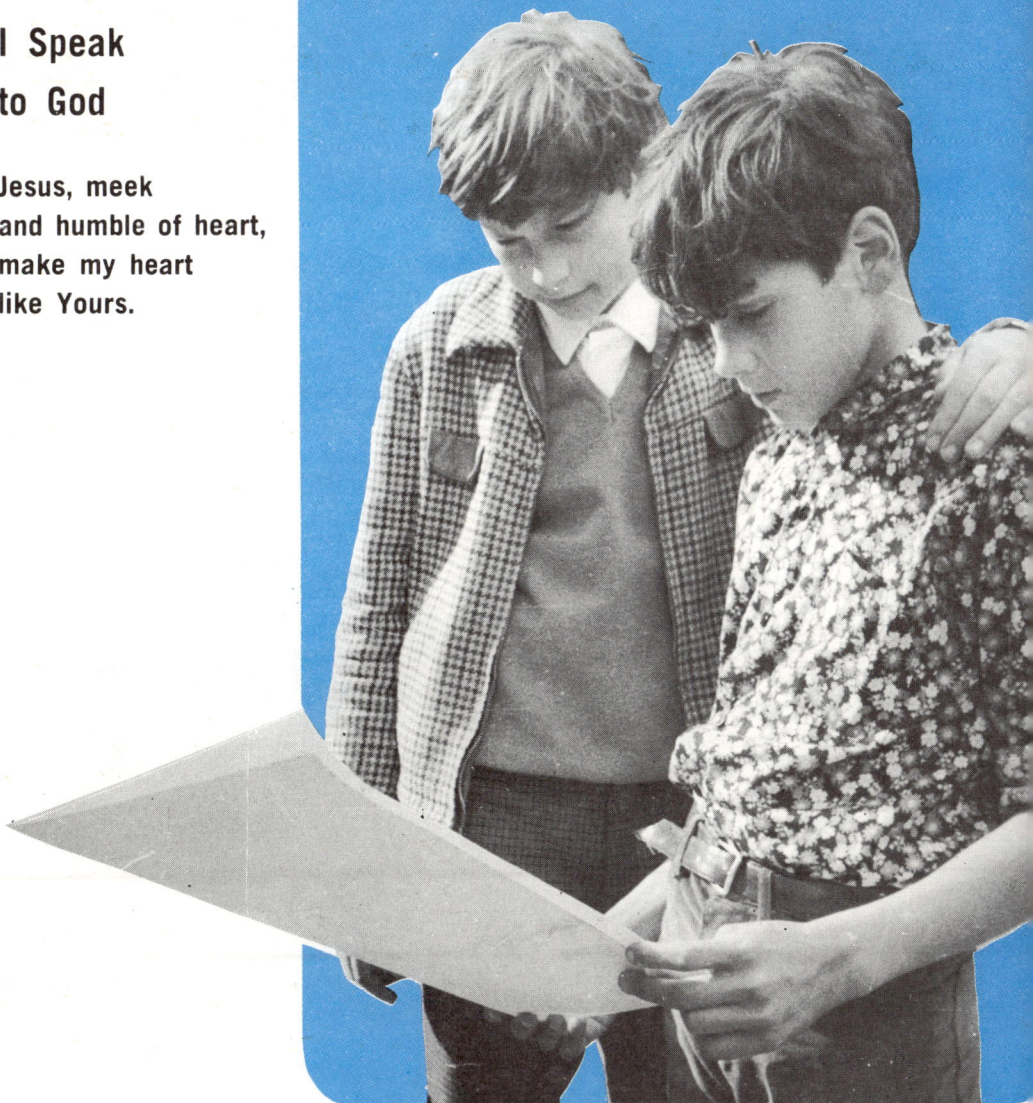

Lord, help me to spread
Your PEACE.

Where there is hatred,
let me bring LOVE.

Where there is hurt,
let me bring
FORGIVENESS.

Where there is sadness,
let me bring JOY.

— St. Francis

The Sixth and Ninth Commandments of God

God has given us many wonderful gifts—our eyes, our ears, our tongue, our whole body—and because He has given them to us, He knows when and how we should use them. He wants boys and girls to be careful not to use or listen to shameful talk or to look at shameful pictures or movies. In this way, God helps us protect our very precious gifts.

The **sixth** commandment of God is:
You shall not commit adultery.

The **ninth** commandment of God is:
You shall not covet your neighbor's wife.

With these
two commandments, God protects
families from much unhappiness. He wants to help
families stay together and never break up.
And He tells everybody
to use
their gifts of body in the right way.

The Holy Bible says:
You should use your body for the glory of God.
1 Corinthians 6:20

When our heavenly Father
made us His children in holy Baptism,
He came to live in us. So we should never **think** anything
shameful, **say** anything shameful
or **do** anything shameful, alone or with others.

14

If boys and girls have questions that are bothering them about their bodies, the best ones to ask are their mother and father.

Our clothes ought to cover our body well. We must stay away from boys and girls who do bad things, and avoid bad pictures, talk, books, and shows. We must be good out of respect for God, who lives in us, and for our guardian angel, who is always at our side.

This is the way to keep God's sixth and ninth commandments.

Whenever bad thoughts come to our minds, let us chase them away with a little prayer and quickly think of something good. We cannot stop them from coming into our minds, but we **can** send them away quickly.

63

Many boys and girls keep holy
pictures or statues
in their bedrooms. They look at them morning
and night. This
helps them to stay good. They read
only good books and magazines,
so that they
will have good thoughts
and will please God.

What does God
tell us in the sixth and ninth
commandments?

In the sixth and ninth
commandments God
tells us
to use the
gifts of our body in the right
way.

Can we stop bad thoughts
from coming into
our mind?

We cannot
stop bad thoughts from coming
into our mind, but we must send them away
quickly, by
saying a quick prayer and thinking of something else.

My Response to God

I will have the courage to walk
away from boys or girls who ask me to listen to or look at
something shameful.

I Speak to God

Sacred Heart of Jesus,
I love You
with all my heart!
Mary,
my holy Mother,
pray for me.

The Seventh and Tenth Commandments of God

15

Our beautiful world, which God made for us to take care of and enjoy, sometimes becomes less beautiful. The air and water may no longer be clean; parks may be littered with paper and cans; buildings and signs may be marked and scarred.

Because God made the world for all of us to use and placed all of us "in charge" of it, we should try to keep it clean and neat.

God wants us to treat all the good things of the earth well—our own things and the things of others. All of them are His gifts to people.

God wants all His children to have food, houses, and clothing.

To protect these for us, He made the seventh and tenth commandments.

The **seventh** commandment of God is:
You shall not steal.

The **tenth** commandment of God is:
You shall not covet anything that belongs to your neighbor.

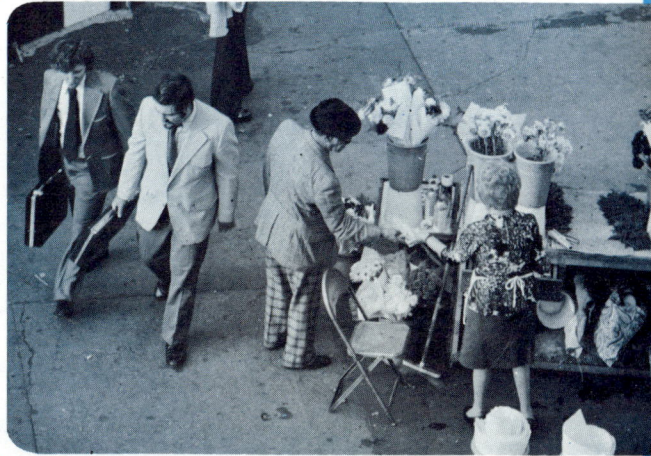

In the seventh commandment God tells us that we must not steal, destroy or spoil what belongs to others; we must not keep what others have lost; and we must not cheat.

The articles on a store counter do not belong to us unless we buy them.
The pens and pencils of a friend are his, not ours, so we must not take them.
Without permission, we do not take the things at home either.

It is wrong to mark up the walls of buildings, to break windows, and worse yet, to set fires.

It is wrong to copy someone else's
test or to cheat in other ways.

If somebody steals or destroys
or damages what is not his, he must make up for it, whenever
he can.

In the tenth commandment,
our heavenly Father tells us not even to **want**
to take or keep things that belong to others. God likes
us to be content with what we have
or with what we can earn. After all, someday we will
die and leave
everything on this earth behind.
Then our real treasure will be the good things we have done.

Of course, it is right for poor people to want to have
enough food and clothing for themselves
and a decent place to live in. But it is wrong to
want to steal
what belongs to others.

A good Christian who owns many good things shares them with
poorer people. This person lives the
way the Holy Bible teaches:

> **Blessed is he who takes pity on the poor.**
> Proverbs 14:21

**What does God tell us in the
seventh commandment?**
In the seventh commandment God tells us that we must
not steal, destroy or spoil what belongs
to others. We must not keep what others have
lost, and we must not cheat.

**Is it enough to be sorry
for breaking the seventh commandment?**
One who has broken the seventh
commandment has to return stolen goods or the amount
they are worth as soon as he can.
He has to repair or pay for damage done on purpose to
the property of others.

What does God tell us in the tenth commandment?
In the tenth commandment
God tells us that we must not want to take
or keep things that belong to others.

My Response to God

If I am tempted to take or want
something that belongs to others, I will remember
the golden rule
of Jesus:

Treat others as you would like them to treat you.

Luke 6:31

I Speak to God

**From his throne in heaven,
the Lord
looks down; he sees
all mankind.
The Lord is just,
and he loves good
actions. Good
men shall see
his face.**

see Psalm 11:4-7

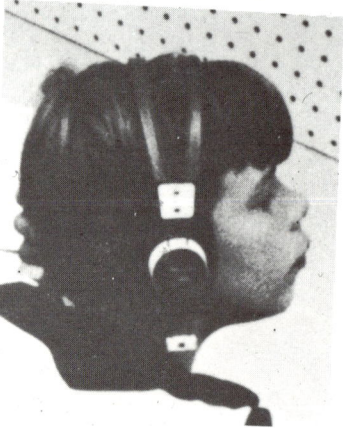

16 The Eighth Commandment of God

Did you ever notice
how much time
we spend every day reading
or watching
or listening or talking?
All of these
things
are called communicating.
Communication
is the way we learn
more and more,
and help others to
learn, too.

To remind us that everything
we tell others should
be **true,**
God our Father gave us the
eighth commandment.

The **eighth**
commandment of God is:
**You shall not bear false witness
against your neighbor.**

Our heavenly Father
gave us a wonderful gift when He gave
us the power to speak. In the eighth commandment, God tells us
never
to use this gift of speech to tell lies.

God also tells us not to talk
about others who do wrong, unless we have a good
reason. He wants all
His children to be able to keep
their good name so that we can all be
happy in
living together.

Our heavenly
Father wants us to speak kindly and
truthfully.
The Holy Bible says:

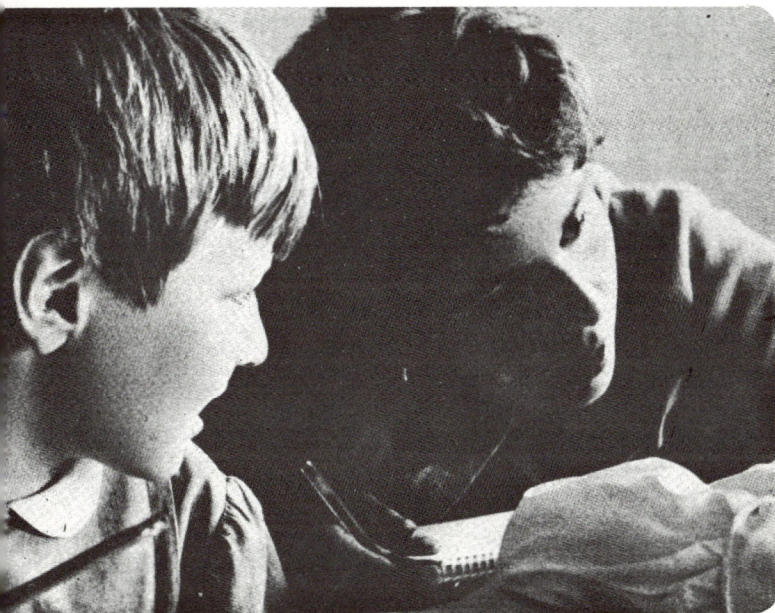

Speakers
of the truth
are
dear
to the Lord
see Proverbs 12:22

If you do
something wrong, and Mother
or Dad asks,
"Who did this?"
answer truthfully,
"I did." Tell the truth
even when it takes courage.
God will bless you for it.

To speak the truth does not
mean that we can always
say everything we know.

Sometimes God wants us to keep a secret to
protect the good name of others.
The important thing to remember is this:
you must always
say the truth
to people who have a right to know the truth.
Such people are
your parents and teachers,
for example.

If we harm a person's good name,
we must do all we can
to make up for the damage we
have done.

**What does God tell us in
the eighth commandment?**
In the eighth commandment God tells
us never to use
the gift of speech to tell
lies or to talk about
others
who do wrong. The Bible says:

"You must speak the truth to one another."
Ephesians 4:25

My Response to God
I will say
the truth even when it
takes courage.

I Speak to God

Jesus Master,
Way, Truth, and Life,
help me to please You by speaking truthfully.

Do you remember how
much you enjoyed
a cold drink that someone
gave you on a hot
summer
day? Or how happy
you were when
someone
came to see you
when you
were sick?

God,
our Father,
wants us to help
one another.
At the end of the
world
Jesus will say
to those
who helped
others:

Come, you whom my Father has blessed.... I was hungry and you gave me food; I was thirsty and you gave me drink; I was a stranger and you made me welcome.

Matthew 25:34-35

We can see that
Jesus considers
whatever good we do
to others as
done to
Himself.
He rewards
us for it.

Actions That Show Our Love

17

The good actions
Jesus
wants us to
do are called the
Corporal
and **Spiritual Works of Mercy.**
Corporal means
"mostly about the body,"
and **spiritual**
means
"mostly about the soul."

If we do not
help our brothers, whom
we see,
how can we say that we love
God,
whom we don't see?

The Holy Spirit
keeps
prompting all of us to be kind
and good to others.
He lives in
us and
gives us the
power to grow more
like Jesus each day. We
act like
Jesus
when we perform
corporal
and spiritual works of mercy.

**The Chief
Corporal
Works
of
Mercy**

The chief corporal
works of mercy are:
to feed
the hungry,
to give drink to the thirsty,
to clothe the naked,
to visit the
imprisoned,
to shelter the homeless,
to visit the sick,
and to
bury the dead.

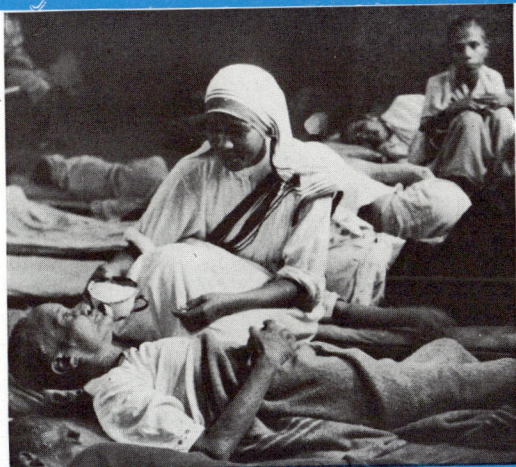

1. To feed the hungry
and
2. To give drink to the thirsty:
We can do this right
at home, first of all,
by **sharing** better — passing
the food and milk or soft drink
to our parents,
brothers and sisters first,
and not eating or
drinking so much that only
a little is
left for someone else.

There are many poor people
in the world today
— people who do not have
enough food. We can
help them
by taking part in
Church campaigns and other
drives to
help the poor and needy.

We can also
perform
another work of mercy by
giving our extra clothes
(if younger brothers
or sisters
do not need them)
to a clothing drive for
the poor.

This third
corporal work of mercy is:
3. To clothe the naked.

Another work of mercy is:
**4. To visit
the imprisoned.**

People in prison are often
very sad and lonely.
They wish
someone would think of them
and care
about them. Boys
and girls
cannot visit prisoners,
but they **can** collect
good books
and send them to a prison.
And they can
always
pray for prisoners.

5. To shelter the homeless

We may not have
a chance to "take in"
someone
who has lost a home,
but we **can**
contribute some of our
spending money
when a fire, flood,
earthquake
or hurricane
has left people homeless. We
can also make our
guests and our parents'
guests
feel "at home"
in our house.

6. To visit the sick

A friendly visit
from us may cheer up a sick
classmate or relative.
Then, too,
there are many
sick people in nursing homes
who never
have any visitors.
If we cannot go to see
them ourselves,
perhaps
we can send
them Christmas and Easter
cards
or small gifts.

7. To bury the dead

Because
the human body is the home
of the Holy Spirit
and because
it will rise one day,
it should
always be treated with great
respect. That is why
the Holy Bible
praises good people who make
sure the dead
are given proper burial.

This work of mercy
includes attending
wakes and funerals
respectfully
and prayerfully.

It also includes
considering
cemeteries as holy places,
to be visited only
in order to pray
for the dead.

The Chief Spiritual Works of Mercy

The chief spiritual works of mercy are:
to admonish
the sinner, to instruct
the ignorant,
to counsel the doubtful,
to comfort the
sorrowful,
to bear wrongs patiently,
to forgive all
injuries, and to pray for the living
and the dead.

1. To admonish the sinner

To **admonish**
means to correct — to let
someone know that
he is
doing wrong. Sometimes just
by not paying attention
to a person
we can make him
realize
he is displeasing God.

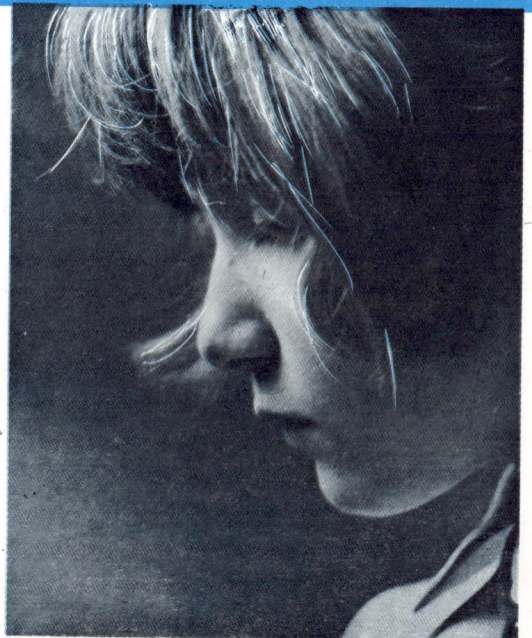

2. To instruct the ignorant

To **instruct** means to teach.
The most important subject we
can teach is our
Catholic Faith, because
it tells us
what to believe and what to do
so that Jesus' life may
grow in us and we may live with
Him forever
in heaven. But first
we must know our religion well
ourselves. Then we
can help others.

There is much good in every
religion, but our Catholic Faith
teaches everything
that Jesus taught and has all
the sacraments that Jesus gave
us in order to grow in His divine
life and keep His law of love.

When boys and girls of
other faiths
ask us about ours, we should be
happy to tell them what we
believe and do in our Church. We
may even invite them to come
to religion class or Mass with us.

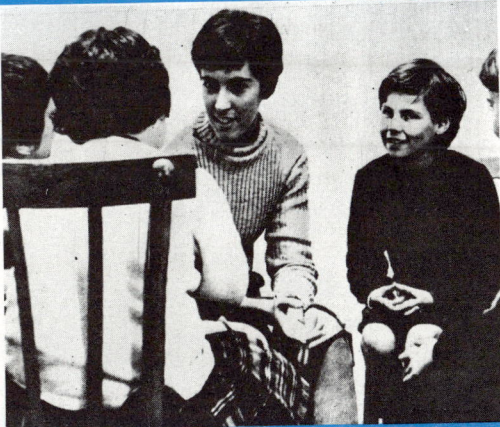

3. To counsel the doubtful

To **counsel** means to tell
a person the right
thing
to do. How do we
know the right thing? We think
of the Ten
Commandments.

For example, if a boy tells
a friend that he should
not take drugs, he keeps
him from
breaking the fifth
commandment
and may save him from
harming
his mind or body for life.

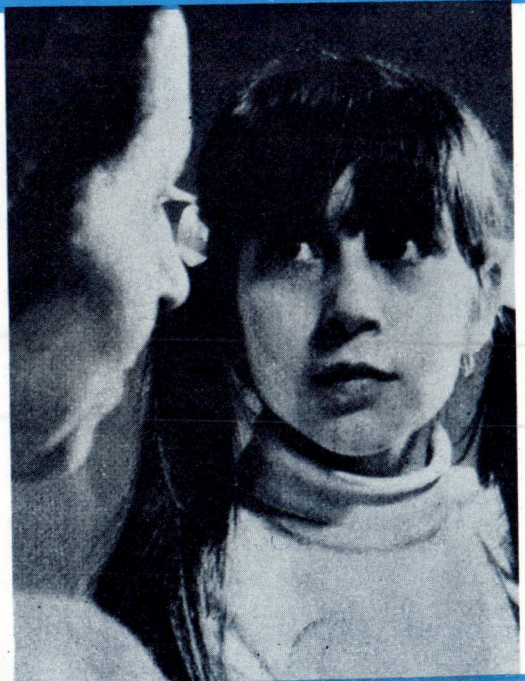

4. To comfort the sorrowful

We can cheer up
those who are sad
by being extra kind to them and
by saying some good words
of encouragement.
We can suggest
that they offer up their
little sufferings
to Jesus,
who died for us, and
we can
remind them that in heaven
we will always be happy.

5. To bear wrongs patiently

This means
not to let our feelings of
anger take over
when someone makes fun
of us
or is mean
to us. At such times
we should keep still,
no matter
how hard it is, and say a little
prayer. A powerful
prayer is:
"Jesus,
meek and humble of heart,
make my heart
like Yours."

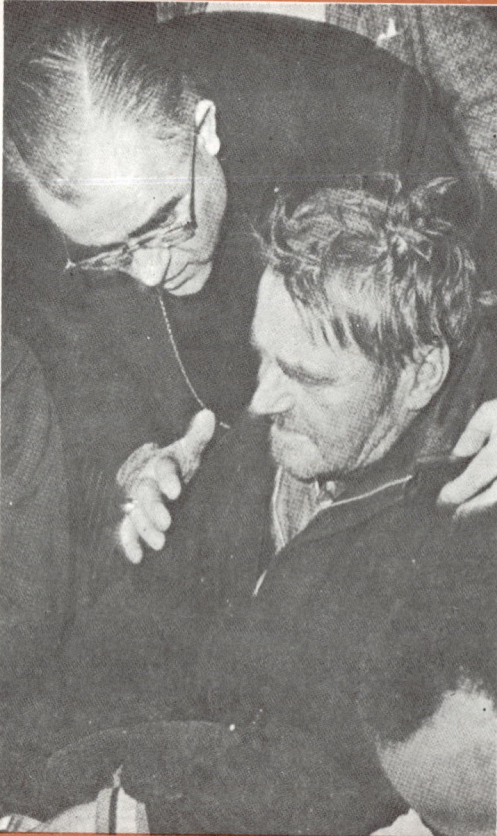

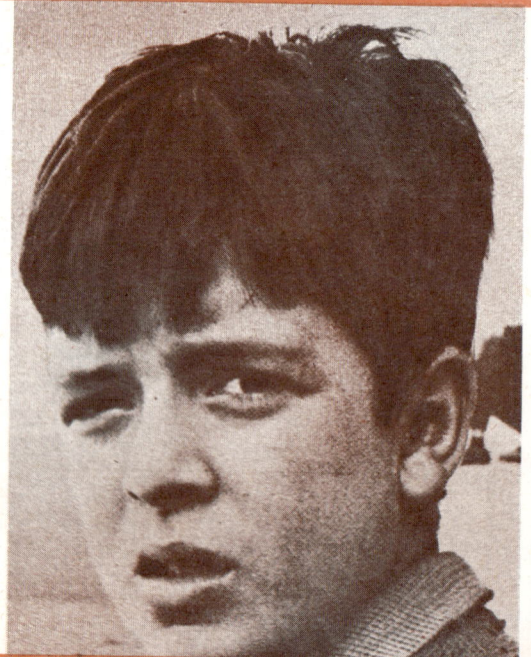

6. To forgive all injuries

This means forgiving from the heart those who hurt us in any way — as we want God to do to us. Every time we say the Our Father, we pray, as Jesus taught us:

Forgive
us
our trespasses
as we forgive
those who
trespass
against us.

7. To pray for the living and the dead

There are many people to pray for besides ourselves and our own family. There is our Holy Father the Pope, and the whole Church. There are our separated brethren — other Christians whom we hope will someday be united to us. There are people who are looked down upon or treated badly because of their poverty, skin-color or nationality. There are people suffering from taking harmful drugs.

There are people who do not know about God and heaven, and suffer terribly in their hearts because they think that life has no meaning. And there are souls suffering in purgatory until they are worthy to be with God forever. We can pray for all these people, even if we do not know them by name.

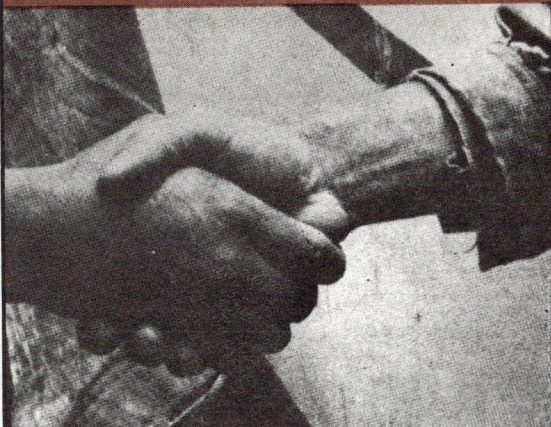

**How do we know that the works
of mercy are important?**
We know that the works of mercy are
important because
Jesus said: "Whenever you
did it for one
of the least of my brothers, you
did it for me."
see Matthew 25:40

**Which are the
chief corporal works of mercy?**
(See the list on page 74.)

**Which are the chief spiritual
works of mercy?**
(See the list on page 78.)

My Response to God

I will practice
the works of
mercy better than I did before,
taking every chance that
comes my way.

I Speak
to
God

Lord Jesus,
may all of us
Christians
freely
help our brothers,
especially
the poorest.
And may we
bring all men
to You.

In His wonderful
Sermon on the
Mount, Jesus gave us the "recipe"
for a good life in the form
of the Eight Beatitudes.
"Beatitude" means
"happiness."

Let us read about these promises of Jesus:

" How blest are the poor in spirit: the reign of God is theirs.
Blest too are the sorrowing; they shall be consoled.
Blest are the lowly; they shall inherit the land.
Blest are they who hunger and thirst for holiness; they shall have their fill.
Blest are they who show mercy; mercy shall be theirs.
Blest are the single-hearted for they shall see God.
Blest too the peacemakers; they shall be called sons of God.
Blest are those persecuted for holiness' sake; the reign of God is theirs. "

Blest are the poor in spirit:
the reign of God is theirs.
The poor in spirit are satisfied with the
things they have and ready to share them
with others. They think more of being
happy with God in His heavenly kingdom
than of having nice things now.

Even though Jesus was God, He chose to be
poor and work hard. To His followers He says:
You will have treasure in heaven.
Matthew 19:21

Blest are the sorrowing; they shall be consoled.

It makes God's good friends sad
to see people who do not seem to love
God or others very much. They pray for these
people. They also feel sorry to see others
in pain or sad or worried.
They do what they can to help.

When they are suffering or lonely or
worried, they remember that God loves
them. They think of what the
Holy Bible says:
He will wipe away all tears from their eyes.
Revelation 21:4.

Blest are the lowly; they shall inherit the land.

The lowly are good people who are not proud. They never think they are better than others.

They are kind and patient and do not complain. They are especially good to people who are poor or are not treated fairly.

Everybody likes a humble person. Jesus said:
The man who humbles himself will be exalted.
Luke 18:14

Blest are they who hunger and thirst for holiness; they shall have their fill.
To be holy means to live as Jesus did, loving God and all our brothers. Jesus will tell everyone who has tried to be like Him:
Come and join in your Master's happiness.
Matthew 25:21

Holy people will be close to God forever and ever in the unending happiness of heaven.

Blest are they who show mercy; mercy shall be theirs.
Merciful people always forgive those who hurt their feelings by saying unkind things, or who push them around, or ignore them. The merciful do not try to get even. Jesus said:
If you forgive others their failings, your heavenly Father will forgive you yours.
Matthew 6:14

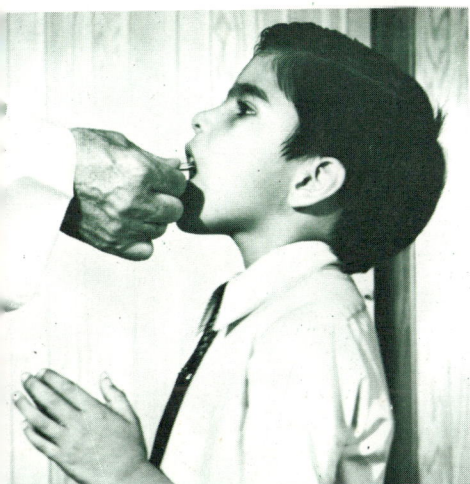

How Wonderful It Is To Live According to the Eight Beatitudes

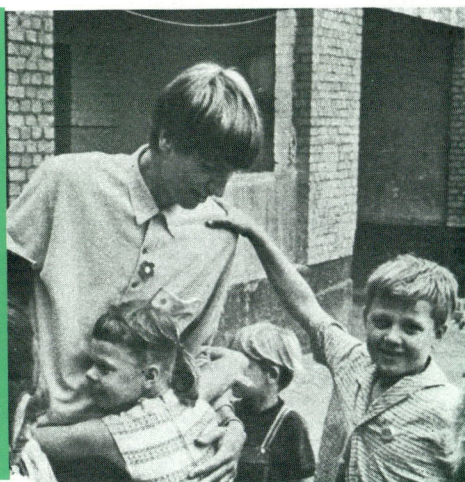

Blest are the single-hearted;
for they shall see God.
We call people "single-hearted"
when they put God before everything
else.

God protects and blesses those who
are always trying to please Him
and do what is right. In heaven
they will see Him face to face.
The Holy Bible says:
Who has the right to stand in God's
holy place? The person who has clean
hands and a pure heart.

see Psalm 24:3-4

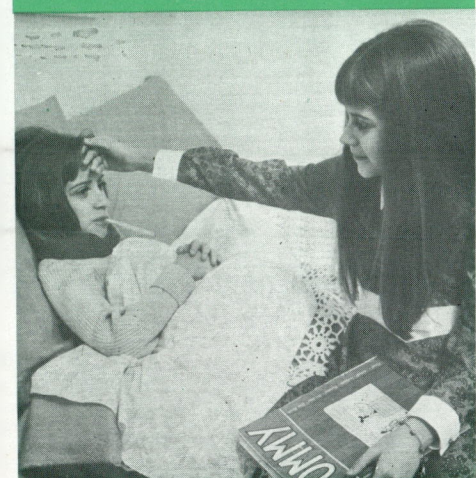

Blest too the peacemakers; they shall be called sons of God.

Peace is very important for our world today. And peace begins "at home"—in our family and among our friends. The peacemakers are careful never to start arguments or fights. And when they see others quarreling, they try to stop them.
The Holy Bible says:
Do all you can to live at peace with everyone.
Romans 12:18

We can see how important it is to make peace, for Jesus said that peacemakers are God's own children.

**Blest are those persecuted for holiness' sake;
the reign of God is theirs.**

Persecution means some kind of suffering caused by others. Some people make fun of others or are unkind to them because they live their religion well.

In this world everyone suffers once in a while. Jesus our Savior suffered much more than we will. If we suffer patiently for the love of Jesus, we will go to heaven one day to be happy forever and ever with Him and all His friends, the saints.

There are a great many saints—even young people—who gave up their lives rather than give up Jesus. They are called martyrs.
The Holy Bible says:
Bless those who persecute you.
Romans 12:14

How wonderful it is to live according to the eight Beatitudes!

What are the eight Beatitudes?
(Say them one by one.)

My Response to God

I will try always to put God first and live according to the eight Beatitudes. Doing this, I will keep Jesus' law of love and be happy.

I Speak to God

Lord Jesus, help me to be poor in spirit, patient in sorrow, humble and holy. Help me to be merciful and single-hearted, a maker of peace. And give me the courage to live up to my Faith always.

Lesson 19, "Mary Shows Us How To Live the Law of Love"

By praying to Mary and trying to be like her, we grow closer to Jesus and become more like Him. **Suggestion:** Encourage the children to begin the practice of saying three Hail Mary's every day for this intention.

Lesson 20, "In God's Family We Love and Help Each Other"

Jesus founded the Church, the new People of God. Guided by their leaders, its members believe and follow the teachings of Jesus and share His life. **Suggestion:** Talk to the children about the good the Church does in the world—the missions, campaigns for human development, local programs to help the underprivileged, etc. If possible, take the family to visit some Catholic charitable institution.

Lesson 21, "The Church Helps Us To Live as Jesus Taught"

Through the Church, the Holy Spirit tells us what Jesus expects of us today. **Suggestion:** Help your child compose a prayer to thank Jesus for giving us the Church.

Preparation for Easter.
Suggestion: On Holy Saturday afternoon or evening emphasize the importance of Easter by decorating your home. Flowers, ribbons in spring colors, colored eggs, paper birds and butterflies all symbolize life, hope and joy. Colorful "Alleluia" posters could be made by the children and Easter cards displayed in prominent places.

Lesson 22, "Our Joyful Meetings with Jesus"

When we receive a sacrament, we meet Jesus and receive His grace. **Suggestion:** Help the children recall some of the joyful meetings with relatives and friends that they have experienced. Help them remember **why** they were joyful, and explain in the same terms why we should be especially joyful at every meeting with Jesus in Penance and the Eucharist.

Lesson 23, "The Wonders of Baptism"

In Baptism we became sharers in God's own life, joined to Christ in His Church, cleansed from sin. **Suggestion:** Help each child prepare for a home celebration of his next baptismal anniversary. (Circle the dates on the calendar so you won't forget!) Decorate a candle and keep it for the family "baptismal party" you will hold on each child's anniversary.

Lesson 24, "The Holy Spirit and His Marvelous Gifts"

The Holy Spirit is God. The Spirit of Truth and Love, He lives in us, making us holy and keeping us joined in love. **Suggestion:** Encourage your fourth grader to make a Holy Spirit poster for his room: for example, a white dove surrounded by seven flames.

Lesson 25, "The Sacrament of Mercy"

In the sacrament of Penance, or Confession, Jesus takes away our sins and draws us closer to Him. **Suggestion:** Read your child the "parables of mercy" (the lost sheep, the lost coin, the prodigal son)—Luke 15:1-24. Have a family discussion about the lesson of God's goodness taught in these parables.

Lesson 26, "The Gift of the Eucharist"

The Holy Eucharist holds first place among all the sacraments. In the Eucharistic Celebration, or Mass, Jesus becomes present under the appearances of bread and wine and renews the sacrifice of the cross in an unbloody manner. In Communion He nourishes us with Himself, so that we may become a people more acceptable to God and filled with greater love of God and others. **Suggestion:** Make up a "family litany" that you may say on the way to Mass, each member offering his work, study, play, etc., of the following week to the Father in union with the sacrifice of Jesus. For example:

(After each prayer, all answer: "Lord, accept our offering.")

Dad: O Lord, we offer You the work that takes us away from home.
Mother: O Lord, we offer You our work at home.
Child: O Lord, we offer You our sports and games.
Child: O Lord, we offer You all our good deeds.
Child: O Lord, we offer You our school and homework.
Child: O Lord, we offer You our hours of traveling, eating, sleeping....

Lesson 27, "My Continuing Response to God"

Religion makes our whole life better. What we have learned from religion study should show in our lives. **Suggestion:** Using the lesson as a guide, help the children draw up a "Christian Life Program" for vacation time.

page for parents

89

Mary Shows Us How To Live

the Law of Love

19

Have you ever tried to be like someone else? This is good, as long as we are careful to choose the right people to be like.

Those great members of the Church called the **saints** became real spiritual heroes by trying to be like our Savior, Jesus. But the person who was most like Jesus was His Mother Mary.

Mary leads us to Christ.
By praying to Mary, we grow closer to Jesus and we become more like Him.

In what ways can we try to be like Mary?

Mary was **humble.** To be humble means to know that everything good in us comes from God and that we should use these gifts to serve God. When the Archangel Gabriel asked Mary to become the Mother of God's Son, she answered,

I am the handmaid of the Lord.
Luke 1:38

Mary was **obedient.** At once she accepted God's invitation to become the Savior's Mother. She said,

Let what you have said be done to me.
Luke 1:38

90

Mary
was
helpful.
As soon as the angel told her that her cousin Elizabeth was going to have a baby, Mary traveled
many miles to help her cousin with her housework.

Mary **trusted** in God's promises.
Her cousin
Elizabeth said about Mary:

**Blessed is she who believed
that the promise
made her by the Lord would be fulfilled.**

Luke 1:45

Mary was **prayerful.**
She thought and prayed over
the words
and actions of Jesus.
The Bible tells us:

**His mother remembered all
these things always.**
see Luke 2:51

All through her
life Mary did what God wanted
of her,
even when it was hard.
How hard it must have been
to watch Jesus dying
on the cross for us!

Do you know the secret
of Mary's wonderful life?
Love of God.
Real love of God makes us
love others, too.
Mary shows us
how to love God and others,
how to live
His law of love.

Jesus is very pleased when we try to love Him as
His Mother did. He **wants** us to honor His
Mother, as He did. He wants us to turn to
this kind Mother of ours
for help whenever we need it.

God the Father
honored Mary by creating her free
from original sin,
so that she would be a worthy
Mother for His Son.
God honored Mary by taking her up into heaven, body and
soul, after her life on earth. He honored
her by making her the queen of heaven and earth and
the Mother of every friend of Jesus. When we honor
Mary, we do what God Himself did.

When we ask Mary to help us become better followers of Jesus, she prays to God for us. No matter what kind of person asks Mary for this kind of help,
Jesus never refuses to answer the prayers of His Mother.

Is the Mother of God
also the Mother of us all?

Yes, Jesus gave us
His Mother to be
our Mother, too. Mary leads us to Jesus.

Is Jesus pleased when we try to be like His Mother?
Jesus is very pleased when we
try to be like His Mother. He is also pleased when we honor
her by praying to her, and He always listens
to her prayers for us.

My Response to God

I will often pray to Mary,
the Mother
of our Savior and
our Mother, too. I will ask her to
help me to be more like her,
and I will thank her for taking
good care
of me.

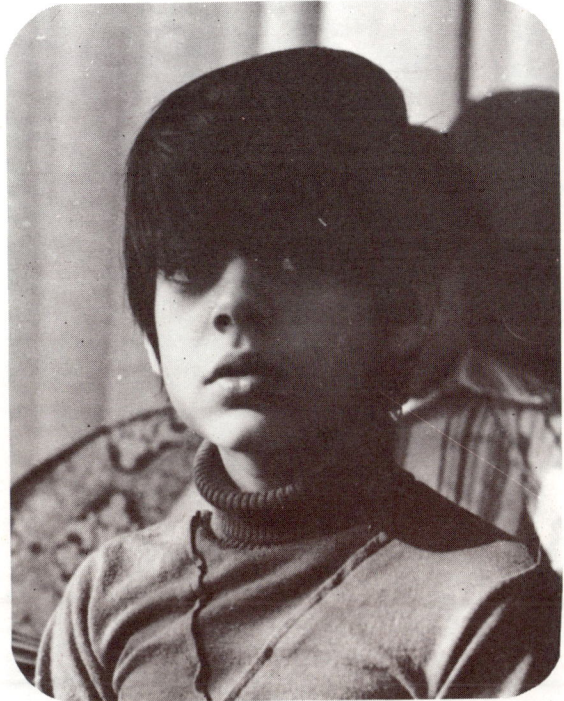

I Speak to God

O Mary,
my Mother,
help me to be like
Jesus and you.

20

In God's Family
We Love and Help
Each Other

You remember that before the Savior came, God chose a special people for Himself and prepared them with a Covenant (or agreement) to make them holy and ready for the coming of the Savior. God planned that when the Savior would come, He would call together a "new" People of God made up of Hebrews and all other nationalities who would believe in Jesus Christ and follow Him.

During His public life, Jesus began to gather a group of followers. This was the beginning of His Church, that is, the Family of the new People of God. Then Jesus chose twelve men from this group. He called them apostles. He made one of the twelve, Simon Peter, the head of the apostles and the chief teacher and ruler of His new people.

Before He
ascended into
heaven, Jesus called all
His apostles
together and gave them
a great share in His power. He
said to them,

"Go and make people
of all nations my followers.
Teach them to obey
all the commands I have
given you."
see Matthew 28:18-19

Jesus promised that He would always
be with His apostles
and with those who
would take their place, so they would always
teach the truth, make us holy and help us to live by
the law of love.

The new People of God
is made up of people of every race,
of all countries of the earth,
because all people
of the earth are children of God, and Jesus
came to save everyone.

In this great Family
we all love one another and help one another
as brothers, no matter
what race or nation we belong to, because
Jesus wants His Family to live by
the law of love. He said,

"I give you a new
commandment:
love one another;
just as I have loved you,
you also must
love one
another."
John 13:34

So we,
the members
of His Family, are to
love one another in Jesus Christ.
The Holy Spirit
helps us to do this.

It is up to everyone in the Church "to be
a missionary." All of us should
share the "good news" of Jesus'
love for us
with as many people as we can.

Through His Church Jesus wants to join all the
world in His love.

The members of a family share many things.
In the Catholic Church,
these are some of the things we share:
we believe the same truths;
we share the life of Jesus, meeting Him
in the same sacraments;
we follow the same leaders—
our Holy Father the Pope and the Bishops,
who lead us in Jesus' name;
we help one another
to keep the same law of love.

Jesus and the Holy Spirit guide the Pope
who takes the place of Jesus as
St. Peter did, and the Bishops,
who take the place of the apostles.
Jesus will
guide the Pope and
the Bishops until
the end of the world, as He
promised the
apostles:

I
am
with you
always;
yes,
to the end
of time.

Matthew 28:20

Priests help the Bishops to lead the Family of God's People.

Men and women called "religious" promise Jesus that they will try to live like Him in obedience, poverty and love for His Father and for everybody in the world. Priests, Brothers, and Sisters spend their whole lives loving God and serving His people everywhere. Jesus stays very close to these special friends of His who do such important work for Him.

Once Jesus said that His Church is like a flock of sheep, led, loved and defended by Him. He said,

I am the good shepherd... and I lay down my life for my sheep.
John 10:14-15

How fortunate we are to belong to the Church!

What is the Church?
The Church is the new People of God. Guided by their leaders, its members believe and follow the teachings of Jesus and share His life.

Who is the head of the Church?
The head of the Church is Jesus Christ. He is our Leader and Brother.

Who is the Pope?
The Pope is the successor of St. Peter and the chief leader of the Church on earth.

Who are the Bishops?
The Bishops are the successors of the apostles. With the Pope, they guide God's People.

My Response to God

I will love the Catholic Church as my family, and I will pray to know how God wishes me to serve Him in it. I will often thank God that I belong to the Church.

I Speak to God

O Jesus, I thank You for the great gift of the Church. Bless our Pope and our Bishops. Give the Church many Priests, Brothers and Sisters. Give them great love for You and for the poor and for everyone who needs their help.

The Church Helps Us To Live as Jesus Taught

21

What a joy it is to be a child of the Church! And just as a good child obeys his parents, so a good child of the Church obeys the Church. When we do what the Church asks us to do, we obey Jesus Himself. In fact, Jesus told His apostles,

"Anyone who listens to you, listens to me."

Luke 10:16

Jesus said that we are to worship the Father. So that we will remember this important duty, the Church asks us:

1. To keep holy the day of the Lord's resurrection.

This means to participate in Mass on all Sundays and holydays of obligation.

The holydays of obligation in the United States are: Christmas Day (December 25); The Solemnity of Mary, the Mother of God (January 1); Ascension Thursday (40 days after Easter); The Assumption (August 15); All Saints' Day (November 1); The Immaculate Conception (December 8).

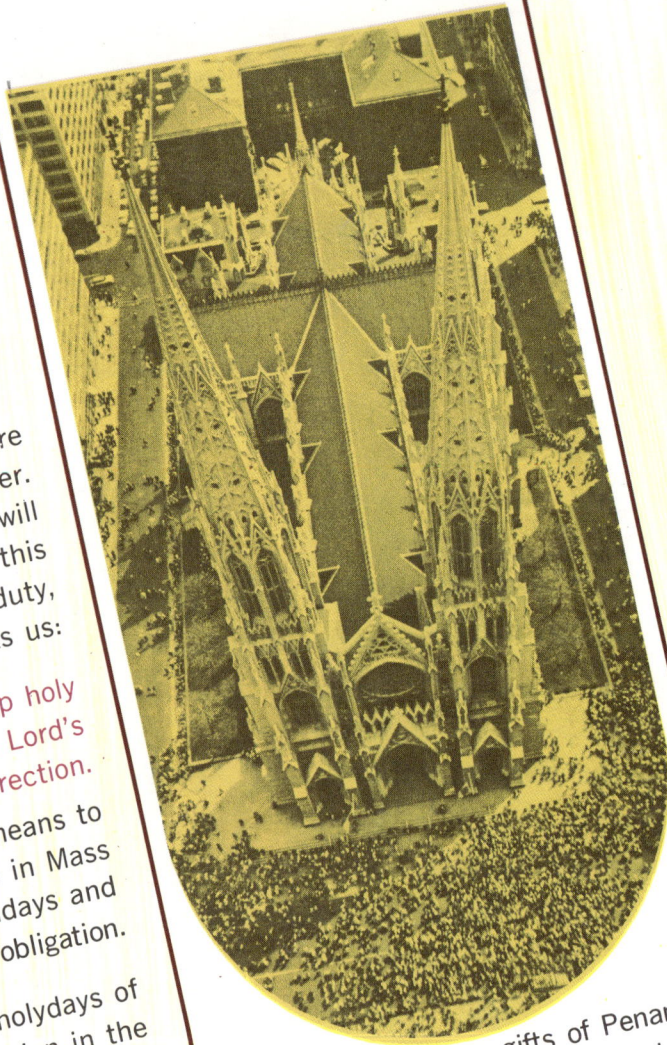

Jesus gave us the gifts of Penance and Eucharist so that we will keep growing in His life. The Church asks us:

2. To receive Holy Communion frequently and the sacrament of Penance regularly.

A person in serious sin must go to confession at least once a year. All of us must receive Jesus in the Eucharist at least once a year, between the first Sunday of Lent and Trinity Sunday. But good friends of Jesus receive these marvelous sacraments very often.

Another duty
of Catholic Christians is:

3. To prepare for the
sacrament of
Confirmation by
studying their Catholic
religion;
To be confirmed;
To keep on studying
their Faith
and spreading it.

So that Catholics who
get married
will be sure to
receive God's blessings
and bring up
their children
in a way pleasing
to God,

the Church asks them:

4. To keep the marriage
laws of the Church;

To give religious
training
to their children;

To use parish schools
and religious
education programs.

God wants us to support
our Church so that the
Pope, Bishops,
Priests and
religious may be able to carry
on the work
of Christ.

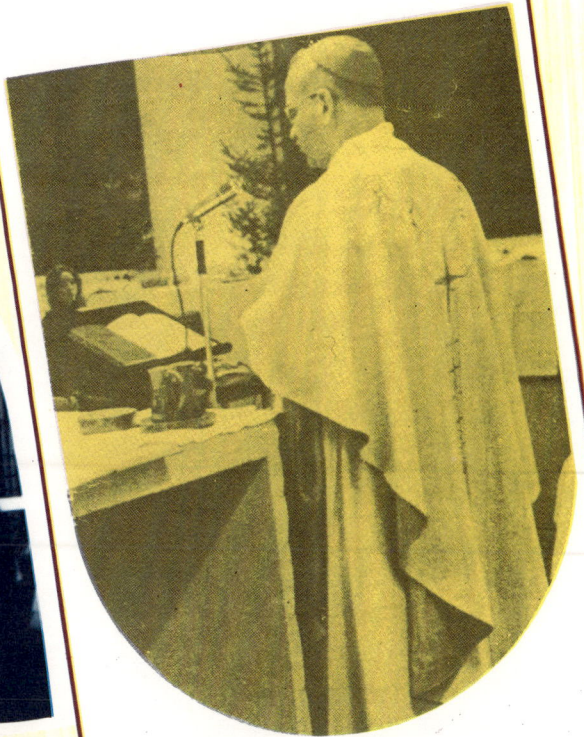

Therefore the Church asks us:

5. To support our own
parish and its Priests,
the worldwide
Church, and our
Holy Father, the Pope.

We do this by contributing
what we can to collections made
for the parish and
for special needs of the
whole Church.

Jesus said we must make
up for our sins.
So that we will remember this
important command
to make sacrifices,
the Church tells us:

6. To do penance;
to fast and abstain on the
appointed days.

To "fast" means to eat
only one full meal
a day,
and to "abstain" means
not to eat meat or
anything made from meat.
The Church asks this on certain
days of Lent to remind
us of the passion
and death of Jesus for our sins.

Because we Catholics have
received the gifts of God in
Baptism and Confirmation, we are
to share these gifts
with others. For this reason,
the Church
reminds her members:

7. To join in
the missionary apostolate
of Christ
and the Church.

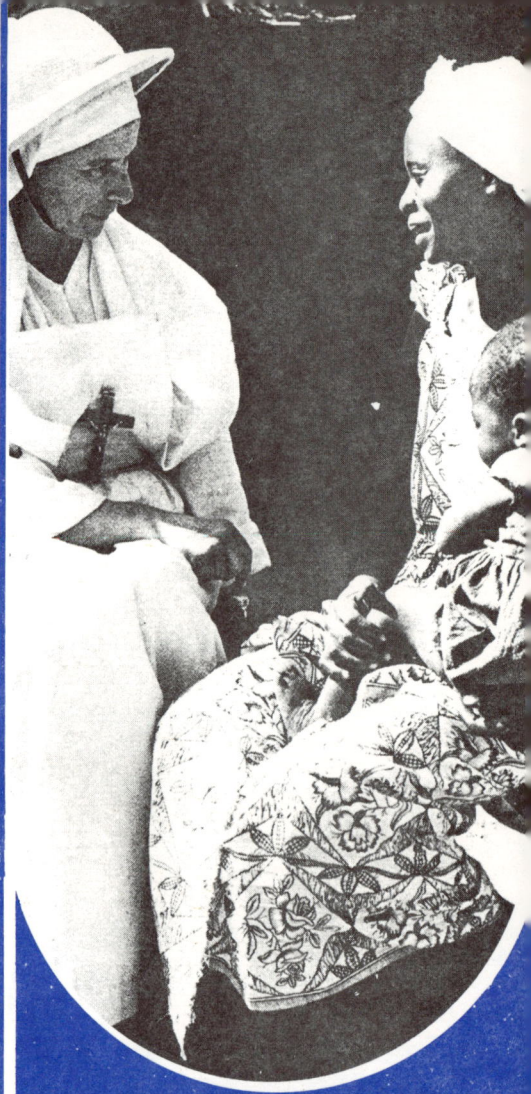

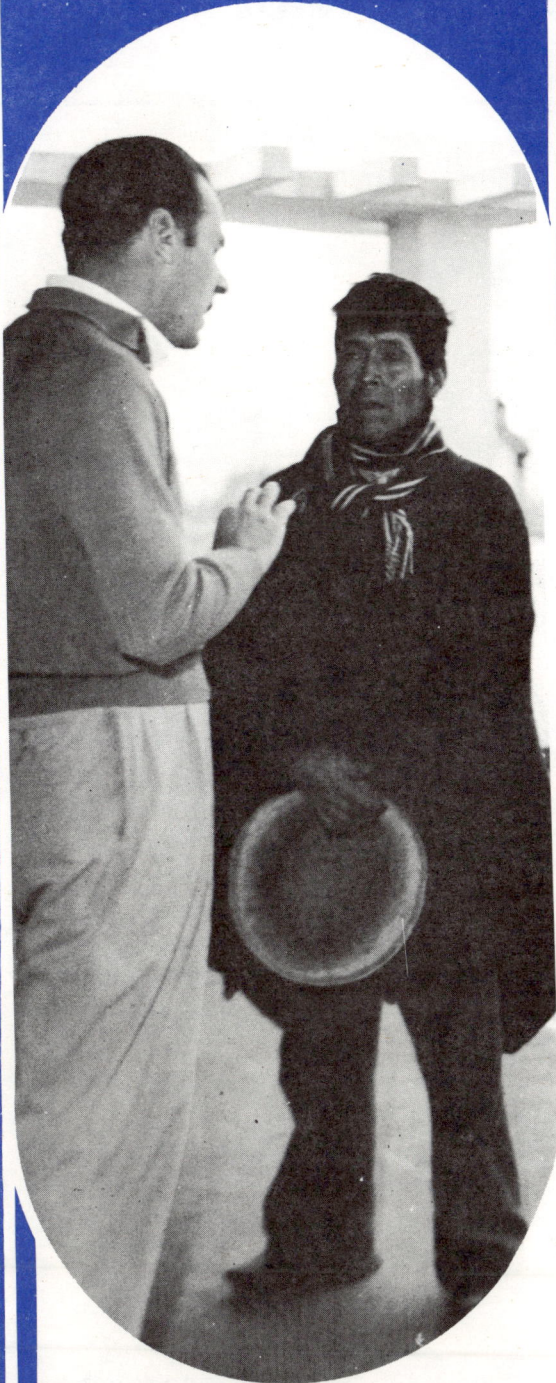

By "missionary apostolate," the Church means showing **everyone** — at home or wherever we may be — how a good Christian lives. Some generous Catholics — even parents and young people — offer to go to other lands to teach about Jesus.

If we always do what the Church expects of us, God will bless us and make us happy.

How do we know what Jesus expects of us today? We know what Jesus expects of us today because the Holy Spirit tells us through the Church.

My Response to God

I will try to give good example to everyone at home, at school, and at play. If I have a chance, I will also speak about my Faith to my friends.

I Speak to God

Lord Jesus, with Your help, may I always love Your Church and do everything it asks of me.

Jesus
is always
working
to save us,
in His Church.
Through
the Gift of the
Holy Spirit,
He makes us holy,
especially by means of
the sacraments.
The sacraments are
precious "meetings"
with Jesus.
When we receive
a sacrament
we really meet Jesus, and
receive His grace. We are sure
of this because He said so.

Through these seven wonderful sacraments
—Jesus shares with us the divine life—grace—that
He won for us when He died and rose
from the dead.
—He draws us close to Himself in love.
—He delivers us from evil.
—He helps us to keep His law of love and to be saved.

When we receive a sacrament, we do not see Jesus or His grace.
We only see and hear the signs of the sacraments—
like the water and the words in
Baptism. But we **know** that Jesus is
there acting to make us more like Himself.
This is our **faith,** and our faith is a very important part
of every meeting with
Jesus in the sacraments.

The names of the seven sacraments are:
Baptism, Confirmation, Holy Eucharist, Penance, Holy Orders,
Matrimony and
Anointing of the Sick.

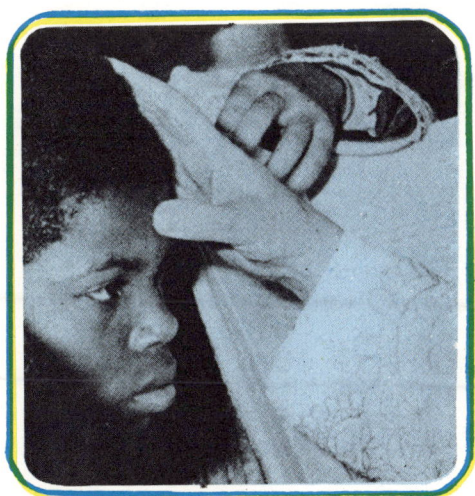

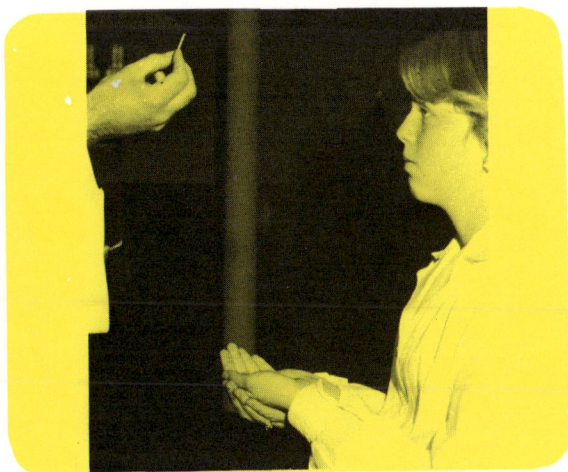

By means of **Baptism,** Jesus fills us with His own wonderful life. He makes us loving children of God and welcomes us into the community of His Church. He frees us from sin and joins us to Himself.

In **Confirmation,** we receive the seal of the Holy Spirit, who is the Gift of God the Father and God the Son. The Holy Spirit prepares us to be strong, grown-up Christians. He gives us the power to be brave witnesses to Jesus. To be a witness means to be like Jesus in all we do and to tell others about Him, so that many others will want to belong to Him, too.

In the **Holy Eucharist,** Jesus gives us His own self as spiritual food. He makes His divine life in us grow stronger and stronger. He draws us close to Himself and to one another.

Penance brings us God's forgiveness for sins committed after Baptism. It helps us get rid of bad habits and become more like Jesus.

By **Holy Orders,** the Holy Spirit comes upon men set apart for the work of the Lord and makes them Bishops and Priests of the Church. Bishops and Priests serve us in the name of Jesus. He helps them teach His gospel, guide us, and make us holy.

In **Matrimony** Jesus blesses a man and woman who take each other as husband and wife for all their lives. They live together in His grace and try to love each other as He loves His Church. He always offers them His help to be good fathers and mothers and to make their home holy and happy.

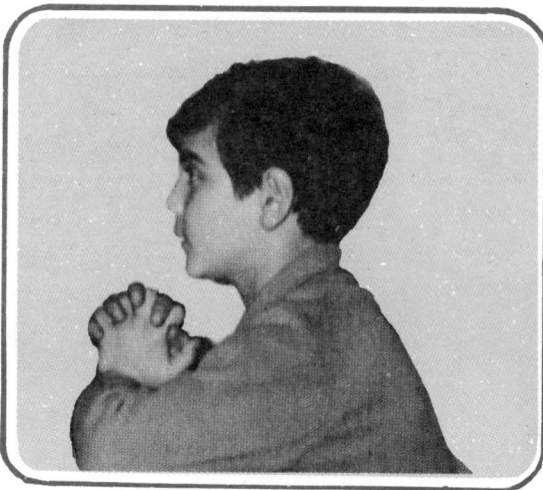

Through the **Anointing of the Sick,** Jesus gives sick people and old people comfort and strength to suffer patiently. By this anointing and the prayers said with it for them to get well, the whole Church asks God to lighten their sufferings, forgive their sins, and bring them to everlasting happiness.

The sacraments always bring us closer to God if we receive them with faith and love. The better we receive the sacraments, the richer we will be in God's life and friendship.

What a wonderful privilege is ours!

Did Jesus come to give His own divine life?
Yes. Jesus said: "I have come so that they may have life and have it to the full" (John 10:10). Jesus gives us His life and increases it through the seven sacraments — Baptism, Confirmation, Holy Eucharist, Penance, Holy Orders, Matrimony and Anointing of the Sick.

What are the sacraments?
The sacraments are the main actions through which Jesus gives His Spirit to Christians and makes us a holy people.
They are outward signs both of God's grace and our faith.

My Response to God

I will live as a true child of God, receiving the sacraments of Penance and Holy Eucharist often with faith in Jesus, in order to grow closer to Him.

I Speak to God

O Lord,
may Your grace
always be with us!

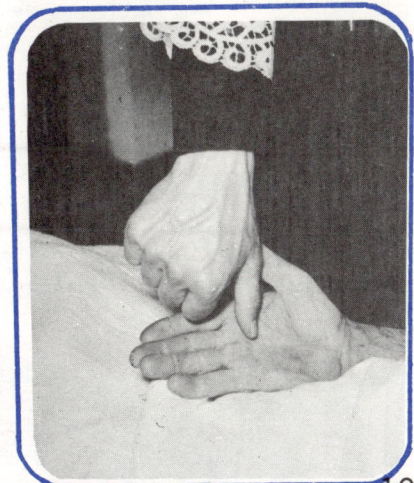

23 The Wonders of Baptism

Did you ever stop to think that
from the very day you were baptized Jesus has been
living and loving in you?

On that great day He gave you the tremendous gift of
His divine life. He made you a child of God,
and He made you holy by His Spirit.
He cleansed you from original sin and brought you into His Church.

How important you are to God!
What great things He has done for you!
At Baptism you became a new and very wonderful person.

A Baptism is a happy celebration. God is happy to have a new
child living by His own divine life.
The Church is happy to have
a new member.

The child's mother
and father,
brothers
and sisters, relatives,
friends
and neighbors
all
rejoice, too.

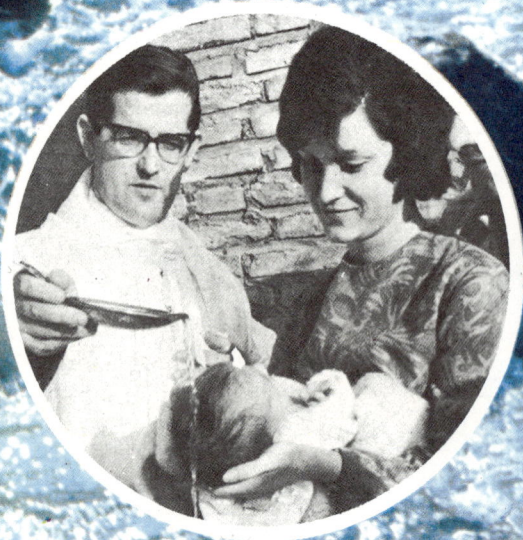

Because you were baptized,
you belong to Jesus in a very
special way.
He has joined you to His own
life, death and resurrection.
He lets you
work for Him and share His
own mission.

Baptism is like a
door into the new Christian
life. Great as it is,
it is just the beginning.
At Confirmation
the Christian is signed with
the Gift of the Holy Spirit, and in
the Eucharist, he receives
the Lord Jesus.

These three sacraments—
Baptism, Confirmation, and the Eucharist
—are called sacraments of initiation.
Through them Jesus acts to
give us the fullness of His life.

Water is what Jesus chose to give us new
life in Baptism and to cleanse us from
sin. In our homes we use water for
drinking, cooking and washing.
Water is really a very important part of our
lives. Every time
we see water let us think of
how Jesus made plain water the means
of giving us
the great gift of divine life.

109

When you were baptized, the
priest poured water on your forehead and said
as he did so:

I baptize you
in the name of
the Father,
and of the Son,
and of the Holy Spirit."

You were signed in the name
of the Blessed Trinity
and became their child.
Now it is up to you
to live up to your great dignity!

What is Baptism?

Baptism is the
sacrament of faith that makes us
sharers in God's own life,
joins us to Christ
in His Church, and frees us from sin.

My Response to God

How beautiful it is to
think that God the
Father,
God the Son and God the
Holy Spirit live within us!
Every morning I will make up
my mind to act as Jesus
wants me to — at home,
at school,
alone and with others.

I Speak
to God

O my God,
I thank You for having created me
and made me a Christian
through Baptism.
Give Your followers the courage
to preach to all nations
and baptize
everyone who believes.

111

24

The Holy Spirit, Gift of the Father

Before He went back to the glory of His Father, Jesus had promised to send the Holy Spirit. On Pentecost, He did send the Spirit, the third Person of the Trinity, to live in His Church and in our hearts.

The Holy Spirit
is God,
like the Father
and the Son.
He is the
Spirit of Truth and of
Love. Jesus told us
that the Holy Spirit
will be with the
Church forever,
making us holy and keeping
us all joined in love.

The Holy Spirit first came to
us in Baptism, to share
the divine life with us.
In Confirmation we are
sealed with the Spirit, and He
even makes us apostles by
giving us special strength
to speak and act
as true witnesses
of Christ.

The gift
of the
Holy Spirit in
Confirmation
is a spiritual
sign and
seal that makes us
more Christ-like and
more perfect
members
of His Church.

113

The Holy Spirit is our light, our joy and
our strength. When we
ask Him for His gifts, we always feel
able to do what is right.
Even what
is hard seems to
become easy. The Holy
Spirit makes us
brave!

**Who is the
Holy Spirit?**
The Holy Spirit
is God, the
third
Person of the
Trinity.
He is the
Spirit
of Truth
who carries
out
Jesus' work
in the world.

**What
does the
Holy Spirit
do for us?**
The
Holy Spirit
fills us with
love
of God
and acts within us
to make
the Church
one and holy.

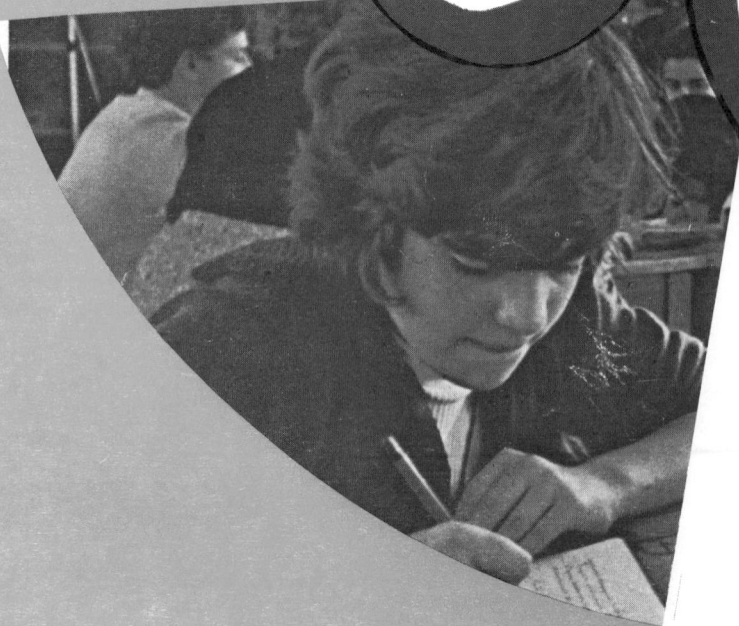

114

My Response to God

I will always let the Holy Spirit
act in me,
so that I will grow in faith,
hope
and love.

I Speak
to God

Come,
Holy
Spirit,
fill the
hearts of
Your
faithful and
light in them
the fire of Your love.

115

25 The Sacrament of Mercy

There are two great sacraments that we may
receive often. Both of them help us to draw closer to
Jesus and be better and
better followers of His. These
sacraments are Penance and Holy Eucharist. Penance is a gift
Jesus gave us on Easter Sunday,
when He said to His apostles and priests:

Receive the Holy Spirit.
For those whose sins you forgive, they are forgiven.

John 20:22

With these words Jesus
gave us the sacrament of Penance, or Confession.

When we are sorry for our sins
and confess them to the priest, Jesus forgives our sins
through the priest.

A good confession is like rising to a new life!
When someone confesses his sins with sorrow,
Jesus takes them away.
If the person has broken his friendship
with God by sinning seriously,
Jesus restores that friendship and gives back the right to
heaven. He also restores
the person's good relationship
with the Family of God, which was hurt by the sin.

If the person has weakened his friendship with Jesus through venial sin, Jesus makes their friendship strong again and enriches the person with more of His divine life.

In every confession, our Savior also gives us the strength to be better in the future. He draws us closer to Him and makes us richer in His love.

A good confession is a real joy!

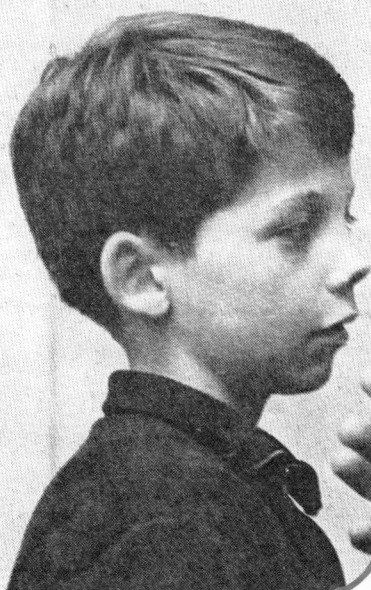

We prepare for confession with a careful **examination of conscience** (on how we have kept the Ten Commandments of God at home, at school, and at play).
We tell Jesus we are really **sorry.** We tell Him we **will do our best** not to sin again.
Then we go into the confessional or room.
We make the sign of the cross and listen while Father reads to us from God's Book, the Bible.
We **tell Father our sins** honestly and clearly.
We listen to him.
We say a prayer of sorrow.
When Father says the words of forgiveness, we make the sign of the cross.
After confession we say or do the **penance** the priest gave us.
We also thank Jesus for forgiving us.

Does God always welcome back a sinner who is sorry for his sins?
Yes. Jesus said: "There will be joy in heaven over one sinner who is sorry." see Luke 15:7

What is the right way to receive the sacrament of Penance?
The right way to receive the sacrament of Penance is this:
First, we examine our conscience. **Second,** we are sorry for our sins.
Third, we make up our mind not to sin again. **Fourth,** we confess our sins to the priest and say a prayer of sorrow.
Fifth, we do the penance the priest gives us.

My Response to God

Jesus brings true joy to His friends. To have His joy for myself,
I will examine my conscience every night
and go to confession often.

I Speak to God

Jesus, Lamb of God, have mercy on us!

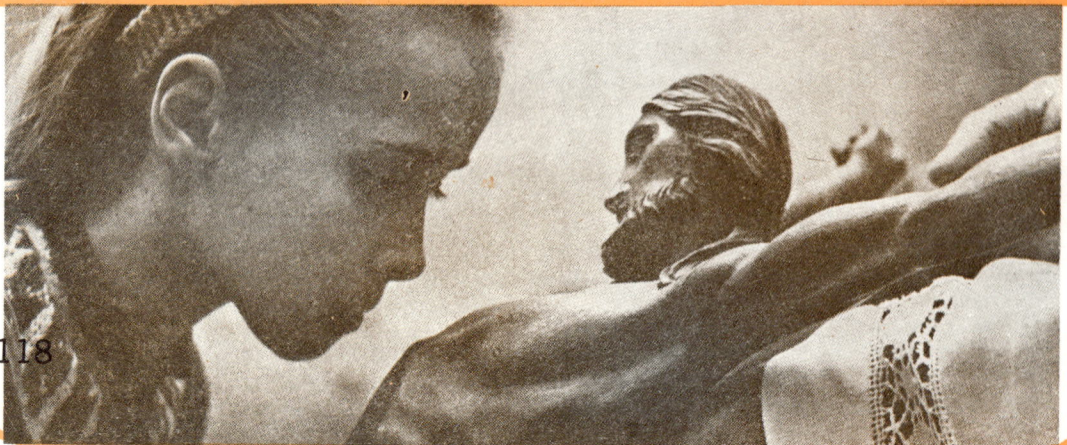

26

The

Gift

of the

Eucharist

First place among the sacraments belongs to the Eucharist. In this marvelous gift of God, we have Jesus Himself,
living and true.

In the Eucharist Jesus

offers Himself
to His Father for us,

gives Himself to us
as our Food,

and stays in our churches so that we can go
to talk with Him.

119

At the Last Supper, the night before He died, Jesus changed bread and wine into His Body and Blood. Then He said to His apostles,

Do this in memory of me.

see Luke 22:19-20

With these solemn words, Jesus made His apostles **priests** and gave them the power to repeat what He had done. He gave them the power to change bread and wine into His own Body and Blood and to offer them in sacrifice to our heavenly Father.

Every hour of the day, all over the world, Jesus' priests offer our heavenly Father the Body and Blood of Jesus in the Eucharistic Celebration, or Mass. Jesus' priests stand for Him at the altar, but the main Person offering the sacrifice is always Jesus Himself. In an unbloody manner, He renews His sacrifice on the cross.

We, the new People of God, have the wonderful privilege of coming together with Jesus our Savior to thank and praise our Father

in heaven. We do this at least once a week in the
Eucharistic Celebration, or Mass, which is the center of the
life of any parish and also the center of the
whole life of the Church.

At Mass, we, the Family of
God, pray together, offer
ourselves with Jesus to
the Father, receive
Jesus in Holy Communion,
and grow closer to Him
and to each other.
The Eucharist is
the great sacrament
of unity.

In the Mass we listen to the Word of God. The First and Second Readings and the Gospel remind us of the love of the Father. The priest explains Jesus' words. We answer our Father's love in song and prayer.

Then with the priest we offer bread and wine to our heavenly Father. The bread and wine stand for our very lives and actions.

During the great Eucharistic Prayer, or prayer of thanksgiving, when the priest repeats the words Jesus said at the Last Supper,
"This is My Body" and **"This is the cup of My Blood,"**
Jesus changes bread and wine into His own Body and Blood. From that moment on, He is really there, true God and true man. And He offers Himself to our heavenly Father for us, as He did on the cross.

At this solemn moment we offer ourselves with Jesus to our heavenly Father and promise Him love and obedience.

How does our heavenly Father respond to our love? He responds by inviting us to the most wonderful and holy banquet that a father

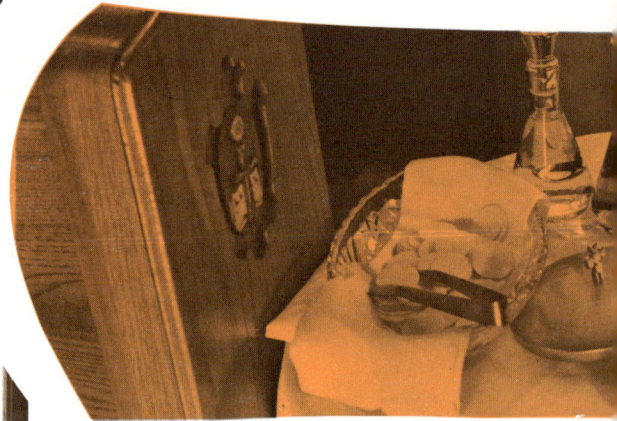

ever gave for his children.
In this banquet, our heavenly Father calls us together as members of His Family and gives us Jesus as our spiritual food in Holy Communion!

When we receive Jesus in the Eucharist, He shares more of His divine life with us and helps us to love Him and each other more. He also gives us strength to become better and to treat **everyone** as a dear brother or sister.

To receive Holy Communion worthily, it is necessary: to be free from mortal sin and to fast from food and liquids (except water) for one hour.

After the celebration of the Mass is over, Jesus remains truly present in the Blessed Sacrament. He loves to have us come to visit **Him** in church, **to** love Him and talk things over **with** Him.

What is the Mass?
The Mass is the same sacrifice as the sacrifice of the
cross. It is a memorial of Jesus' death,
resurrection and ascension,
and a holy banquet in which we receive Jesus Himself.

**How do we know that Jesus wants us to receive Him
in Holy Communion?**
We know that Jesus wants us to receive Him in Holy Communion
because He said: "He who eats my flesh and drinks my
blood lives in me and I live in him."
John 6:56

My Response to God
I can repay Jesus' great love by going to Mass faithfully and taking active part in it; by receiving Jesus in Holy Communion; by visiting Him in the Blessed Sacrament.

I Speak to God
O Lord, I do not deserve to have You come to me,
but say the word and I shall be healed.

27 My Continuing Response to God

This has been an important year for you, hasn't it? In **all** your school subjects, you have learned many new things.

And your religion study has been especially important this year, because you realized that religion is not just the memorizing of some truths and rules.

Our religion enriches our whole life — what we think, say, feel and do. It makes us better people, and when **we** become better, our families, school and whole community become better, too. If everyone knew our Faith well and lived by the law of love, our world would be full of peace, brotherhood and happiness for everybody.

How will you show your love for God and others during the summer vacation?

You may have a chance to help younger boys and girls. Then, you will be patient and kind, explain carefully, teach them to do things together happily, without fighting, lead them in a prayer once in a while, speak sometimes of God, our Father....

There are so many ways you can live by the law of love while looking after younger boys and girls.

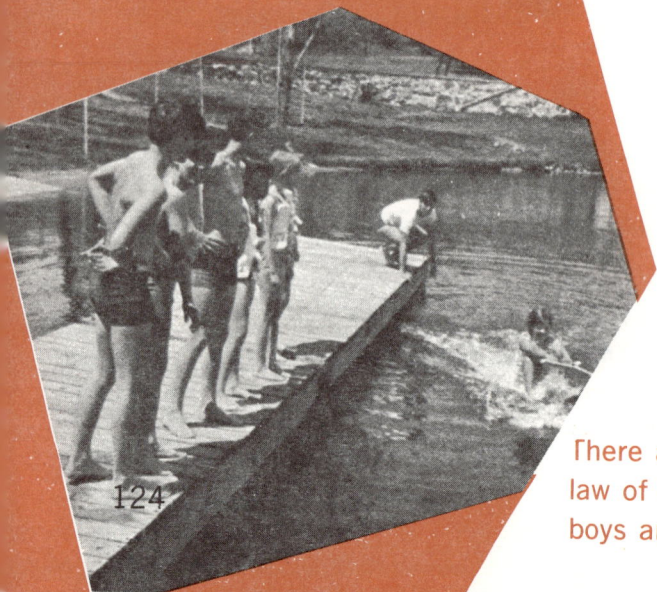

124

You may have a chance to help your parents around the house and on family outings. You may have a "job," such as mowing lawns or running errands. Whatever you do, you will respect everyone's opinion, belongings and property, and work well. This is a wonderful way to prepare yourself for your future as an adult.

You may be spending the summer with boys and girls your own age or a little older. St. Paul once wrote that nothing could separate him from the love of Christ. We should feel that way, too. We should never let anyone coax us into taking a drug or into looking at or listening to something shameful or into damaging someone's property. Being with our friends is a **challenge.** Let us lead them to enjoy good, clean sports and to help others. This is the way to stay happy.

God wants us to show our love for others. But, first of all, we should show our love for Him, because He gave us everything we have and everything we are. We will have many chances to speak heart-to-heart to our heavenly Father. Every Sunday we will participate in the Eucharistic Celebration. And as often as we wish, we will meet our Best Friend, Jesus, in Holy Communion and in the sacrament of His mercy.

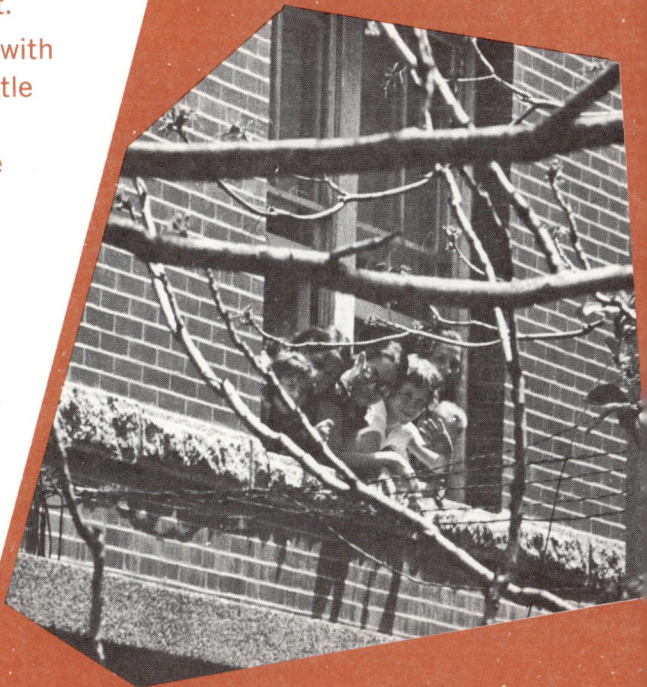

Make this a summer of real Christian witness!

Glossary

A

abstain — not to eat meat or anything made from meat.

angels — very intelligent spirits with no bodies.

anoint — to sign with oil, which stands for power or healing.

Anointing of the Sick — the sacrament through which Jesus gives comfort and strength to sick people and old people.

apostles — a group of Jesus' close followers, to whom He gave a great share in His power.

Ark of the Covenant — a wooden chest, lined with gold, in which the Hebrews carried the Ten Commandments during their journey to the Promised Land.

B

Baptism — the sacrament through which God makes us sharers in His own life, joins us to Jesus in the Church, and frees us from sin.

Bible — the holy Book in which God speaks to us through the writings of good men who wrote what He wanted them to write.

Bishops — the successors of the apostles who, with the Pope, guide God's people.

Blessed Sacrament — another name for the Eucharist, which has first place among the sacraments.

blessings — all the gifts God gives us.

C

Christ — another name for Jesus, showing that He was the Messiah, or Savior.

Church — the new People of God, who believe and follow Jesus' teachings, meet Him in the sacraments, share His life, and follow the leaders (the Pope and Bishops) He has given us.

Communion — the receiving of Jesus in the Eucharist.

Confirmation — the sacrament through which we are sealed with the Holy Spirit, who gives us a special strength to speak and act as Christ's true witnesses.

Covenant — an agreement between God and the Hebrews: He would guide and protect them as long as they kept His commandments.

create — to make something out of nothing.

crucifixion — nailing on a cross — the way Jesus died to save us.

D

devils — angels who turned against God and now tempt human beings to turn against Him.

E

Eight Beatitudes — promises of happiness for following Jesus in a more perfect way.

Eucharist—the sacrament in which Jesus Himself is really and truly present, under the appearances of bread and wine.

Eucharistic Celebration—also called Holy Mass: the renewal of Jesus' sacrifice on the cross in an unbloody manner; the holy meal in which we receive Jesus and celebrate our unity in Him.

F

faith—belief in everything God has told us.

Faith—our religion.

fast—to eat only one full meal a day.

G

God—the all-powerful, completely perfect Creator and Ruler of the whole universe.

God the Father—the first Person of the Trinity, who watches over us as a real Father.

God the Son—the second Person of the Trinity, who became man to save us; He is the God-man, Jesus Christ.

God the Holy Spirit—the third Person of the Trinity, given to us by the Father and the Son to live in us, help us, and share God's life with us.

Gospel—the four most important books of the Bible; they tell us about the words and actions of Jesus.

grace—God's gift to us of a sharing in His own life, by which we become His children and can hope to join Him in heaven.

H

heaven—everlasting life and happiness with God.

Hebrews—the people descended from Abraham, Isaac and Jacob, to whom God gave the Commandments and promised the Savior.

hell—everlasting suffering and separation from God.

holy—belonging to God or close to God.

Holy Orders—the sacrament through which Jesus gives His Spirit to men to make them priests and bishops.

holydays of obligation—special days besides Sundays on which Catholic Christians are expected to celebrate the Eucharist.

I

Immaculate Conception—the special privilege of Jesus' Mother, Mary: she came into life free from original sin.

J

Jesus—the name of the Second Person of the Trinity after He became man. "Jesus" means "Savior."

judgment—moment at which Jesus will tell a person what reward or punishment he will receive for the good or bad he has done.

L

lowly—humble and kind; not proud.

M

martyr—a person who gives up his life rather than give up Jesus.

Mary—the name of Jesus' holy Mother.

Mass—another name for the Eucharistic Celebration.

Master—a name given to Jesus by His followers; it means "great teacher."

Matrimony—the sacrament through which Jesus blesses a man and woman who take each other as husband and wife for all their lives.

means of salvation—helps God gives us so that we may enter into His happiness after we die.

miracle—a marvelous action, above and beyond the laws of nature, done by the power of God.

missionary—a person who shares with others the good news of Jesus' love for us.

mortal sin—a serious disobedience to God, done knowingly and on purpose; this drives God's life out of a soul.

Mount Sinai—a red granite peak near the tip of the Sinai Peninsula; there God spoke to Moses from a burning bush and later gave him the Ten Commandments.

N

neighbor — someone who lives near us; also: everyone in the family of mankind.

O

original sin — the lack of God's life in us when we are born.

P

penance — sacrifices made to make up for sins; also: prayers or good actions to be said or done after confession.

Penance — the sacrament through which Jesus forgives our sins, draws us closer to Himself and gives us the strength to do better.

Pentecost — the day the Holy Spirit came upon the apostles, to remain with the Church forever.

People of God — another name for the Church, the great worldwide Family of Jesus' brothers and sisters who believe and follow His teachings and share His life.

persecution — suffering caused by others because they are against what a person stands for.

Pope — the successor of St. Peter and the chief leader of the Church on earth.

prayer — talking to God with our minds and hearts, and often with our voices and actions.

priests — men to whom Jesus gives the power to act for Him in offering the Mass and forgiving sins.

Promised Land — the land called Canaan, or Palestine, into which God brought the Hebrews.

prophet — a man chosen by God to be His special messenger.

purgatory — a place of suffering after death where people make up for their sins before they enter heaven.

R

religious — men and women who promise to be poor and obedient and to live only for God and others, as Jesus did.

resurrection — our Lord's return to life after His death on the cross.

S

sacraments — the chief actions through which Jesus gives us His Spirit and makes us holy; they are signs of His grace and our faith.

Sacred Scriptures — "holy writings" — another name for the Bible.

saints — people who followed Jesus closely and are now happy with Him in heaven.

Samaritans — people who lived near the Hebrews but did not worship God in the same way that the Hebrews did.

Sermon on the Mount — sermon in which Jesus gave us the Eight Beatitudes and made the Ten Commandments more complete and perfect.

sin — disobedience to God.

soul — the unseen part of us by which we live, think, and make decisions.

spirit — a real and living being that cannot be seen, felt, etc.

T

temptation — attraction to commit sin.

Ten Commandments — ten great rules of behavior which show us how to love God and others.

Trinity — the mystery of one God in three divine Persons, Father, Son and Holy Spirit.

V

venial sin — a less serious disobedience to God that weakens a person's friendship with Him.

W

witnesses of Christ — people who share Jesus' teachings with others and show His goodness in their own lives.

works of mercy — good deeds we do to others because we love God and them.

worship — offering God the gift of ourselves, especially in the Mass, but also by praying to Him, believing Him, and doing what is right.